Teleology

Teleology

Andrew Woodfield

Lecturer in Philosophy, Merton College, Oxford

Cambridge University Press

CAMBRIDGE

LONDON · NEW YORK · MELBOURNE

Published by the Syndics of the Cambridge University Press
The Pitt Building, Trumpington Street, Cambridge CB2 1RP
Bentley House, 200 Euston Road, London NW1 2DB
32 East 57th Street, New York, NY 10022, USA
296 Beaconsfield Parade, Middle Park, Melbourne 3206, Australia

Library of Congress catalog card number: 75-44574

ISBN 0 521 21102 6

First published 1976

Printed in Great Britain by
Cox & Wyman Ltd
London, Fakenham and Reading

Contents

Preface

This book is a comprehensive investigation into teleological explanations, their varieties, their logical structure, and their proper uses. The subject of teleology crops up in many different fields of inquiry, and in various guises. It raises problems not only for philosophers, but also for biologists, psychologists, social scientists, theologians, and even for engineers. Indeed, I hope that the book will be of interest to anyone who is intrigued or puzzled by the concept of purpose.

My treatment of the subject does not fall clearly under any single heading in contemporary philosophy. It straddles various branches. If I had to locate it, I should say that it lies roughly at the intersection of philosophy of science, metaphysics, and philosophy of mind. When I first started to think about teleology, the ideas I had were terribly jumbled, but I thought there must be a way of fitting them together, like pieces of a jigsaw, to produce a coherent overall picture. Many times a picture seemed to be emerging, only to disintegrate on closer inspection. For long periods I was captivated by models that turned out to be completely wrong. So although the theory presented here seems to me now to provide the best framework for understanding teleology, in fact the only framework that gives due consideration to all factors, it wouldn't surprise me to learn that there are other, very different, ways of looking at the matter. Teleology, like all important philosophical issues, can be approached from many angles and on many levels.

There exist several good books dealing with selected aspects of teleology, for example, with goal-directed behaviour in animals and men, but as far as I know there is no other work which tries to trace all the ramifications of the subject systematically. Much of the recent work on teleology has appeared in the form of articles in philosophical journals, which are not easily accessible, and which many readers might not know about. I have made a point, therefore, of including references to such work in the text. The bibliography is by no means exhaustive, however. It could have been at least twice as long as it is.

I should like to thank all the friends and colleagues who have read parts of this book and have discussed the topic with me, in particular, Robert Adams, Joanna Bosanquet, David Bostock, Philippa Foot, Bill Frerking, Patrick Gardiner, Ros Godlovitch, Stan Godlovitch, John Mackie, Robin McCleery, Colin McGinn, Marie McGinn, Alan Montefiore, Denis Noble, David Pears, Trevor Phelps, Archie Smith, and Brandon Taylor. I owe a special debt of gratitude to my thesis supervisors, David Pears and John Mackie, for their help and encouragement.

Finally, I should like to thank the Senatus Committee of Edinburgh University whose generosity, in the form of a Postgraduate Studentship which financed my doctoral studies at St John's College, Oxford, enabled me to write the thesis on which this book is based; and Linacre College, Oxford, which gave me a Junior Research Fellowship in order to complete the book.

Los Angeles   A.W.
January 1976

PART ONE
INTRODUCTION

I

What is teleology?

If you ever look closely at an ants' nest, you will see an intricate network of pathways and chambers teeming with activity. Ants scurry around like frantic workmen trying to meet a deadline. Some carry twigs, or bits of grass, or white eggs as big as themselves. You will probably see columns of ants marching in single file into or out of the nest, or passing lumps of food back down the line. The impression is inescapable that there is a purpose in what they are doing.

People in the desert sometimes experience a feeling of awe when they look at the night sky. The black background is alive with stars. Each one is millions of miles away, and there are uncountably many. When one thinks how minute the earth is compared to the whole galaxy, and how small human beings are compared to the earth, one's personal concerns begin to seem insignificant. In such a cosmic setting people sometimes find themselves wondering whether the universe as a whole has any overall purpose.

Reflections like these are teleological. In the *Oxford English Dictionary* 'teleology' is defined as 'the doctrine or study of ends or final causes'. This definition contains a technical term, 'final causes', not much used nowadays. A more familiar word would be 'purposes'. Questions about teleology are, broadly, to do with whether a thing has a purpose or is acting for the sake of a purpose, and, if so, what that purpose is. Such questions can be raised with respect to *anything*: twigs, people, schools, ants' nests, ceremonies, stars, the universe as a whole, et cetera.

In everyday life, questions about the purposes of people and things crop up all the time. We often need to know why so-and-so did something, or what such-and-such a thing is for. Occasionally, deeper, more general questions are raised about whether a kind of thing, especially a natural thing, has a purpose. These can be extremely difficult to answer, and very often, opinions differ. At times it may seem that there is no right answer, but that it depends on one's world-view.

Consider two extreme theses about teleology: one says that nothing whatever has a purpose, the other says that everything has. If we take the first at face value, it is false. Chairs, tables, and so on have a purpose; men often do things on purpose. Nevertheless, depressed people can come to think that in a deep sense everything lacks purpose. It isn't just that they think their own lives are meaningless. From their depressed perspective, the whole world and everything in it appears utterly pointless. Before we can say whether they are right or wrong or neither, we need to know what it means for a thing to lack, or to have, a purpose in this allegedly deeper sense.

Many would hold that the second thesis, that everything has a purpose, is equally incorrect. Surely pebbles on a beach, for instance, are not there for a purpose, nor do they act purposively. However, some Christians uphold it because they believe that God does nothing in vain. If God has created a thing, He must have had a reason, and His reason gives the thing a purpose. Nor need the motive for adopting the thesis be a religious one. An atheist could hold that although pebbles have no God-given purpose, they exist for the sake of some future goal. The evolution of the universe, he might say, is a goal-directed process in which even the most insignificant objects have a part to play. Thus there are at least two ways, and possibly more, of construing the thesis. In fact, it would be better to say that there are two quite different theses here, which happen to be expressed in the same words. Furthermore, it may be that each one is itself open to a variety of interpretations. How are we to take the claim that evolution is a goal-directed process, for example? It might be put forward as a necessary truth, or as a scientific hypothesis, or as the expression of a non-objective teleological *attitude* to things. Perhaps the speaker is not committing himself to any factual claim, but is saying merely that he views the present in a future-oriented light. If it is intended as a factual claim, however, what sort of evidence would count for or against it? Does it imply that the future influences the present by somehow pulling events towards it? Many people have thought that teleology involves some such assumption of backward causation, or of a *vis a fronte*. Or does it assert that the universe is *trying* to reach some ultimate end, such as Teilhard de Chardin's Point Omega? Clearly, before one can weigh the evidence for or against any hypothesis, or judge of its truth or falsehood, one needs to be clear about what it means. But this is precisely the problem. Getting clear about the meanings of teleological claims is, in fact, the main aim of this book.

The subject of teleology has figured prominently in Western philosophy since Aristotle. To trace its ramifications properly one would have to write a complete history of metaphysics, epistemology, theology, science and ethics. Such a task would be beyond the power of a single author. It goes so far beyond mine that I thought it would be better for me not to try a historical approach at all. But I think it is worth while to look very briefly at one historically important theme. It will help to locate the subject, and also to show why we need an analytical approach if these problems are ever going to be solved.

Modern science is on the whole hostile to teleological explanations. That they are obscurantist and unempirical has been the dominant view among scientists ever since the Renaissance. One of the most eloquent advocates of the new inductive method was Francis Bacon, who gave aphoristic expression to this opinion In *De Augmentis Scientiarum* (1623), Book III, ch. 5: 'nam causarum finalium inquisitio sterilis est, et, tanquam virgo Deo consecrata, nihil parit'. (Inquiry into final causes is sterile, and, like a virgin consecrated to God, produces nothing.) But Bacon was writing at a time when the prevailing philosophy of nature was still Aristotelian. Because of the different background, some of his reasons for rejecting final causes were different from ours.

The most common criticisms of teleological explanations nowadays are either that they are animistic, i.e. they assume that the thing being explained has a mind, or that they tacitly invoke a supernatural being who directs the course of events. Take 'The apple fell off the tree in order to reach the ground' as an example. If this implies that the apple chose to fall, or wanted to reach the ground, it is animistic and invalid. The explanation is wrong in principle, because apples can't choose or want anything. Of course, if it had been 'The *child* (deliberately) fell off the tree in order to reach the ground', the explanation would, logically speaking, be perfectly all right. If, on the other hand, we take the explanation to mean that the apple fell because God intended it to be on the ground, it explains a natural phenomenon by reference to a supernatural cause. There is nothing wrong with that from a logical or theological point of view, but it is not scientific. There is no way of checking its truth-value experimentally.

While Bacon and Galileo would probably have agreed with these criticisms, they had other criticisms as well. The sentence about the apple need not be interpreted either animistically or supernaturally. It could mean that reaching the ground was an Aristotelian final cause. If so, it could be attacked on the grounds that this very notion is suspect. Renaissance scientists who rejected final causes were reacting against a concept which lay at the heart of Aristotelianism. It is difficult for us, conditioned as we are by their success, to imagine how things looked before the scientific revolution.

According to Aristotle, the universe is composed of five elements, and each element has a natural tendency to move in a characteristic way. The stars, made of aether, travel around the earth in perfect circular orbits, and never stop. The four sublunary elements, earth, water, air and fire, move in straight lines and eventually stop at their natural resting places, if they get that far. Earth, being the heavy element, tends to move downwards. Fire goes upwards, and water and air are intermediate, in that water tends to sink relative to air, but to rise relative to earth. These elements combine, through processes like heating, cooling, compacting and rarefying, to form material objects. Objects are either natural or artificial; natural objects are either living or non-living. All objects have both matter and form: their matter is what they are made of, their form is the way the matter is organised, and is what makes them the kinds of things they are. This is a relative distinction which can be applied on different levels of decomposition.

A flower, if it has the form of a rose, *is* a rose for that reason. Thus the form of a thing is intimately bound up with its essential nature, with what the thing really is. It is also connected with the idea of actuality and of being fully developed. Although a rosebud is not actually a rose, but only potentially, in calling it a bud of a rose we identify it in terms of what it is naturally going to become. To that extent the rosebud has potentially the form of a rose.

The main thing that a scientist had to explain was movement. Aristotle's word *kinesis* actually covers growth and alteration as well as local motion, so perhaps 'change' is a better word. To explain why a change occurred is, quite generally, to cite some reason or explanatory factor in a 'because' clause. Aristotle thinks there are four main types of 'because': material, formal, efficient and final. In answer to the question 'Why did this building come to be as it is?', we can say 'Because of the bricks and mortar' (material cause); 'Because it is a house' (formal cause); 'Because the builder made it' (efficient cause); or 'Because it is for living in' (final cause). It is clear from this example that the final cause of an artefact is its intended function. But Aristotle thought that final causes operate in nature too. For him, it is an obvious fact that natural objects and processes are *for* something, just as much as artefacts. The clearest cases are to be found in biology. Who can doubt that the eye is for seeing, the ear for hearing, and so on?

The things that are teleologically explained, i.e. the *explananda*, fall into a variety of different categories. First there are the several kinds of change that have been mentioned. One can also explain an object, or the existence of an object. The object may be regarded as a whole thing, or as part of a bigger thing, or as an earlier version of a later thing. In all cases the *explanans*, the explaining factor, is a *telos* or end. However, *tele* fall into several categories too. They may be objects, or states, activities, or products of activity, and various *tele* may be offered for one and the same explanandum. For example, the roots of a tree are for absorbing nourishment from the soil (*Physics* 199^a 29–30), but also for the whole tree. A plant grows leaves to protect its fruit, and the leaves themselves exist for the protection of fruit (*Physics* 199^a 26–9). A half-grown plant develops in order to become a full-grown one; for 'coming-to-be is for the sake of being, not being for the sake of coming-to-be' (*D.P.A.* 1, 640^a 18–19). Every living thing acts for the sake of ends proper to its type. Plants live the life of growth and reproduction, animals have sensation and appetite on top of these, and man has all these plus reason. A man might walk for the sake of his health (*Physics* 194^b 32–5), or in order to get to Athens, or as a means to some virtuous action. For all deliberate human action is, or should be, aimed at the good (*Nic. Ethics* 1094^a 1–3). This is quite an assortment. There is obviously great scope here for imposing some sort of classification upon teleological explanations. One pattern which we shall be particularly interested in later is where the explanandum is an action, and the *telos* is an end to which the action is a means.

The final cause of a natural movement is closely connected with its formal cause. This comes out especially clearly when the movement in question is growth. To give the formal cause of a rosebud's growth is to explain it by reference to the essence or actuality of the rosebud. To explain it teleologically is to cite the end towards which it is naturally tending. But the actuality of the rosebud, and its *telos* under one description, are identical: the fully developed rose. Again, the two kinds of explanation are equivalent whenever the explanandum is a thing that is *defined* in terms of a function it performs. This holds for both artefacts and natural organs. If we define the eye as the organ of sight, or define a house as a building for living in, then the question

'What is this for?', asked about an eye or a house, amounts to the same as the question 'What is this?'. Whenever it is part of the very nature of a thing to move or act in a certain way, that movement or action can be explained in terms of the thing's form. This is true of all things, including the basic elements (*De Caelo* 311ᵃ 1–14).

The most distinctive feature of Aristotelian teleology is that it is *immanent* in nature (Ross, 1923). This means that the source of a thing's end-directed movement is to be found within the nature of the thing itself, not in some external agency. Given that striving for its end is something that an object does naturally if it does it at all, it would be quite wrong to accuse Aristotle of invoking the supernatural. He had no use for demiurges who actively control what goes on in the world. And it would be unfair to regard his teleological explanations as animistic. They are certainly not intended to be. Aristotle thinks he has dispensed with the idea that a thing needs a mind if it is to act for an end. If an object behaves teleologically, it does so because it is in its nature to do so, whether it be animate or not.

How far does he wish to extend teleological explanations? Certainly, not every movement of every thing is end-directed. A tile does not slide off a roof in order to hit the man standing underneath, nor for any other purpose. But he thinks that every natural thing will, if the opportunity arises, perform *some* movement which is end-directed, namely, that one which is natural to it. He thinks this about both inorganic and organic things. Admittedly, his actual examples are usually biological, but this is because biological teleology is easier to see. His arguments are aimed at establishing the view that teleological tendencies are present in everything. There is plenty of indirect evidence that he took this view. For one thing, there is the connection already noted between final cause and formal cause. For another, he thinks non-living and living things form a continuum, with no sharp dividing line (*D.P.A.* IV, 681ᵃ 12 and *H.A.* VIII, 588ᵇ 4). But most importantly, his defence of the teleological method in *Physics* Book II, ch. 8 does not restrict itself to the movement of living things. He concludes that 'action for an end is present in things which come to be and are by nature' (*Physics* 199ᵃ 7–8), on the grounds that such things are or come to be always or for the most part. He says, indeed, that rain does not fall in order to water the corn. But it does, on his principles, fall for the sake of something else, such as reaching its proper place in the universe. Most commentators agree that the tendency of inorganic substances to move to their proper places is not just *de facto* for Aristotle, but teleological. Their natural places are their natural goals.

This doctrine was one of the prime targets in the Renaissance assault on Aristotelianism. Two main lines of attack stand out, the first and best-known being the criticism of phoney 'natural tendency' explanations. The argument is simple, and it applies to any spurious invocation of a natural tendency, whether it be a tendency to be, to become, or to move. Suppose that an explanation is required for the fact that ripe apples fall off trees. A possible place to look for an answer is in the apples themselves. If we could discover something about apples which causes them to fall when certain circumstances occur, this would count as a perfectly good explanation, on a par with explaining why sugar dissolves in water in terms of its molecular structure. Consider, however, the claim that apples fall because they have a natural tendency to fall. Let us assume that there is no evidence for this apart from the fact that they do fall, and that the claim is construed in such a way that no more evidence is either possible or necessary. Given this assumption, the explanation is vacuous. The natural tendency is masquerading as an internal property which makes them fall, whereas in fact it is just a redescription of the phenomenon to be explained. Pseudo-explanations of this kind seem to have been common among Scholastic philosophers and quack doctors, their circularity often being disguised by technical-sounding terms like *vis viva*, and *virtus dormitiva*. Galileo was well aware that inventing names for unknown causes can lead to a comfortable illusion of understanding. The name 'gravity' was a case in point. (See his *Dialogue on the Great World Systems* (1631), page 250 of the Santillana edition.)

The nub of the criticism is that appeals to natural tendencies are non-explanatory unless there is or could be evidence for them which is independent of their alleged manifestations. However, the examples cited so far have nothing to do with *purposes*. The argument is directed not against final causes specifically, but against any explanation that has a question-begging explanans. It has not been established that all final cause explanations are of this type. So the argument knocks out only those final cause explanations which fall into a special proscribed class, and it hits them for being circular, not for being teleological.

An illustration will make this point clearer. Take the question 'Why do apples seek the ground?' It demands an explanation for an alleged phenomenon which is already assumed to be teleological, inasmuch as the description employs the teleological word 'seek'. The answer

'Because they have a natural tendency to seek the ground' might be classed as teleological for the same reason. But it is not vacuous through being teleological. It is vacuous for the same reason as before, i.e. because the explanans is merely a redescription of the explanandum. Indeed, it is doubtful whether this should count as a teleological *explanation*. The mere presence of a teleological word is not enough. What is required is that there should be a distinctive mode of dependence of the explanandum upon the explanans such that the former is said to be for the sake of the latter. No such connection is asserted here.

It seems, therefore, that this first line of attack does not address itself to the teleological explanatory pattern *per se*, though it does destroy a certain kind of typically Aristotelian pseudo-explanation. Some explanations which assume final causes are of this invalid kind, but their fault is that they are of a question-begging form. What needs to be shown, in order to refute Aristotle's doctrine of final causes, is that there are no final causes of the sort in question. This problem is prior to, and encapsulated within, the problem we have just been discussing, for it has to do with how to *describe* the phenomenon we wish to explain. It has to be shown that apples do not *seek* the ground, they just fall on it.

This brings us to the second line of attack. The main reason why Aristotle's doctrine faded out is simply that the new men of science stopped asking teleological questions. To them, final causes were scientifically irrelevant. A number of factors conspired to bring about the change of perspective. Aristotle's cosmology was being steadily undermined by new discoveries in astronomy. Observations made with the aid of the telescope tended to support Copernicus's theory. In dynamics, Aristotle's theory of gravity was shattered by Galileo. A cannon ball dropped from the leaning tower of Pisa does *not* reach the ground sooner than a musket ball. Also it became clear that the theory of natural resting places had to go, though the full story had to wait for Newton. The natural thing for a freely moving body to do, wherever it might be in the universe, is to carry on moving until acted upon by an external force. As these and other discoveries weakened Aristotle's physics, so they weakened the metaphysics with which it was intertwined. The new philosophy ushered in a new experimental method, with the emphasis firmly upon exact description and measurement of observables. In his capacity as a *describer* of phenomena, Galileo studiously avoided all speculation about their underlying reasons and causes. 'He set himself to discover not *why* things fall, but *how*: in accordance with what mathematical relations, a great development of scientific method' (Dampier, 1929, pp. 130–1.) He held that when one is ignorant of the cause of a thing, it is far better to be candid about it and say 'I don't know'.[1] Where *final* causes are concerned, he probably would have said that we not only don't know, but we cannot know. He might have added in private that he didn't care. To confess one's ignorance unashamedly on this topic has been a standard motif in scientific writing ever since. Darwin was expressing much the same idea, and in the same spirit, when he told Lyell that the question of the ultimate purpose of evolution was 'beyond the human intellect, like "predestination and free will" or the "origin of evil"'. (Letter from Darwin to Lyell, April 1860, in F. Darwin (1888), vol. II, p. 304.)

The second line of attack, then, was not a reasoned refutation of the doctrine of final causes, but rather a switch of interest away from it. Philosophically speaking it is no more conclusive than the first line. Suppose it were conceded that the investigation of purposes is a sterile and unfruitful procedure for scientists to follow. The concession would be over a purely heuristic matter, to do with the advantages and disadvantages of the procedure. To go deeper, one has to ask: *Why* is there no advantage to be gained? The most intellectually satisfying explanation of this fact would be, surely, that it is because natural phenomena do not *have* purposes. Generally, the best reason why it is unfruitful to believe a certain proposition P is that P is false. But no independent reason has yet been given for thinking that the doctrine of final causes is false. Of course, no good reason has been given for thinking it to be true either. The point is simply that none of the considerations so far has refuted it.

Although it was no longer possible in the seventeenth century to stick to Aristotle's physics without flying in the face of known facts, there were plenty of people who carried on viewing the world teleologically. The reason for this is, I think, that they treated the thesis of final causes as a metaphysical principle, immune to falsification by new empirical discoveries. The principle helped to structure their view of the world and whatever facts it might contain, without committing them to any specific empirical claim. A good example of such a person is Leibniz (1646–1716), one of the most learned men of his day, and thoroughly up-to-date with the latest scientific developments.

[1] See, for example, *The Assayer*, Stillman Drake translation, p. 241.

It is important, when discussing Leibniz, to remember a distinction which has already been hinted at between two kinds of teleology. Throughout his life, Leibniz believed that God had designed the world according to the best possible plan. 'God has chosen that world' – he writes, in the *Discourse on Metaphysics*[2] – 'which is the most perfect, that is to say, which is at the same time the simplest in its hypotheses and the richest in phenomena.' Each thing has its God-given role, and the ultimate purpose of all parts of the system is to form a world that is perfectly harmonious and well-ordered. There are two methods, therefore, of investigating nature. You can observe events, and try to discover by experiment what made them happen. This is the method of efficient causes. Or you can try to work out what the simplest and most perfect laws are, secure in the knowledge that particular events will in fact obey them. 'Both methods are good, both can be useful not only for admiring the skill of the great workman but also for making useful discoveries in physics and in medicine' (Loemker, pp. 487–8). As an example of the second method, Leibniz mentions Snell's work on refraction, which uses the hypothesis that light takes the easiest path. He calls it 'the method of final causes', including under that title both the search for harmonious laws and the search for particular good consequences such as might have been expected on the hypothesis of a benevolent designer.

So Leibniz certainly believed in final causes, in this sense. But God-given functions are conferred upon things by an agent who is outside nature; this kind of teleology derives from an external source. What we are really interested in just now is *immanent* teleology. Did Leibniz believe in that too? The two kinds are logically distinct, since a thing with an immanent purpose would have it even if it had not been designed for a purpose. The difference is sometimes difficult to see, especially if you hold the view that all things, including things with purposes of their own like animals and human beings, are designed by God. You may be tempted to think that if God makes a thing that has a purpose, then God makes it have a purpose. In a sense, of course, this is true. If God created an animal whose goal in life was to catch mice, the fact that it had that goal would be traceable to His workmanship. But catching mice is not God's goal; it belongs to the animal itself. The truth of the statement that the animal has it does not depend on facts about the animal's origin. To confuse the two kinds of teleology is to attribute the purpose to the wrong logical subject. It is like confusing

[2] In *Philosophical Papers and Letters*, edited by L. E. Loemker, p. 470.

'God made the animal move' with 'God made the animal in such a way that it would move'.

All theists would agree that, whatever the world is made of, God made it be like that. But what is the world made of? What are its basic constituents? On this question of metaphysics theists may differ; Leibniz, in fact, changed his mind about it. As a young man he rebelled against Scholasticism and opted for the new materialism of Hobbes, Descartes and their followers. In a letter to his thesis supervisor, he wrote (1669): 'I maintain the rule which is common to all these renovators of philosophy, that only magnitude, figure, and motion are to be used in explaining corporeal properties.' (Loemker, p. 146.) The world consists ultimately of indivisible atoms, i.e. solid, extended, moving particles. Observable objects are aggregates of atoms, and all changes are the result of mechanical interactions between them. But matter is essentially passive; it won't move unless something else moves it. The first cause of motion, therefore, is not matter but mind. There is no need to ascribe minds or incorporeal souls to all bodies, however. That would be a return to 'heathen polytheism'. Their movements can be adequately explained as after-effects of God's initial push, which take place in accordance with the laws of motion. 'There is in fact no wisdom in nature and no appetite; yet a beautiful order arises in it because it is the timepiece of God.' (*Ibid.*, p. 158.)

But Leibniz soon ceased to believe that the building blocks of the world were extended corpuscles. His mathematical work led him to conclude that any extended thing, however small, can be divided into smaller parts, since there is no limit to the number of points on a line. Therefore there are no such things as atoms, defined as the smallest possible extended things. Secondly, individual substances cannot be Cartesian bodies possessing just shape and size, because such bodies have no true individuality. Two could be perfectly similar to each other, and this would contradict his principle of the Identity of Indiscernibles. Both these points are made in *First Truths*, written around 1680–4. (Loemker, p. 416.) Cartesian dynamics was wrong too, in particular the principle of the constancy of the quantity of motion. Leibniz argued, in *A Brief Demonstration Of a Notable Error of Descartes And Others Concerning a Natural Law* (1686), that what is conserved is the quantity of motive force. Mistakes in dynamics and physics generally are bound to arise if natural philosophers 'believe that they need to use only mathematical principles, without having any need either for metaphysical principles, which they treat as illusory, or for principles of the good, which they reduce to human morals; as if perfection and the good were only a particular result of our thinking and not to be found in universal nature.' (*Tentamen Anagogicum,* Loemker, p. 778–9.)

In place of materialism Leibniz developed a tight metaphysical system whose key concept was that of an individual substance, or monad. To us the system seems fantastic, but it is important to realise that Leibniz thought it followed logically from half a dozen or so basic principles which were necessarily true. That there are such things as monads was, for him, a logical requirement of our conceptual scheme, just as, for Wittgenstein in the *Tractatus Logico-Philosophicus*, the logic of our language required that there be simple objects named by logically proper names, though it was impossible to produce any. He sums up the position as follows, in *A New System Of The Nature and Communication of Substances* (1695):

> To find these real unities, therefore, I was forced to have recourse to a formal atom, since a material being cannot be at the same time material and perfectly indivisible, or endowed with a true unity. It was thus necessary to restore and, as it were, to rehabilitate the *substantial forms* which are in such disrepute today, but in a way which makes them intelligible and separates their proper use from their previous abuse. I found then that their nature consists of force and that there follows from this something analogous to sense and appetite, so that we must think of them in terms similar to the concept which we have of *souls*. (Loemker, p. 741)

Monads are perfectly simple units, each one different, and each able to reflect the world around it from its own distinctive point of view. This ability he calls 'perception'. They also have 'appetite', an innate tendency to pass from one state to another. The state of a monad at a given time is its perception of the total state of the world at that time; and all its changes of state are pre-programmed. Monads do not interact with each other causally, but follow their own predetermined paths of development. Although no human being can ever know a monad well enough to get a complete concept of it, the complete concept of a substance would contain every predicate that has been, is, and will be true of it. Certain monads perceive things more clearly than others, and these dominant ones may be regarded as 'spokesmen' for the general point of view held by those near to it. When a lot of monads are grouped together in this way, they create the appearance of a material object. Causal interaction between material bodies is a mere 'phenomenon'; what really happens is that the groups of monads change their states according to their own fixed plans, but the separate plans are orchestrated and harmonised so that synchronised patterns of change occur. The observable result is that material objects appear to move and to affect one other.

As far as our present discussion is concerned, the most interesting feature of monads is that they are essentially *active*. The true concept of substance is the concept of activity or force concentrated at a metaphysical point. Furthermore, Leibniz makes it quite clear that he regards this activity as immanently teleological. 'Active force,' he writes in 1694, 'differs from the mere power familiar to the Schools, for the active power or faculty of the Scholastics is nothing but a close possibility of acting, which needs an external excitation or a stimulus, as it were, to be transferred into action. Active force, in contrast, contains a certain action or entelechy and is thus midway between the faculty of acting and the action itself and involves a conatus. It is thus carried into action by itself and needs no help but only the removal of an impediment.' (*On the Correction of Metaphysics and the Concept of Substance*, Loemker, p. 709.) The end to which each substance tends is the progressive actualisation of its potential. Since the seeds of its future development are already to be found within it, its present state is 'pregnant with the future'.

In spite of his frequently saying that monads are like souls and are alive, his theory is not like traditional versions of vitalism. A vitalist is someone who tries to account for the difference between living and non-living things by postulating a vital power which is present only in the former. The vital principle or 'entelechy' or 'élan vital' is conceived as a non-material entity which, when added to the inert physical body, makes it come alive. Leibniz constantly criticizes this doctrine for being 'in part impossible and in part superfluous' (*On Nature Itself, or On the Inherent Force and Actions of Created Things* (1698), Loemker, p. 810). God doesn't need to add life to organic bodies by a special act, additional to the act of creating the bodies, any more than he needs to intervene in purely physical processes to keep them going. He created the bodies with life already built into them. But Leibniz *is* a vitalist in the sense that he thinks all substances are alive. He holds that 'it is consistent neither with the order nor with the beauty or the reason of things that there should be something vital or immanently active only in a small part of matter, when it would imply greater perfection if it were in all' (*ibid.*, p. 820).

Every object that has genuine unity and individuality, like a plant or an animal, as opposed to a mere aggregate, like a heap of stones, has a substantial form or soul. The soul of a composite substance is identified with the dominant member of the group of monads of which it is composed. Leibniz is an animist without being an anthropomorphist: he endows plants and inorganic substances with analogues of souls that are appropriate to their lowly status in the chain of being, not with human thoughts or feelings. Thus, when he defines the 'appetite' of a monad as 'the striving from one perception to another' (Loemker, p. 1077), he does not mean conscious striving. Aristotle, as we have seen, was not an animist. But in most other respects, Leibniz's teleology of nature was thoroughly Aristotelian.

Most people today would agree that the thesis of universal animism, in so far as it makes empirically testable claims, is quite false. In the generally accepted senses of the words 'think', 'feel', 'want', and so on through the whole list of psychological verbs, it is not true that houses think, mountains feel, or books want anything. If Leibniz's theory claimed the contrary, then it is empirically untenable. He probably would have agreed with this verdict, but would have argued that the words have a metaphysical meaning in which the claims he makes are not only true, but necessarily true. However, I am not too concerned with what exactly he would have said. The reason for this excursion into his views has been just to illustrate the point that one could still adopt a teleological metaphysical system even if one lived in a post-Galilean era. If I am right about this, it raises a rather disturbing question. Mightn't it still be open to *us* to embrace a systematically teleological world-view? Is there any rational reason why we should not switch back to an Aristotelian conceptual framework? In recent philosophy of science, there has been a tendency to regard scientific revolutions as social phenomena influenced to a great extent by non-rational factors. Fundamental changes of outlook have often been due to a chance mixture of two ingredients: an individual with great force of personality and powers of persuasion, and a community of scientists who, for various social and economic reasons, are receptive to change. Rational argument plays a relatively minor part. In several branches of science today there are competing paradigms, that is, competing views about what the science should be concerned with, what a good experiment should look like, what methods to use, how the field should develop, and so on. There are plenty of paradigms, especially in biology and the social sciences, which lay great emphasis on the usefulness of teleological explanations. Systems theory is one example. Many people hail it as a new metaphysic which will supersede the worn-out, atomistic and mechanistic paradigms that have been dominant for so long. In many respects, its basic concepts and methods hark back to Aristotelianism.

A further point, even more disturbing, is raised by our discussion of Leibniz. Given that Aristotle's opinions had such a profound influence on the entire development of Western thought, might it not be possible that our science retains traces of his teleology even today? Perhaps hidden teleological assumptions lie behind some of our most basic physical concepts, such as action, force, energy, work, and so on, though we don't realise it. A. J. Bernatowicz (1958), in an article deploring the use of teleological language in scientific textbooks, sees examples of it practically everywhere. Tell-tale signs of it, so he thinks, are the use of the infinitive verb in such contexts as 'The ammonia molecule can attach a proton to itself, to form an ammonium ion, NH_4+', and the preposition 'for' as in 'Each (molecule) bounds back and forth more and more vigorously in the little space left for it by its neighbours'. He quotes Erwin Schrödinger's view that the notion of force is a dangerous relic of animism. '"Force"', says Bernatowicz solemnly, 'a cornerstone of Newtonian physics, a word and a concept that pervade our language and our thinking – if this is suspect, then what of the vocabulary of the less exact sciences?'

I hope it is clear by now that the topic is important, and has far-reaching implications. It is also fraught with difficulties. To avoid needless confusion, one's first task, surely, is to be absolutely clear about what teleology is. What is it exactly to view a phenomenon teleologically? What is a teleological concept, and what is teleological language? How can one recognise when a word or phrase is being used teleologically? In the next chapter, I shall describe the method of analysis that I have chosen, and set out the plan of the book. Before doing so, however, I need to explain two basic assumptions, on which the method depends. There are lots of different ways of approaching this subject. I don't claim that my way is the only way. But I hope the reader will find these assumptions plausible, whatever his philosophical standpoint.

The first assumption is that there is a difference between saying that a movement is teleologically directed to a certain end and saying that the movement just happens *de facto* to go toward that end. The second is that one way, indeed the standard way, of offering a teleological explanation of why an event occurred is to say that it occurred *in order that* a second event should occur, or *in order to* produce a certain result. The explanation so offered may be false, invalid or totally inappropriate, but it *counts* as a teleological one in virtue of that form of words.

Anyone who asserts that a sequence of events was teleologically directed to the end at which it stopped takes himself to be making a substantive claim which goes beyond the claim that the sequence did in fact end at that point. He is claiming not only that the earlier parts led to the end, but that there was a press of events in that direction, such that the later event provides an understanding of why the earlier events occurred. This is the main characteristic of teleological explanations, and is what makes them so interesting and problematic. A teleological sequence of events is therefore clearly different from a coincidental sequence. But it is also different from an ordinary causal sequence, such as a hurricane causing a tree to fall down. A chain of events may unfold in accordance with strict causal laws, so that if you knew the laws and the initial conditions, you would be able to predict exactly how the chain would end. In such a case there is a sort of pressure for events to follow each other in that way, given that the whole process is governed by laws. But this is not enough to make the sequence teleological. Given the hurricane, the tree had to fall down, but the hurricane did not blow in order that the tree should fall down.

This point indicates that there is an ambiguity in Leibniz's dictum 'The present is pregnant with the future'. On one interpretation it is teleological, on the other it is not. If the universe obeyed deterministic laws, its total state at any time would determine all its subsequent states. Every present would, in a sense, be pregnant with what it is necessarily going to become. Someone who knew all the laws could view the present in the light of later events to which it must give rise, just as God can see in each monad its total future course of development laid out. However, Leibniz did not believe that monads just sit back and wait for their destiny to unfold. He thought that they actively strive after it. Monads have appetites, which are analogous to animal desires. They are therefore pregnant with the future in the stronger sense that their present state obtains *for the sake of* the future.

In order to clarify the concept of a teleological sequence, it is essential for me to have a 'base vocabulary' in which I can formulate propositions that are agreed to be non-teleological, as well as a vocabulary for formulating teleological propositions. Otherwise it would be impossible to express the contrast. I often use the terms '*de facto* movement' and '*de facto* tendency' for this job, when I want to describe a movement or a tendency without implying that it is for anything. I shall also use the verbs 'cause', 'lead to', and other active verbs which don't have built into their meaning that the actions they name are purposive.

What, though, of the suggestion that large chunks of our vocabulary may retain hidden teleological connotations? I agree that some verbs are implicitly teleological, e.g. 'seek', 'aim', 'try' and so on, but not all are, and certainly the non-specific verb 'to act' is not. Aristotle believed that all genuine action was end-directed because this was part of his concept of action. But it is not part of ours. If anyone wishes to define 'action' in this way, he may; but it means that he has to know whether a thing is end-directed before he can ascribe actions to it. However, using the word 'action' in the way it is commonly used, we do not need to know whether the subject is end-directed, or commit ourselves either way on this issue. I treat 'action' as a term that applies whenever anything does something. Thus, when the hurricane blew the tree down, it performed an action on the tree. A man who knocks over a vase thereby causing it to shatter has performed the action of breaking the vase, whether he intended to do so or not.

Nevertheless, the suggestion about hidden teleological assumptions deserves to be taken very seriously. It leads us to make a necessary distinction between overtly teleological statements, which explicitly assert that a connection between two things holds such that one is for the sake of the other, and covertly teleological statements, which imply or presuppose such a connection without asserting it. Not only statements but also words and phrases can be implicitly teleological; also a term can, without itself being implicitly teleological, be used in a particular context to convey a teleological implication. Such uses are difficult to identify – even the speaker may not be aware of the implications of his words. Clearly, the first thing to focus on is the nature of the teleological connection, so our attention must be turned to those forms of words which explicitly assert such a connection. That is why I make the second assumption. Other locutions would have done just as well, but I find it convenient to concentrate on sentences containing 'in order to' or 'in order that'. Their grammatical complexity mirrors the relational nature of teleology. A thing or event is described in the main clause, which is then further described, hence explained, by being related to the purpose cited in the subordinate clause.

The main clause may itself be implicitly teleological, as in the sentence 'Ripe apples seek the ground in order to find a place of rest'. This sentence can be used to assert an explicitly teleological explanation of the alleged fact that apples seek the ground. To show that it is incorrect, one would have to show a flaw in the relation between two terms, the explanans and the explanandum. It would not be enough to look at the explanandum alone. When one does look at the explanandum alone, however, one finds that it is roughly equivalent to 'Ripe apples fall in order to reach the ground', which is itself an explicit teleological explanation of the fact that apples fall. In general, if a thing being explained is already described in a way that has teleological overtones, and one wishes to query the validity of this description, one can always replace it by a sentence containing 'in order to' which is roughly equivalent in meaning. This brings the teleological relation into the open, and helps one to pose the relevant question: does this relation in fact hold? Having a standard form of words helps to locate the problem.

Apart from these two assumptions which underpin my method, I also take countless empirical facts for granted. It is impossible to list them all and give the grounds for believing them, nor is it necessary to do so, since they are undisputed. For instance, I assume that the world contains animals, vegetables and minerals; that some animals fabricate things, e.g. nests; that objects which are normally called 'inanimate', such as knives and forks, sticks and stones, really are inanimate; and so on. The method relies on accepted truths about many matters of fact in order to reach the truth about certain matters of meaning. At the end of the book, when the meanings of 'in order to' sentences have been worked out, we shall have a method by which to determine the truth-value of any particular teleological claim. We shall know how to set about answering big questions like 'Does everything in the universe have a purpose?', 'What is the purpose of life?', and 'Is evolution a goal-directed process?'. In some cases, where all the necessary factual information is already available, we shall actually be able to give a definite answer.

2

The method of analysis

The main idea behind my approach can be put very simply. I aim to understand teleology by teasing out the correct conditions for *describing* things teleologically. The raw materials required for this task are a range of sentences, plus a set of intuitions and arguments about when it is appropriate to use them. The sentences in question are those that contain 'in order to', 'in order that', 'for the sake of', 'for the purpose of', 'so as to', or simply 'to' where it is used as an abbreviation of 'in order to'. I call these *teleological sentences*. That is, I stipulate that if one of these linguistic expressions is present in a sentence in the right place, then the sentence is teleological. It is usually an easy matter to convert any such sentence into an equivalent sentence containing 'in order to' or 'in order that', so for convenience I take these as the standard form. Here are some examples:

(1) The man ran in order to catch the train.
(2) The cat opened the door in order to get the cream.
(3) The thermostat turned the heater off in order to stop the water going above a certain temperature.
(4) Witchcraft persecutions occur among the Navaho in order to lower intra-group hostility.
(5) The heart beats in order to circulate the blood.
(6) Knives have blades in order that they may cut.

At the end of the book I offer guidelines for paraphrasing such sentences into ones that do not contain 'in order to' or any of the other expressions, and which reveal the meanings of the originals in a perspicuous way.

The procedure for arriving at the paraphrases is to work on *teleological descriptions* (abbreviated to 'TDs'), i.e. statements that could be made by means of teleological sentences. By conducting thought experiments I try to discover the general conditions in which such statements are true. Once I have isolated a set of conditions which seems to be necessary and sufficient for the truth of a TD, I hypothesise that the TD asserts that the set of conditions holds, and that the sentence used to state the conditions is a paraphrase of the sentence used to make the TD. I take statements made by 'in order to' or 'in order that' sentences as the standard kind. Henceforth, it will always be these that I am talking about when I speak of 'TDs'.

Of course, every individual statement has its own individual truth-conditions. But generalisations can be made about their truth-conditions if one generalises over different kinds of subject-matter. The best way of abstracting from inessential differences between statements is to use *schematic TDs*, expressed by teleological sentences containing various letters of the alphabet as place-fillers for subjects and predicates of various types. For example, sentence (1), 'The man ran in order to catch the train', will be represented by the sentence-schema 'S did B in order to do G', where 'S' stands for a subject, 'B' stands for a bit of behaviour, and 'G' stands for a goal. But sentence (2) can be represented by the same schema, and so perhaps can (3). Strictly speaking, schematic TDs are not statements but forms of statements. One can speak, however, of the truth-conditions of a schematic TD, meaning the general conditions that must be satisfied by any particular TD of that form, and one can speak also of the meaning of a schematic TD.

But there is a limit to how far the abstracting process can go. TDs have to be grouped into types, because different *types* of conditions are satisfied by different TDs. Each type has to be represented by a *separate* schematic TD. Sentences (4) – (6), for example, will not be represented by the same schema as (1) – (3). The fact that each type has its own distinctive set of truth-conditions entails that each type has its own analysans or paraphrase. This does not necessarily mean that 'in order to' is ambiguous – the differences might be due to differences in the other components of the sentence.[1] It might depend on the category of the items which the schematic letters stand for. But even if it should turn out that 'in order to' is not univocal, it might be possible to trace affinities between its various senses. This is the next best thing to univocality.

In what sense does this enterprise amount to a theory of teleology? On the face of it, the exercise might appear to be purely linguistic. It starts with intuitions about the meanings of sentences, and ends up

---

[1] A similar point is made by Roger Wertheimer (1972, ch. 2, pp. 63–4). He argues that differences in paraphrasability may be due to factors other than the meaning(s) of a certain word, since 'the information (not the meanings per se) carried by the rest of the sentence may suggest one rather than another paraphrase of the word.'

with explicit paraphrases of them. I think the main interest, though, lies in what goes on in between. Although the analyses will not, I hope, be counterintuitive, the method of deriving them is not by direct intuitions of synonymy, but through a detailed investigation of necessary and sufficient conditions of the truth of TDs. Teleological sentences are frequently used in daily life; people evidently believe that the statements they make with them are often true. My method takes it for granted that TDs *can be true*, so that I can examine what in the world would make them true. The clearcut linguistic criterion of a teleological sentence enables me provisionally to demarcate the range of teleological phenomena, but I take teleology to be primarily a feature of the phenomena themselves. It is the fact that *they* are teleological which makes it appropriate to use teleological sentences to describe them. To have a clear understanding of what makes a TD true is to know what teleology really is; if there are several types of TD, this is because there are several types of teleology to be described. I am not trying to reduce teleology to anything else. Although the sentences that I offer as paraphrases will not count as teleological sentences by my linguistic criterion, and nor therefore will statements made by them count as explicit TDs, nevertheless the facts which make such statements true will show what teleology really is, since they will be the same facts that make TDs true.[2]

I do not think that anything controversial is being claimed here. A theory of teleology is presumably something that provides an answer to the question 'What is teleology?'. The most natural way of interpreting the question, initially at least, is as a request for an explanation of what the technical, unfamiliar word 'teleology' means. It is not the name of an entity but of a pattern of relations. After it has been settled exactly what the relations are, there may be nothing further that the questioner needs to know. Later he may wonder how things can get into such relations, or he may speculate about how often they are exemplified, but these are further questions that go beyond, and presuppose an answer to, the first question. The case would be different if one were considering, say, the questions 'What is colour?' or 'What is heat?'. The words 'colour' and 'heat' are not philosophers' jargon; every normal English-speaker knows what they mean. It is

---

[2] Compare L. J. Cohen's approach in 'Teleological Explanation', (1950), where he treats the presence of 'in order to' or its cognates as the grammatical sign of teleology. My treatment owes a great deal to Cohen's sophisticated paper.

natural, therefore, to interpret the questions differently, as requests for a scientific explanation or reduction of properties that are already identified. One can cite the date when scientists first discovered that heat is mean molecular kinetic energy, but one cannot say when scientists first discovered what teleology really is. That is not something that ever needed to be settled by an empirical investigation. The main problem is to define it.

A corollary of my approach is that it is absurd to suppose that scientists might discover that there is no such thing as teleology, in the same way that they discovered that there was no such thing as phlogiston. A philosopher or linguist might analyse the meaning of the theoretical term 'phlogiston' unconcerned about whether there exists any substance answering to that name. 'Teleology', however, does not purport to name a substance. There must be teleology if teleological descriptions are sometimes true.

The semantic investigation is linked, via realism, to metaphysics. At each level there is an analytical component and a taxonomic component to the investigation. On the level of language I ask 'What is it to describe things teleologically, and how many types of TD are there?'. On the level of reality I ask 'What is teleology, and how many types of it are there?'. There is also a third level on which the business may be conducted – the level of concepts. One might say that my two tasks were to analyse the concept of teleology, and to work out how many subconcepts there are. But this is slightly obscure. It is not clear whose concepts are being referred to, nor is it clear what a concept is meant to be. Since I often speak of concepts, especially when pursuing topics that stray far from explicit TDs, a few remarks are needed.

I take it that to have the concept of, say, a triangle, is to be able to think about or be aware of triangles. The evidence of concept-possession is recognising, discriminating, classifying, and, where applicable, using words correctly. Each individual's concepts are his own, but as we learn from and communicate with each other, our habits of classifying and naming tally to a great extent. Insofar as one can speak of *the* (shared) meaning of the word 'triangle' in English, one may also speak of *the* concept of a triangle shared by people who communicate their thoughts in English. Indeed, one can pool the concepts of all the people who speak a language that has a word for triangle, or who recognise a similarity in kind between triangles. One can speak of their, or our, or *the* common concept of a triangle. A person does not need to be able to state what 'triangle' means, or to state by what criteria he groups things together as triangles, in order to have the concept of a triangle. But he may be able to state the criteria. If he can, he not only has the concept, he can also make it explicit. Analysing concepts, in one sense, is simply attempting to make explicit the criteria for application of words that everybody knows how to use.

But not every word or phrase corresponds to a concept. Normally the word has to be a noun or noun-phrase. It would be inappropriate to speak of the concept of *to*, or the concept of *in order to*. Nor is it possible to analyse our shared concept of X, if 'X' is not a word in common use. The word 'teleology' is not in common use. There is, however, an enterprise that might be called 'analysing our *implicit* concept of teleology'. The first step is to announce that everybody who uses sentences containing 'in order to' has, *ipso facto*, an implicit concept of teleology. The second step is to assert that the process of making explicit the rules which people conform to in their use of such sentences counts as analysing the shared concept(s). On this interpretation, conceptual analysis is identical with analysis of the meaning of TDs.

There is, however, a subset of the past and present population that does use the word 'teleology', in their writings if not in speech. It comprises, principally, some philosophers and theologians and a few scientists. Would it not be possible to analyse *their* implicit concept of teleology in just the same way that one can analyse our implicit concept of a triangle? Certain complications would attend such a task. The main factor is that these writers, aware that the word is technical, usually try to explain their use of it for the benefit of the readers. They may give an explicit definition, or they may indicate that they are taking a certain definition for granted. This shows that they themselves have a more or less explicit concept of teleology, which a reader is able to discern straight off. A writer who reflects about the meaning of a word is unlikely to use it in a way that conflicts with his stated definition. Conflict is not impossible, of course; the reader may have to interpret what the writer says he means in the light of other indirect evidence about what he means. The fact that the word 'teleology' tends to be used in a self-conscious way changes the nature of the task of analysis.

It is unreasonable to suppose that different writers' *explicit* concepts can be pooled together to yield a single shared concept. On the contrary, there is every reason to expect antagonisms and incompatibilities. In philosophical literature, the word nearly always appears in the context of a discussion *about* the nature or status of teleology. These texts are often reactions against, or endorsements of, previous views. Each philosopher who has his own opinions on the subject may be said to have his own distinctive concept. One can analyse Aristotle's, or Leibniz's, or Kant's, but now 'analysing' just means studying what they each say.

I conceive my task of analysing TDs as a process of theory construction, the conclusions of which are empirical hypotheses about what TDs mean. I would not like it to be thought that I have simply invented meanings. I claim that these meanings, these conclusions about what teleology really is, are actually implicit in our usage. This claim may be wrong; perhaps I have ignored crucial data, or generalised poorly from such data as I do consider. Perhaps someone else will construct a simpler, more elegant theory out of the same data. The procedure that I follow is a straightforward synthesis of current techniques. The *basic* method is as follows: Adopt tentatively and provisionally a scheme of classification for TDs, peferably one that is currently accepted. Invent a hypothesis, or borrow one from some other philosopher, to the effect that a TD of a certain type is true if and only if conditions A, B, C . . . hold. Test it by trying to think of counterexamples. Try to imagine situations where a TD of that type is false even though the conditions hold, and situations where the conditions do not hold, but where a TD is true. If such situations can be envisaged, refine the hypothesis by adding more conditions if the proposed set is insufficient, or by subtracting some if not all of them are necessary, or by changing some. This creates a new hypothesis which is tested in the same way in new imagined situations. If necessary, it too is refined, turned into a new hypothesis, which is then tested . . . and so on, until one reaches a set of conditions that is necessary and sufficient for the truth of any TD of that type in any imaginable situation. Hypothesise that the reason for this is that the conditions explicate the meaning of the TD.

A similar process is gone through for each type of TD. It may prove impossible to distil out such a set of general conditions in every case. If that happens, one must assume that the schematic TD that one has been taking as respresentative of a single type actually represents a mixture of two or more types. Working on the principle that it is desirable not to multiply types unnecessarily, one must try to assimilate the anomalous TDs to other types. If this is impossible within the confines of the original classification scheme, one must think of revising the scheme, creating a new one that is more economical on types. Since the best scheme is the one that recognises only as many types as there are autonomous sets of truth conditions, the taxonomical and analytical tasks proceed hand in hand. Each type of TD is analogous to a biological species. A species contains a number of varieties; separate species do not interbreed: but species of the same genus exhibit family resemblances. Similarly, TDs of the same type have a variety of truth-conditions, but their truth-conditions are all of the same type; different types of TD do not share truth-conditions with each other; but they may be said to belong to the same genus, if there exist similarities between their respective truth-conditions.

However, this is a somewhat oversimplified account. On top of this, there are certain principles, concerning the relative weighting of data, the conditions under which first intuitions may be overriden, and what to do when intuitions conflict. They enter the picture when one makes decisions which the data do not dictate. In the main, I think they are adaptations, tailored to specific circumstances, of very general principles of scientific theory construction, such as the principle of parsimony and the principle of simplicity. The analyses given in chapter 12 will be the end result of a process of adjusting, trimming and polishing, guided by a desire for system. I want them to be acceptable as paraphrases, but I also want them to reveal underlying structural affinities between different types of TD. Takèn together, they should show what the different uses of 'in order to' have in common. The whole process should count as a unified theory of teleological description.

Because teleology is a rather intricate topic, the actual working out of the programme necessarily involves discussing some side-issues. It may be difficult at times to see how parts of the argument fit into this overall structure. Much of the discussion is conducted in the object-language, and may not appear at first to be about the meaning of TDs at all. For example, I ask in Parts Two and Four what features are necessary and sufficient in order for behaviour to count as goal-directed. But this is just a shorthand way of asking what the behaviour must be like in order to be *truly described* by means of a certain type of 'in order to' sentence.

The question of objectivity

I now turn to an important issue that needs to be resolved before the programme can begin. My aim of discovering the truth-conditions of TDs is predicated on the assumption that TDs *can be* objectively true or false. But is this assumption correct? Some philosophers have believed that teleology is not an objective feature of things and events, but that it arises out of the way we, the conceptualising observers, view them. Their position would be that TDs are not empirical statements. TDs are not false, nor are they reducible to non-teleological descriptions; the question of truth and falsity just does not arise. Their role in discourse is to express a way of looking at the world that does not make any empirical claims, although it may be suggestive of them.

In our earlier discussion of Leibniz, it was said that his theory about the teleology of monads was not empirically testable. This was because monads are supposed to be purely metaphysical entities that lie forever beyond the world of actual or possible observations. No empirical tests can touch them. Their existence is supposed to be guaranteed by reason, not by experience. For Leibniz, the proposition that monads strive after their ends is necessarily true. But the view we are now considering does not say this. It says that teleological statements are not true at all, but are merely interpretative. The view presupposes a distinction between descriptions, which can be either true or false, and interpretations, which are neither true nor false, but it does not entail any particular view about what objects there are to be described or interpreted.

The question to be settled is: Where is teleology really located – in reality, in language, or in the mind? I have presumed that the presence of teleological connectives in descriptions is to be justified by reference to the presence of objective features in what those descriptions describe. The alternative view, which I shall call *projectionism*, is that TDs project on to things a 'property' which the things do not really possess. The average man does not know this. He thinks he is saying something about things when he uses teleological sentences. According to projectionism, this is an illusion. What he is really doing is metaphorically projecting his own teleological attitudes on to the world. He is saying, in effect, 'It looks to me as if an intelligence has been at work here'. His utterance masquerades as a categorical assertion about reality, but really it expresses his own state of mind. Probably the most illustrious proponent of a theory of natural teleology which is basically projectionist was Kant. It is crucial for me to face up to projectionism, because my search for truth-conditions would be futile if TDs couldn't ever be true.

To clarify the issue, we need to make some distinctions and establish a provisional classification scheme. Every TD ascribes a *purpose* to the entity that it describes. The man running has the purpose of catching the train, the knife has a blade for the purpose of cutting, and so on. However, 'purpose' seems to be used in different ways in these two examples. The man's purpose is his intention or goal, but a knife blade or a knife does not have intentions. Knives have a purpose in virtue of the fact that men create and use knives for a purpose. Men desire to cut, they make tools which enable them to cut, and then they cut with those tools. Knives play such an important role in the cutting that we shift the responsibility for the job on to them by saying that *they* cut. By a parallel process, the standard purpose of users and makers of knives becomes transferred to the knives. In general, the purposes that artefacts have are borrowed from the purposes of their users and designers, and they 'have' them in a different sense. Let us restrict the term 'purpose' to its first context of employment, and speak of 'functions', instead of 'purposes' in the secondary employment. The most familiar kinds of purposes are human intentions, the most familiar kinds of functions are ones that are bestowed upon objects by human intentions.

The class of items with functions conferred by human intentions is not coextensive with the class of man-made artefacts. Human beings exploit things that they find as well as things that they make. For a thing to have a function conferred by human intention, the criterion of intentional use may be sufficient. Moreover, the fact that a thing is a man-made artefact is not enough to give it a human function. Some products, e.g. works of fine art, are not designed to fulfil any function. Still, both the design criterion and the use criterion involve relating the thing to human intentions in one way or another. I shall say that functions conferred by human intention are functions on the 'artefact-model'.

However, some of the things that humans find seem to have functions *already*, independently of human intention. First, some things in the world are artefacts created by species other than man. These seem to have functions for those species in roughly the same sense that man-made artefacts have functions for man. The relationship between a spider and its web, for instance, is similar to that between a fisherman and his net. The spider makes the web, the fisherman makes the net; the web helps the spider to catch food, the net helps the fisherman to catch food. The fisherman's net has the function of catching fish because the man uses the net to further his purpose of catching fish. It is tempting to explain in a parallel way why the web has the function of catching flies. The web has that function, we may say, because the spider uses it to further his purpose of catching flies. We simply generalise the relevant relationship between the user and the tool. This explanation commits us to ascribing purposes to spiders. So long as sense can be made of *that*, there is no problem about making sense of the functional ascription through the artefact model.

The second category of items with functions that are not humanly intended presents a bigger problem. These items are *parts* of animals, of plants, and of other organic wholes, including human beings. For example, the heart of an animal has a function for that animal, but animals neither create their own hearts, nor do they use them intentionally to further their purposes (except in exceptional cases).

It has already been mentioned that an animal or vegetable may be given a function by human beings when they use it as an instrument. This applies to animal and vegetable *parts* too. It may be extended, by the analogy above, to cover cases where species other than man use animal or vegetable parts as instruments. But these cases are quite different from the ones intended here, where the part performs a natural function for its owner. Nearly all living components have functions in this sense, regardless of whether they serve the purposes of any beings other than their owners.

So the sense in which organs have functions cannot be related directly to human intentions, nor indeed, if such be admitted at all, to animal intentions. Those who wish to stick with the artefact model are forced to cast around for other sources of intention, such as God, or Mother Nature.

Suppose though that a god existed and that all the things in the world (in particular living things) were his *creaturae*. Suppose that he designed the parts of each organism so that they would fit together harmoniously each with its own special job. The job assigned to each organ would be its function in the familiar sense. But how could we ever be sure that an organ was doing what the god intended it to do? We should need a way of identifying the god's intentions that was independent of how things actually happened. Until we had such a line of access, functional hypotheses would be unverifiable. So the appeal to a god's intentions does provide an account of what it *means* to assign natural functions, but at the price of making it impossible to identify any with certainty. And, of course, it relies on that initial assumption of the god's existence.

Artefact-modellers in search of something more sophisticated – Kant, for instance – gravitate towards projectionism at this point. They say that to talk of natural functions is to speak *as if* natural objects had been designed, without committing oneself on whether they actually were designed. If we personify Nature, we can imagine anything in nature to be an artefact of Nature. When we think of, say, a river as something that Nature intended should exist for its own sake, we think of it, to use Kant's terminology, as an End of Nature (*Zweck der Natur*), possessing 'intrinsic finality' or 'internal teleology'.[3] If we think of the river as something that Nature created as a means to some other end, e.g. 'to facilitate international intercourse in inland countries' we think of it as having 'extrinsic finality' or 'external teleology', relative to that imagined end. A thing has extrinsic finality only if it actually is a means to something which is an end of nature, but there are no empirical constraints on what may be supposed to be an end of nature.

Kant believed, however, that there is a certain class of things, organisms, which it is especially inviting to think of as ends of nature. Indeed, he says (p. 24) that 'organisms are ... the only beings in nature that, considered in their separate existence and apart from any relation to other things, cannot be thought possible except as ends of nature'. There are two reasons for this. First, according to Kant, we cannot conceive of any way in which organisms could have arisen except by design, because their parts are so intricately fitted together. We naturally presume that a conception of the whole, i.e. a plan, guided the assembling process. Secondly, Kant says that the parts of the organism influence each other's development in such a way that the form of the whole is maintained. This is a phenomenon not found in human artefacts. Clearly, a maker of organisms would need far greater powers than a watchmaker. These are the two criteria in virtue of which organisms count as '*Naturzwecke*' ('physical ends'), and afford the first idea that there really are such things as ends of nature.

Now what exactly is the status of the judgment that an organism is

[3] Kant (1790, trans. J. C. Meredith, 1928). All references are to the Meredith edition.

a physical end? The judgment involves, by the first criterion, the claim that an organism is an end of nature, i.e. that nature intended that it should exist. Since nature does not literally have intentions, this claim is not objective. *No* judgment that a thing is an end of nature can be objective, whether the thing be a river or an organism. The second criterion, on the other hand, is extremely obscure. The parts must 'combine of themselves into the unity of a whole by being reciprocally cause and effect of their form' (p. 21). If this were simply a matter of efficient causation, it would surely be objective. But Kant believes that the idea of *final* causation is involved here, since 'the thing that for the moment is designated effect deserves none the less, if we take the series regressively, to be called the cause of the thing of which it was said to be the effect' (p. 20). To understand the dynamic interrelations between the components of an organism, we need to think of the whole as somehow guiding and co-ordinating the various causal processes that take place inside it. But this is not an objective matter either. A whole cannot really determine the disposition of its own parts. The idea of the whole is functioning here as 'the epistemological basis upon which the systematic unity of the form and combination of all the manifold contained in the given matter becomes cognizable for the person estimating it' (p. 21). By thinking of the activities of the parts as done for the sake of the whole we can systematise a mass of otherwise disparate observations.

By neither criterion is it an objective fact that an organism has intrinsic finality, and nor, therefore, is it an objective fact that organs have functions (extrinsic finality). We, the conceptualising observers, project teleology on to an organism by subsuming it under the concept of a physical end. 'The concept of a thing as intrinsically a physical end is, therefore, not a constitutive conception either of understanding or of reason, but yet it may be used by reflective judgement as a regulative conception for guiding our investigation of objects of this kind by a remote analogy with our own causality according to ends generally, and as a basis of reflexion on their supreme source ... It may be that the ends in question only reside in the idea of the person forming the estimate and not in any efficient cause whatever' (pp. 24–5).

There are many points of interest in Kant's theory which I cannot go into.[4] The main point here is that it is a version of projectionism. Kant concludes that teleological judgments are not 'constitutive',

---

[4] For a more detailed account, see J. D. McFarland (1970).

but are 'regulative' or heuristic. Under Kant's influence other philosophers have built a reference to how things seem to an observer into
their definitions of teleology. Broad (1925, p. 82), for example, defines
a 'teleological system' as one 'composed of such parts arranged in such
ways as *might have been expected* (my emphasis) *if* it had been constructed by an intelligent being to fulfil a certain purpose which he had
in mind', and such that 'if we use this hypothesis as a clue to more
minute investigation, we continue to find that the system is constructed
as if the hypothesis were true'. Broad builds an epistemological element
into the *content* of the judgment that a thing is a teleological system.

However, Kant's arguments afford no reason for thinking that *all*
teleological judgments are non-objective. He argues that to see a
thing as teleological is to view it as if it were designed, leaving open the
question of whether it was designed. But if later it were discovered that
the thing really had been designed, surely this would make it objectively teleological. It would be absurd to maintain that an object
designed by an intelligent being for a purpose does *not* have a function,
on the grounds that it goes beyond *seeming* to have been designed for a
purpose. Thus there is at least one kind of teleological judgment that
has objective empirical content, namely a judgment about the function of a known artefact. The issue of whether or not an object is
teleological in this sense is quite independent of how we the judgers
conceive the object, although, of course, it is crucially dependent upon
how the designer or user conceives it. Functionality is not a proper
property of the object like size or structure; that the object has a
function depends on its standing in certain relations to other things.
But relational properties are not necessarily subjective. It may well be
an objective fact that the object does stand in the relevant relation to a
designer or user.

Kant's problem about objectivity arises only in connection with
natural functions. It arises because Kant does not wish to make his
theory depend on a *commitment* that organisms are artefacts. He
therefore analyses the concept of a natural function as the concept of
an apparently intended function. For him, 'X has a natural function'
means 'X seems to have an intended function'. Let us be clear, however, that if bodily parts really had been designed for a purpose, then
they really would have functions in the same *sense* that familiar artefacts have functions. It would make sense to ask whether they really
have the intended functions that they seem to have. Anyone who
construes natural function statements as analogical is committed to

holding that artefact function statements are literal. It is the literal use of the word 'function' which identifies the *kind* of teleology in question. An analysis of TDs would pin down the key features of this *kind* of teleology by examining what makes statements about the functions of artefacts true.

Actually, Kant's view that natural function-statements are meta-phorical because they borrow their sense from the artefact-model may not be correct. Although *some* biological function-statements may seem metaphorical, some seem to be literally false (e.g. 'Noses exist in order to support spectacles'), and some seem literally true. We often think that we can identify the function of an organ despite the fact that we do not know whether the organ was intended to do that by a designer. There appears to be a different type of teleology here, not assimilable to the artefact-model. In Part Three I try to clarify this. Whatever the correct analysis of these TDs may be, there is a strong presumption that they make at least *some* objective claims on reality.

A second type of projectionist thesis concerns the ascription of *purposes* to animals. It can be dealt with along similar lines. The thesis is that whenever we judge that an animal has a purpose or goal, we are not putting forward an empirical hypothesis, but are adopting an anthropomorphic attitude towards the animal. We are viewing it as if it had a mental state similar to one that a human being might have, and thereby making it more intelligible to ourselves. For example, when we say that the spider weaves its web in order to catch flies, we imagine the spider intending to catch flies, though the spider does not literally intend this, or anything else.

Suppose, for the sake of argument, that this view were correct. Would it show that *all* purposiveness resided in the mind of the con-ceptualising observer? On the contrary, given that the metaphorical ascriptions of purposes borrow their meaning from central cases which are not metaphorical, there must be literal ascriptions of purposes. An analysis of this *kind* of teleology would concentrate on TDs of human behaviour first, work out their objective truth-conditions, then show how situations where not all the conditions hold may yet be inter-preted on analogy with situations where all the conditions do hold. I take it that the statement that a fisherman made his net in order to catch fish can be literally true, and analysis might reveal that one of the necessary conditions of its truth is that the fisherman intended to catch fish with it. Whether the fisherman had that intention is an objective matter, even if intentions are, as some would say, subjective entities, i.e. states of mind. Having established this, we may turn to more problematic TDs, like 'The spider wove its web in order to catch flies'. If we decide that this one is indeed metaphorical, as the projectionist claims, then we cannot say that it has a set of necessary and sufficient truth-conditions. But we can treat it as having the same semantic structure and components as literal TDs from which the metaphor is presumably derived. Then we can say that it has something analogous to a set of truth-conditions, which stands in the same relation to a set of genuine truth-conditions as the relation between the whole TD and the TD about the fisherman. The analysis will lead us to say that part of its meaning is that the spider intended to catch flies, but that this is a metaphor, just as the whole was. Indeed, this component is the main source of the metaphor. The other components of the meaning of the TD, as distilled out by the method of parallel analysis, may turn out to be non-metaphorical. This method has the virtue, therefore, of locating the factors which prevent certain TDs from having a truth-value. It enables us to explain *why* these TDs are metaphorical.

A general reply, then, can be given to any form of projectionism. Even if ascriptions of purposes to a lot of things are analogical, it must be the case that ascriptions to some things are literal, because the analogues derive their meaning from the literal ones. My method is not undermined, because I focus on the literal ones, and I take these as defining the *kind* of teleology under investigation.

I remarked earlier in passing that the projectionist view of natural functions was implausible anyway. The extreme projectionist view of animal goals, that all ascriptions of goals to non-human animals are anthropomorphic, is equally implausible. It is plain that chimpanzees, for example, have goals, even though they cannot (with a few exceptions) communicate them linguistically. No doubt there are some species whose members do not literally have goals. Certainly, to ascribe them to *plants* would be anthropomorphic. But as we go up the animal evolutionary scale there is more justification for thinking that animals exist which really do have goals of their own, and would have even if no human being thought it so. Large chunks of this book are devoted to the analysis of goal-directed behaviour, which I assume to be objectively present in higher animals. It is interesting that the two main problem areas, goal-directed behaviour and natural functions, both fall under the heading of *immanent* teleology, as it was defined in chapter 1.

Topics that are bypassed

A number of issues which have been associated with the problem of teleology in other discussions are omitted from mine. These issues fall roughly into two groups: ones that are irrelevant to teleology as I conceive it, and ones that are relevant but outside my scope. An example of the former is the issue of backward causation.

Many of the traditional problems about teleology sprang from the peculiar conceptions of it that prominent thinkers had, or from erroneous opinions about it which became uncritically accepted. Some writers have believed that all teleological explanations must be false, on the grounds that final causation is defined as a kind of efficient causation where the cause happens after its effect, and no such reversed causal connection ever obtains. Some would say that backward causation is *logically* impossible, while others would say that it could happen, though as a matter of fact it never does. It is not necessary for me, however, to investigate the matter. Backward causation is a red herring in the present discussion, since final causation is not defined in that way.

Suppose, for the sake of argument, that backward causation not only makes sense, but happens quite frequently. What bearing would this have upon our analysis of TDs? Teleological explanation cannot possibly be committed to any reversed causal hypothesis, for a very simple reason. The hypothesis that a certain type of event which occurs at t_1 is efficiently caused by an event of a certain type which occurs at a later time t_2 asserts or presupposes that an event of the second type does occur at t_2. If t_2 is in the future relative to the time the hypothesis is made, it asserts or presupposes that an event of the relevant type will occur. The failure of such an event to occur would conclusively falsify the hypothesis, or render it void. But TDs are capable of being true whether or not the event cited as the purpose *occurs*. It may be true that the man ran in order to catch the train, though he failed to catch the train; a knife may be made for the purpose of cutting, yet it may never actually cut; and so on, for all types of TDs. It is impossible, therefore, to construe the concept of a purpose as the concept of an efficient cause of a temporally antecedent effect. This would be so even if it were the case that on every occasion when the purpose does occur, the event which is the purpose of the earlier action or event happened also to be a retroactive efficient cause. The concepts would still be completely different. Since the truth of any TD about a sequence of events is unaffected by whether or not backward causation was operating in that sequence, I feel justified in bypassing that vexed topic completely.

I turn, finally, to certain issues that are relevant, but outside my self-imposed scope. The first has to do with a limitation that is inherent in my method. Suppose that, as the analysis progressed, it revealed that every kind of teleology grows out of the kind which involves intentions. A stage is eventually reached where the analysans of every kind of TD makes some reference to an intention. A general question then arises about how far an analysis can or should go. Might it not be possible to paraphrase statements of intention in turn by stating *their* truth-conditions? Now an analysis of this kind cannot continue beyond statements of intention unless there is some method, available to any competent maker of such statements, of identifying and describing the state of affairs that constitutes a person P's intending to do A, independently of the identification and description of it as 'P's intending to do A'. But the concept of intending may be primitive. We may not be able to state what conditions need to hold in order for it to be true that a person has an intention. Even if neurologists discovered the relevant conditions, to state them would not count as analysing what is meant by 'P intends to do A'. At the point where truth-conditions cease to be discoverable by pure thought and reflection on usage, the revealing of truth-conditions cannot contribute towards meaning-analysis. So statements assigning intentions or equivalent states of mind may well represent a limit for analyses of this type.

My method relies on the fact that explicit TDs, like that expressed by 'The man ran in order to catch the train', are *not* conceptually primitive, but are complex propositions containing or implying simpler component propositions. The proposition that the man intended or wanted to catch the train may turn out to be one of the embedded components. The analytical process is complete when every clause of the paraphrase contains a sentence whose meaning cannot be further analysed by the same method. The final aim is to identify what these clauses are, and how they are connected. Perhaps it is superfluous to add that my method does not require the analysans to be a *truth-function* of its constituent propositions. In fact, at least one of the connectives in it is going to be non-truth functional. This does not prevent the analysans, as a single, integrated statement, from being either true or false.

Other topics, like the nature of efficient causation, and the relations between teleological explanations and other types of explanation, just have to be omitted through lack of space. Both of these raise wider issues which go beyond the study of teleology. As far as the former is concerned, I have had to assume that the concept of cause is familiar enough to be employed without being analysed in this context. The word 'cause' crops up in many places; indeed, a causal clause will figure in the analysans of every TD. My interpretation of the meaning of causal statements is not esoteric – on the contrary, I agree with the standard empiricist neo-Millian account, as elucidated by Mackie (1965). But it is not possible or necessary for me to delve into the nature of causation when my aim is to elucidate teleology. A reader may agree (or disagree) with what I say about the role of the causal clause in the analyses, whatever his views about causal necessity, causal laws, etc. may be.

There is a great deal in current literature about the role and status of teleological explanations in science, especially biology. Much of it is directed to the question whether teleological explanations are reducible to causal explanations. Many philosophers regard this as the most important problem in the whole area. Although my analysis implicitly provides an answer, I try not to approach the question directly. To answer it properly, one would need to subject the concept of *reduction* to thorough analysis. What is supposed to *count* as reducing one form of explanation to another? Would it be to pair every teleological explanation with a causal explanation that had the same explanandum, or to replace every teleological explanation by a causal explanation that explained the same explanandum *in the same way*? Would it be like reducing one *theory* to another? The term 'reduce' has many different uses. I try to avoid it as far as possible, in the hope of avoiding attendant confusions.

In any case, it is impossible to say whether teleological explanations are reducible to causal explanations unless one knows exactly what a teleological explanation is. I prefer to call 'in order to' statements teleological *descriptions* rather than teleological *explanations*, only because it shows that I am concentrating on the cognitive meaning of such statements, and not worrying too much about their explanatory force. Admittedly, in this context the terms 'description' and 'explanation' are more or less interchangeable. TDs are intrinsically explanatory statements; to determine what they mean *is* to determine in what way they are explanatory. I am not concerned, however, with whether they are scientifically respectable, or conform to the deductive-nomological pattern.

The method may now be summarised. First I demarcate the area of study provisionally by a *grammatical* criterion, giving the name 'Teleological Description' (TD) to any statement made by a sentence containing the words 'in order to' or 'in order that' or cognate expressions. This step provides a simple linguistic procedure for identifying teleological explanations which is independent of any considerations about their meaning. Second, I take it that some TDs are capable of being literally true. Statements like (1) – (6) are usually made by people in the belief that they convey factual information. The ordinary speaker of English might not be able to state in precise terms what such TDs mean, but he is sure that they make some objective claims about reality. Third, given this basic premiss that TDs can be objectively true or false, one can raise the question 'Under what circumstances is a TD true?' One aims to elucidate their meanings, not by the route of direct paraphrase, but by discovering the necessary and sufficient conditions for their truth. TDs can then be grouped into different types according to the different types of truth-conditions they need to satisfy. My approach is antagonistic to the 'projectionist' or 'subjectivist' view that TDs are necessarily anthropomorphic, metaphorical or animistic. Some are, and some are not; there is nothing about their *form* which prevents them from being literally true. The following TD is clearly a metaphor: '. . . the glass case where five little dolls with pendent bare legs awaited the impact of a coin in order to come to life and revolve'.[5] But metaphors borrow their force from cases in which purposes are ascribed literally. None of the sentences (1) – (6) is metaphorical, in any case.

The following chapters are arranged into four sections, corresponding to the kinds of teleology that are dealt with in them. Part Two examines the theories of Braithwaite, Sommerhoff, Nagel and Taylor, which are attempts to characterise goal-directedness in behavioural terms. They are criticised on the grounds that they provide neither necessary nor sufficient conditions of goal-directedness, and that they give an incorrect account of the way TDs explain. The various arguments are generalised in chapter 6, and two pathways for further research are indicated. Part Three is an analysis of TDs which ascribe functions, as distinct from goals. Particular attention is paid to biological functions, and to the way natural functional explanations

[5] Vladimir Nabokov, *The Defence*, p. 15.

work. Part Four returns to goals, and explores the two pathways of externalism and internalism that were distinguished earlier. The reason why things have to be done in this order is that externalism builds upon the notion of function that is developed in Part Three. In the end, however, internalism proves to be the better approach. Chapters 10 and 11 are devoted to finding out which version of internalism is the true one. Part Five brings all the analyses together, and exhibits their structural similarities. The parallels are striking enough to justify the conclusion that the different types of teleological explanations are variations on a single theme.

PART TWO

GOAL-DIRECTED BEHAVIOUR

3

Braithwaite's plasticity theory

When behaviourism started to be a dominant trend in psychology, in the first two decades of this century, its theoreticians were pressed to supply objective, non-mentalistic criteria of purposive action. Men like Watson and Perry felt that unless a behaviourist account could be given any reference to human or animal purposes must be methodologically unsound. The objections would be, roughly, that ascribing purposes to animals is anthropomorphic, and that reports on human purposes rely upon introspective evidence. If these objections are valid (they thought) all descriptions couched in teleological language should be expunged from behaviourist psychology. But to banish those phenomena which naturally call for teleological descriptions would deprive the new science of a large part of its subject-matter.

In biology at about the same time, tedious and conceptually confused disputes were still raging between mechanists and vitalists. They spurred on scientists like L. von Bertalanffy, E. Rignano and E. S. Russell to produce a synthesis which would make the two factions obsolete. These men felt that the investigation of so-called final causes can and must be reconciled with the study of efficient causes, because both perspectives are essential for the full understanding of biological processes. They believed that teleology, so far from necessarily implying a transcendent mind that controls the organism from above, need not even involve assigning a mind to the organism itself.

Thus it was that behaviourist psychologists and organismic biologists converged, in a manner that was illustrative of the teleology they were seeking, upon the same idea: that the hallmark of a goal-directed process is the constancy of the final state in the face of variations in the initial conditions and starting-points. This property is objective, and empirically testable. It can be used to explain why teleology was often felt to be a kind of backward causation. One may use knowledge of the result to forecast which way the process will go, as if the future were dragging the process towards it. Also the property is very prevalent throughout the living world. Organismic biologists believe that since consciously purposive behaviour seems to be merely a special case of it, the discovery of this teleonomic property helps to unify the study of man with the study of other organisms.

Various attempts to describe the property were made, but the first *formal* characterisation was provided by R. B. Braithwaite. He took his cue from the biologist E. S. Russell.

'There are,' says Russell, 'certain general or normal characteristics of all goal-directed activity (whatever its biological end) which may be summarised as follows:

(1) When the goal is reached, action ceases; the goal is normally a terminus of action.

(2) If the goal is not reached, action usually persists.

(3) Such action may be varied:

(a) If the goal is not reached by one method, other methods may be employed;

(b) where the goal is normally reached by a combination of methods, deficiency of one method may be compensated for by increased use of other methods.

(4) The same goal may be reached in different ways, and from different beginnings; the end-state is more constant than the method of reaching it.

(5) Goal-directed activity is limited by conditions, but is not determined by them.' (Russell, 1945, p. 110.)

In his 1946 paper 'Teleological Explanation', and in ch. X of his book *Scientific Explanation*, Professor Braithwaite focusses his attention on the non-conscious goal-directed behaviour of organisms. The theory claims to be able to deal with the goal-directed behaviour of certain inanimate systems too, like pilotless planes. He recognises that the mere fact that a piece of behaviour comes to a definite end is not enough to warrant a teleological description of it; indeed, he criticises Bertrand Russell's theory of desire in *The Analysis of Mind*, ch. 3, for its failure to provide an adequate criterion of the end of a behaviour-cycle. Not all states of temporary quiescence are teleological ends, so to distinguish those that are from those that are not, 'it is necessary, I think, to look at the whole causal chain and not merely at its final state'.[1] Thus

---

[1] Braithwaite, *Scientific Explanation*, p. 329. All page references are from the 1964 edition.

characteristic (1) is obviously needed, but it is not enough. It has to be supplemented by (2), (3) and (4). The anti-determinist fifth condition is allowed to lapse. If the main criteria for goal-directed behaviour are persistence (condition (2)) and plasticity (conditions (3) and (4)), then by characterising these properties in a formal way, Braithwaite aims to make teleology amenable to scientific treatment.

The paradigm he works with is a repeatable behavioural process where the following features are taken as read: What will count as attaining the goal is laid down in advance and easily recognisable (e.g. eating food). The item of behaviour being explained is also specified in advance. The goal is always attained sooner or later, at the end of every relevant chain of behaviour. In fact, goal-attainment is essential for individuating the chains that count as relevant. The beginning of a chain is also unproblematic, since there is never any reason to take as the initial state anything earlier than the explanandum itself. Finally, the whole sequence can be relied on to recur several times, in different circumstances, and can be recognised as the same. This is important, because a great deal hangs on the possibility of observing several separate chains.

Braithwaite's theory may be summarised as follows. The basic unit of analysis is a causal chain of events c, in a system b, determined, given the 'ordinary determination assumption of physical science', by the initial state e of the system and by the external stimuli or field-conditions f. The set f contains all the field-conditions that impinge on b during the time c lasts. All causal chains which end at an event of type Γ are said to contain the Γ-goal-attaining property, and the class of such chains is called the Γ-goal-attaining class γ. The variancy ϕ with respect to given b, e, and Γ is then defined as 'the class of those sets of field-conditions which are such that every causal chain in b starting with e and determined by one of these sets is Γ-goal-attaining'. In other words, ϕ is the class of those f's which uniquely determine those c's which are members of γ.

Now we view as *plastic* those chains of which the variancy has more than one member. That is, plasticity equals 'getting to the goal in a variety of circumstances'. Plasticity is linked to persistence in an obvious way. If one route to the goal is unavailable, a plastic system may be able to capitalise on a different route, and is to that extent persistent in its journey to the goal.

For Braithwaite, plasticity is first and foremost a property of causal chains, though 'not in general a property of one teleological causal chain alone', but it is convenient to speak of it as a property of the organism, or of the behaviour of the organism, when the behaviour comprises plastic causal chains. When behaviour is plastic with respect to Γ, the animal, or the behaviour, is *goal-directed* to Γ.

Plasticity, hence goal-directedness, is defined with relation to a specified end-state. In the examples he considers, the end-state is presumed to be known. It is unproblematic, for example, that the goal of the rat struggling through a maze is to get to the food-box. However, there will be situations where the animal's goal is not known in advance. The procedure for discovering the goal is, first, to observe a certain persistence in the behaviour and hypothesise that there *is* a goal, then to vary the circumstances and observe whether the behaviour is plastic with respect to the hypothesised goal. Plasticity with respect to an end-state furnishes a criterion of the directedness of the behaviour towards it, and hence provides an implicit definition of goalhood.

It may happen that there are two or more candidates for the title of goal, where the observed behaviour appears to be plastic to all of them. Very often, further observation and experiment will make clear which one is the goal, if the behaviour later is not plastic to the others, and if it can be assumed that the goal has not changed. But it may not always be possible to decide between the candidates. Israel Scheffler has argued in his important paper 'Thoughts on teleology' (1959), that if an event Δ always immediately precedes (or succeeds) Γ, and the behaviour is plastic with respect to Γ, then it cannot help being plastic with respect to Δ. This is part of what he calls 'the difficulty of multiple goals'. For instance, when a rat runs through a maze under different conditions, there are many chains of events that converge upon the event of eating the food in the food-box. The chains also converge upon the rat's touching the food with its snout. Couldn't its goal be to touch the food, as far as Braithwaite's theory is concerned? I think he would have to admit that if further experiments were incapable of deciding between the two goal-hypotheses, then either the rat has two goals at once, or his theory is inadequate, and something other than plasticity must be involved in defining what makes an event a goal. But it is not clear that experiments could never decide in cases like this. Would the rat still run if its reward were food received through a gastric fistula? If so, food is the goal; not tactile stimulation. So plasticity still provides the criterion.

The term 'goal-directed' is, perhaps, ambiguous. It could mean 'directed to a goal', rather as 'homeward-bound' means 'bound for home'; or it could mean 'directed by a goal', in the way that 'hand-made' means 'made by hand'. On the second interpretation the goal causally influences the direction, whereas the first leaves the causal influence open. To say that the goal plays a part in causing the directed movements would be to prejudge the issue of how to explain phenomena that are goal-directed merely in the first sense. This is undesirable for Braithwaite's purpose; he uses the word 'directed' to imply a direction but not to imply a director (see p. 323). So he must mean 'goal-directed' in the first sense. But the behaviour must be directed teleologically, not just coincidentally. The requirement that there be more than one f in the variancy is brought in to minimise the possibility of chance convergence.

But does the requirement rule out non-teleological convergence? Has Braithwaite succeeded in demarcating our intuitive boundary between genuine teleological behaviour and the aimless movements or stabilities of inanimate objects? He seems to think that teleology admits of degrees, so perhaps there is no clear dividing line. This, I think, is ominous. No doubt some movements are more manifestly goal-directed than others, and no doubt intensity of striving can have degrees, but there is a clear dividing line between behaviour that does have a goal and behaviour that does not. Surely an analysis should provide the conceptual cut-off point.

Assessment of the theory is hampered by its unfortunate notation. Each causal chain c has its corresponding set of field-conditions f. The set f may contain many members, comprising the field-conditions that obtain at the start e, and the new conditions that arise during the unfolding of c. The chain consists of causally connected events, each one of which, together with the field-conditions obtaining at that instant, determines the next. Constituents of the chain include not only the system's responses to stimuli, but also the stimuli themselves. If the system manipulates an object in the environment, causing the object to change in some way, and then reacts to the change, the trajectory of c goes from the system to the object and back again.

Given the assumption of determinism, any difference between two causal chains that begin at e and end at $\varGamma$ must lie in a difference between their respective sets of field-conditions. As plasticity implies a variancy with more than one member, one would expect it to imply more than one chain. This is not the case, however, for Braithwaite says that 'the variancy may have many members and yet there be only one nomically possible chain' (p. 331). Such a case is clearly possible whenever there is an *irrelevant* difference in field-conditions. For example, a stimulus may have different intensities on different occasions, yet so long as it is above the animal's perceptual threshold, it elicits the same response in the chain. But Braithwaite has quite a different case in mind. His examples are of temperature regulation in mammals and automatic navigation devices in pilotless aeroplanes, where a constant state is maintained by a homeostatic mechanism. When he says that in these cases there is only one nomically possible chain, he cannot simply mean that given the field-conditions that obtained, the system had to react in the way it did, for this is true of all cases, indeed it follows from the ordinary determination assumption. He must mean, therefore, that in the case of a homeostatic mechanism, the same *type* of chain occurs under different conditions. What, however, are the criteria for the type-identity of causal chains? We know that 'for given b and e, the causal chain c is uniquely determined by f', but this must not imply a denial that a difference of *reaction* to different f's makes a difference to the composition of a causal chain. When, then, are two reactions different? It would be begging the question to say that a type-difference between two reactions will have been captured already by a relevant type-difference in the sets of field-conditions. We must be able to type-identify the c's independently in order to be able to say they can be the same under different f's.

The fact that causal chains are represented as single units instead of being decomposed into their constituents forces us to skim over structural differences between chains. Events that occur in the animal are not kept separate from events that occur outside it. There is no room to make the distinction between active and passive systems, which Rosenblueth, Wiener and Bigelow[2] find useful. Consequently Braithwaite has a less powerful basis for demarcating systems that appear to be relatively independent of environmental constraints (Russell's condition 5).

In fact, the lack of any general guidance in deciding when one set of field-conditions is relevantly different from another, and hence for judging the size of the variancy, makes it easy to trivialise the theory. If minute differences in the environment entail differences in field-conditions, then the variancy of the conditions under which, say, a boulder rolls downhill will provide overwhelming evidence of plasticity. But boulders do not *seek* the bottom of the hill. Obviously not all

[2] In 'Behaviour, purpose and teleology', 1943. See also chapter 11 below.

features of the environment are to count as relevant field-conditions. Only those whose presence or absence affects the system causally are to count. But even so, there is too much room for manoeuvre among causally relevant variables. Rivers flowing to the sea, the tide rising up to the beach, the wind blowing the leaves off trees, in fact, any natural process that exhibits stability or persistence in the face of potential external disruptions would count as goal-directed. If plasticity in this sense is a necessary condition of goal-directedness, this is only because it is a necessary feature of any natural process. Every causal regularity can tolerate some variation in the conditions under which it operates.

I think the central cases which Braithwaite has in mind are those where there are a number of different types of causal chains, starting at e and ending at Γ. It would seem natural to describe this as a type of case where there is more than one means or method of getting to the goal. It can be represented on a diagram which I call the 'lens pattern'.

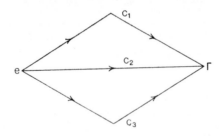

His example of Lashley's rats that can either run, crawl or lunge through a maze is of this type. He does say that 'the essential feature, as I see it, about plasticity of behaviour is that the goal can be attained under a variety of circumstances, not that it can be attained by a variety of means'. However, the difference between 'a variety of different circumstances' and 'a variety of different means' is somewhat academic, since the basic unit of analysis, the causal chain, consists of events that result from both the organism and the environment. The means adopted will depend on the circumstances that obtain, and the circumstances that obtain will depend on the prior movements. The set of field-conditions is chronologically ordered. What the animal does at t_0 may determine whether it is exposed to a given field-condition at t_1.

However, plasticity in this sense is subject to the same kind of trivialisation as before, since we are in no better position to decide whether two movements on separate occasions count as responses of different types and hence that the causal chains are of different types, than to determine whether two sets of conditions count as different types. A rolling snowball can either surmount obstacles (within certain size limits), or roll around them, or incorporate them into its mass. Does this imply that it has a variety of methods for getting to the bottom of the hill?

A third sort of plasticity may be constructed which reflects the basic idea. It may be represented by the 'fan pattern'.

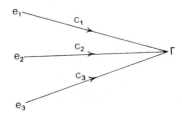

Here there are a number of initial conditions from which the system can start, and can get to the same terminal state. The difference in starting-points guarantees a difference in chains, and so automatically we may say there is a variety of different circumstances and a variety of methods. It is quite easy to see that this kind of plasticity can be trivialised too. All three are variations on the same theme. The criticism is always basically the same, namely that any straight line representing a causal process can be bulged out in the middle or opened up like a fan, simply by choosing more refined criteria of type-identity for the middle or the start of the chain than for the end.

Criticism of this kind, which depends on showing that the plasticity patterns are relative to a level of description or conceptualisation, is liable to provoke a subjectivist or projectionist view of teleology. On such a view, whether a process is teleological or not depends on whether it is *being viewed as* an exemplification of the lens or the fan pattern. If it is, then it is teleological; if not, it is causal; but the process in itself is neither one nor the other. In this context, such a position might seem absurd, and certainly Braithwaite would not espouse it. I shall say no more about it here, because it crops up in more sophisticated disguises in chapters 4 and 5.

The difficulty of goal-failure

Does anything really serious hang on the fact that plasticity is vague and underspecified? After all, 'what has been drawn is only an outline sketch which will need much working on to make a convincing picture' (p. 341). Let us suppose that the notation can be tightened up, so that the behaviour of the rats definitely does count as plastic, in a non-trivial sense. Would the new plasticity be a genuine necessary condition, and not just trivially necessary, as the old plasticity was?

Even without knowing the exact character of new plasticity, we may be certain that the theory still won't work as it stands. It is susceptible to Scheffler's difficulty of goal-failure. It is a plain fact that animals and men often do not succeed in attaining their goals, for they may be prevented by some obstacle, or they may just give up. When this happens, it does not become false that their actions were goal-directed in the first place. Braithwaite, however, identifies a sequence of behaviour as directed towards Γ by virtue to its belonging to a class of sequences that end in Γ. If a given chain does not end in Γ, there is no question of its being plastic with respect to Γ.

It might seem that a slight modification could put things right. Perhaps the criterion for including a chain into γ could be loosened in such a way that it became unnecessary for a chain actually to have the goal-attaining property so long as it was sufficiently similar to other chains which had it. The explanation 'The animal ran in order to escape from the predator', for instance, may be correct although the animal gets caught, provided that its behaviour is sufficiently similar to that of other animals which have escaped from similar field-conditions, or sufficiently similar to its own behaviour on occasions in the past when it escaped. Goal-attainment needs only to be statistically probable, so long as there is good evidence that causal chains of that type are plastic.

The modification does not go far enough though, because goal-attainment might not be probable. It might even be impossible, as in Larry Wright's example (1968), of a fish struggling to escape from a net but becoming more entangled. Perhaps no fish have ever succeeded in escaping, but a teleological explanation of their struggling might be true. Scheffler gives the example of a dog trapped in a cave by an avalanche, pawing ineffectually at the entrance in order to get out. Such a situation may never have occurred before, so there does not exist a class of relevantly similar Γ-goal-attaining chains.

In order to cope better with such cases, the plasticity theory needs an overhaul in two connected respects. First, it becomes essential to distinguish plasticity possessed by a single, possibly unique, causal chain, from plasticity the evidence for which is culled from past chains that ended in Γ. Braithwaite believes that we need inductive evidence that the animal has got to Γ several times before we can say it is directed to Γ, for otherwise, if Γ occurs once only, it might be pure coincidence. However, coincidence can be ruled out in another way. There is something about behaviour on a particular occasion which tells us that *if* other tests were done, the behaviour would lead to Γ again. And even when Γ is not reached, we are often in a position to hypothesise that *if* the conditions had been different, the goal would have been reached.

Second, it is necessary to revise his remarks about the relation between teleological explanation, inductive evidence and prediction. The next section will be devoted to this. The two weak points are intimately connected. The failure of an animal to reach its goal is often due to the presence of an obstacle among the field conditions, or to the absence of a necessary field-condition. Yet sometimes we can still explain the behaviour teleologically, for we are sure that if the conditions had been favourable, the goal would have been reached. This proves that it is not the case that teleological explanations predict that the field-conditions will fall within the variancy. Braithwaite's reason for claiming that they do can be traced to his belief that teleological explanations are grounded on inductive evidence of plasticity, based purely on observation of past sequences that ended in Γ. For, obviously, if such chains have occurred, then necessarily they occurred in conditions that fell within the variancy.

Let us try to redefine plasticity as a property of single causal chains rather than a property of a class. Such an attempt is desirable in any case, since it is more natural to call a class plastic because its members are plastic, than to call causal chains plastic because they belong to a plastic class. It is really very easy to make the switch. Instead of requiring that a variety of chains should actually have occurred, we say that a single chain is plastic when there is a variety of hypothetical alternative chains that could occur. If field-conditions f_1 obtained, chain c_1 would occur; if f_2, then chain c_2 would occur, and so on. A single trial can inform us that the behaviour is plastic, because we can manipulate some of the field-conditions during the course of the performance, and observe the concomitant changes in response.

Changing a field-condition midway is like actualising a chain that used to be hypothetical. The rest of the course that was being followed now becomes hypothetical. From this point onwards, it should be represented on the lens diagram by a dotted line rather than an unbroken one. But dotted lines are just as effective for symbolising the direction of a chain, and so we can construct a diagram of the same type as before, representing a class of possible chains.

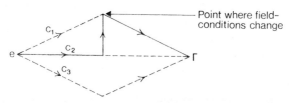

Dotted lines mean that the chain has been inferred or extrapolated from the known behavioural capacities of the animal. The number of hypothetical alternative chains depends on the number of true subjunctive conditionals of the form 'If field-conditions f_x were to obtain, the animal would get to Γ.' These conditionals are based, of course, on inductive evidence, but not necessarily of past behaviour that ended in Γ. The causal chain is broken into stages, and for each stage there may be separate evidence. The links in the chain are like building blocks made out of reliable stimulus-response pairs, which can be combined in different ways to form different chains. The rules for combining are no doubt very complicated, and themselves rely on inductive evidence about the intelligence and learning capacity of the animal in question. Evidence that a great variety of chains could and would occur, even if none has occurred complete, is good enough to establish plasticity.

The difficulty of goal-failure can now be accommodated by invoking counterfactual conditionals of the form 'If obstacles o_x had not been present in field-conditions f_x, which otherwise fall within the variancy, or if an essential member of the set f_x had not been absent (we may call this an obstacle too), the behaviour would have ended in Γ'. The truth of such a conditional is enough to save a teleological explanation, provided there is positive evidence of plasticity. The counterfactual is grounded upon inductive evidence which may consist either of past sequences in which the obstacle was not present and the behaviour did end in Γ, or of separate behavioural building blocks that can be moulded into such a sequence. The sequence is hypothetical, but we know it could have occurred, and we believe it would have occurred if given the chance. This conjecture is based on extrapolation from the known extent of the plasticity of the animal.

On this scheme, the role played by inductive evidence is more complicated but more realistic than in Braithwaite's original. A teleological explanation can be true when the goal is not reached, provided there is an indefinite range of conditionals of the form, 'If obstacles o_x had not been present, the goal would have been reached'. This range of conditionals plots the limits of excusable goal-failure. Goal-failure does cast doubt on the teleological explanation, however, when an obstacle is a field-condition that falls within the variancy. For the organism would have surmounted it, had the explanation been true.

The above is a rudimentary sketch of a way to convert the theory into a theory of plasticity for single chains, which recognises that goal-failure may occur provided there is an appropriate excuse. Plasticity is defined in terms of a hypothetical variancy, marked out by a class of true conditionals of the form 'If the set of field-conditions were f_x, (where f_x is a variable ranging over different sets from that which actually obtains), a different chain c_x would occur which would end in Γ'.

Even if plasticity were so defined, it is still doubtful whether it is a *sufficient* condition of goal-directedness, however. Imagine a very simple phototropic organism with legs, eyes and the innate goal of approaching sources of light. All it has to do is locate a light, point itself in the right direction, and walk. Although it can follow a moving light, it cannot make detours round obstacles that lie between it and the light. Consequently there are many types of situations where goal-failure would be tolerated. Are there many types of situation in which it achieves goal-success? It depends, of course, on our taxonomy of reactions whether walking north when the light is to the north counts as a different type of response from walking south when the light is to the south, given that both are instances of the same response-type 'approaching the light'. But let us say there *is* a variety of different ways in which the organism can get to the goal. Behaviour of this sort counts as plastic in a non-trivial sense. Now compare it with the behaviour of an iron-filing in the presence of a strong magnet. If we place the magnet to the north, the iron-filing moves to the north; if we place it to the south, the iron-filing moves south. Since we said that the two situations 'light to the north' and 'light to the south' were different, we can hardly avoid saying that 'magnet to the north' is a different situation from 'magnet to the south'. If the phototropic organism shows plasticity, then so does the iron-filing. Since the iron-filing is not goal-directed, plasticity is not a sufficient condition. It looks as though the concept is still too crude to discriminate between genuine teleology and magnetism.

One further point about the adequacy of plasticity as an index of teleology needs to be made. No doubt sensitivity to changed conditions is a good sign of goal-seeking ability in general. But is it possible to identify on that basis which particular goal is being sought on a given occasion, when the animal is thought to have more than one? The second part of Scheffler's difficulty of multiple goals asks us to imagine a cat crouching before a mousehole. If a mouse were to emerge, the cat would catch it. But equally, if a bowl of cream were to be placed nearby, the cat would forsake the mousehole and drink the cream. Is the cat crouching before the mousehole in order to catch the mouse, or in order to drink the cream? There seems to be nothing to choose between the two goal-hypotheses, since each one is supported by a true counter-factual, and we may assume the cat is plastic with respect to both goals. To generalise the difficulty, the behaviour of a cat at a given moment can be incorporated into different causal chains that show plasticity with respect to different goals. Since plasticity defined in terms of a *hypothetical* variancy is present with respect to all of them, the notion does not help us to identify which goal is being aimed at.

One factor which could help us to choose is knowledge of the cat's past experience. If she has been conditioned to the mousehole by a cream reward, she crouches there for the sake of the cream. If she associates the mousehole only with a mouse, she waits there in order to catch the mouse. Background evidence may favour Γ over Δ, but, as noted above, the evidence need not be of sequences that actually ended in Γ. However, the difficulty of multiple goals raises problems about time-sharing between competing drives, which are of a higher order of complexity than those with which Braithwaite's theory can deal without further modifications. More will be said about this later.

Teleological explanations and prediction

It was suggested above that Braithwaite misdiagnoses the role played by inductive evidence in backing up teleological explanations. By the same token, he holds strange views about their predictive power, and their status *vis-à-vis* causal explanation. For example, he believes that a teleological explanation predicts that the animal will get to the goal. How does this mistake arise?

In order to understand his position fully, we must adopt an epistemological standpoint. Let us suppose, along with Braithwaite, that a warranted present-tense teleological explanation relies on evidence that the goal has been reached in the past. Now, it is analytic that a chain that ends in Γ occurs in conditions that fall within the variancy, whatever the variancy may be. One is justified in predicting that the conditions on a particular occasion will fall within the variancy, only if one has some independent evidence of what the variancy is. First, one finds out that the conditions are going to be such and such; second, one assesses whether conditions of that sort come within the hypothesised variancy. If they do, one can justifiably assert a present-tense TD on that basis. We predict that the goal will be attained on that occasion by uttering the TD.

What is the independent evidence on which we judge whether conditions such and such come inside the range within which the system can adapt? It consists of knowledge that past sequences which ended in Γ occurred in conditions that were similar. So we have only a rough idea of the range. Our hypothesis that conditions such and such fall within ϕ is not based on complete knowledge of the structure of the system and the environment and the laws governing their interaction. If we were in a position to predict that the goal will be reached because we had complete knowledge, it would in Braithwaite's view, be disingenuous to predict it by asserting a teleological explanation. He thinks it would be misleading, because by seeming to rely on the teleological explanation, i.e. on the inductive evidence on which all teleological explanations are based, we conversationally imply that we do not know the exact limits of the variancy, hence that we are not 100% sure that the present conditions do fall within the variancy.

Now it follows from all this that when we assert a teleological explanation with justification, we must believe that the goal will be reached on this occasion, for we believe that the present conditions fall within the variancy. The two beliefs are equivalent. The evidence on which they are based is what justifies the teleological explanation. Of course, the explanation may be wrong, because we have misidentified the variancy, but it was at least justified on the available evidence. According to Braithwaite, a teleological explanation predicts the future behaviour of the animal, and the prediction is based on this inductive evidence.

But is it true that when an experimenter explains that his laboratory rat is running through the maze in order to get food, he is thereby predicting anything at all? One thing seems clear: he is not necessarily predicting that the rat will get food. He may know that the rat will not get food, because there is none in the food-box. In this case, he has certain knowledge both that the goal will not be attained and that the field-conditions do *not* fall within ϕ.

Earlier, Scheffler's difficulty of goal-failure forced us to modify Braithwaite's theory. It now asserts that a teleological explanation entails not that the goal will be reached, but that it would be reached if nothing blocked it. On the epistemological level, the theory must be modified in a corresponding way. When a teleological explanation is justified, it must be based on evidence that in the given circumstances the goal would be reached if nothing blocked it. However, one may know perfectly well that one of the field-conditions will block it. The reasonableness of a hypothetical prediction of goal-attainment does *not* depend on 'the reasonableness of believing that ϕ is large enough to contain every set of field-conditions that is at all likely to occur' (p. 332). We must separate very clearly the two kinds of evidence that Braithwaite mentions, the evidence upon which we base our knowledge of the variancy, which is general, and the evidence we have about the field-conditions that are likely to obtain on a given occasion.

Once we separate them, and make the adjustment to the theory, it matters little how the knowledge of the variancy is obtained. An inventor may know the exact size of the variancy of a goal-directed mechanism he has designed, yet still find teleological explanations of its behaviour useful. He may be lecturing to an audience, and the complete mechanical explanation may be too complicated. He is free to choose the type of explanation that is most appropriate to the questions being asked. The *meaning* of a teleological description is the same, whether it is asserted on the basis of past behavioural evidence or deduced from knowledge of the structure.

Braithwaite believes that it is built into the use (and meaning?) of a teleological description that it is based on less than conclusive inductive evidence. As scientific knowledge increases, and we become able to make the same predictions on surer authority, teleological explanations will presumably drop out. But this is a complete misconception. It derives from the idea that the prediction in question is a prediction that the goal will be attained. Such a prediction is never entailed by a teleological description, whatever evidence it may be grounded upon.

Not even the inventor himself can give a 100% guarantee that a mechanical tortoise which is now heading back to base will ever get there. The tortoise might be struck by lightning as soon as the description is uttered.

Of course, entailed predictions are not the only sort we make. An inventor may, in fact, predict that the tortoise will get back to base, and he may be in a better position than the people in the lecture-hall, who may be reluctant to accept that it *can* get back. But then, the man in the front row may be in a position to know what no one else even suspects, that he is about to prevent this from happening. Predictions which depend on beliefs about what conditions will in fact obtain are irrelevant to the meaning of the description.

There remains the question whether the hypothetical prediction 'if nothing blocks it, the goal will be reached' is entailed. This is a difficult question, because it is difficult to determine whether a conditional of this sort is part of the meaning of a teleological description, or whether it is an inference licensed by very general contingent truths. I shall discuss this in chapter 6. Whatever the right answer may be, however, I should have reservations about calling this conditional a prediction. It seems, moreover, that there are no other kinds of straightforward prediction entailed by a present-tense teleological description. The only other plausible candidate seems to be 'The animal will get some way towards the goal', which can no more follow logically than can a full-blown prediction of goal-attainment. So Braithwaite's theory seems to fail for several different reasons.

4
Sommerhoff's theory of directive correlation

Let us turn to a more sophisticated theory. In 1950, G. Sommerhoff published *Analytical Biology*, an original work which sought to define goal-directedness rigorously and to apply the definition to a wide range of living things. He belongs in the tradition of organismic biology in his desire to accommodate teleological phenomena while not assuming any non-empirical properties. Sommerhoff proposes that goal-directedness is an 'objective system property' that can be discovered by observing the behaviour over time, without postulating any hidden mechanisms or mental states. In my view, the book deserved more attention than it in fact received. If it had not been for Nagel, whose well-publicised theory of directive organisation was based on it, *Analytical Biology* (hereafter referred to as *AB*) might have been forgotten. As things turned out, very little comment or criticism appeared, with the result that Sommerhoff's later expositions[1] of the concept of directive correlation add only a few minor modifications into substantially the same framework.

There are three broad categories of goal-directed behaviour, Searching, Aiming and Keeping. A Searcher typically has the goal of finding an object which is not present to his senses. He explores the surroundings until he either gives up or sees what he wants. His explorations may be systematic or random. Once he sees it, or finds out where it is, his behaviour switches into the Aiming pattern. This category is perhaps the broadest, since it includes cases where the goal is an event or achievement, as well as ones where the goal can be described as an object. When the goal is an object, there is always some closely associated achievement, which may be said to be the goal too. Moving towards a destination, bringing a part of one's body in contact with something, and causing one object to impinge on another, are typical forms of 'aiming'. When its goal is to hit an object, the

---

[1] The first of these is a paper entitled 'The abstract characteristics of living systems' (Sommerhoff, 1969). The second is in a book with much wider scope, *Logic of the Living Brain* (1974), ch. 4.

behaviour exemplifies Canfield's 'Target-schema'.[2] In the third category, Keeping, the goal is a state of affairs that already obtains. It may also be described as an activity, namely 'keeping the state of affairs in being'. In so far as behaviour directed towards this end may itself be described as 'keeping' no rigid distinction between the goal-activity and the goal-directed activity can be made here. Balancing on a tightrope and keeping ahead in a race are examples. Thermostats are often cited as machines capable of this sort of behaviour, which falls under Canfield's 'Furnace-schema'.

Since Sommerhoff first illustrates his theory with an Aiming model, it is worth noticing certain general features of this kind of behaviour. First, it is clear that the goals to which it is directed may be of several kinds. The goal can be a momentary event, or a process, or a state; when there is a goal-object, like a target, this object may be stationary or mobile. Secondly, aiming itself is a process that takes time. It is typically followed by a quick action like firing or hitting. The quick aimed response also takes time, of course, but in many cases it is irrevocable once it has begun. This distinction between the aiming process and the aimed response is not the same as the distinction between processes and achievements. The latter is logical and grammatical, being marked by differences in the use of the verbs; the former is an empirical distinction between actions that are controlled while they are going on, and all-or-none actions which cannot be checked in midstream. Both types of action are present in typical cases of Aiming.

It is important to see that actions defined by their results, such as pressing a bar, hitting a target, and achievements in general, are not necessarily goal-directed. That a bar be pressed is a logically necessary condition for any action to count as a bar-pressing. Since this result can be secured by a variety of different methods, there are lots of ways of performing the act. But a rat may press a bar accidentally. Classifying an act as being of a type defined by reference to an end-result is quite different, therefore, from explaining an act, which may or may not be type-identified in terms of its result, by saying that it occurred for the sake of that result.

Sommerhoff's basic notion of 'directive correlation' is illustrated in *AB* by a man firing a gun (or an automatic gun firing itself) at a moving target. At the time of firing, t_1, the position & velocity of the target (Et_1), are causally dependent on its position & velocity, at some prior time t_0. Its earlier position & velocity are called the 'coenetic variable'

[2] See Canfield's Introduction to *Purpose in Nature* (1966).

(CVt$_0$). The response, (Rt$_1$) is also causally dependent on CVt$_0$, as the gunman needed to take account of it when he took aim. If the line of fire is appropriate, the target is hit at t$_2$. This event is the goal or 'focal condition' FCt$_2$. The target's actual position and velocity at t$_1$ represent just one out of a range of values that the variable E could have taken, and would have taken had the value of CV been different. For each of these possible values, there is one possible effective response. The response that actually occurs is said to be appropriate, rather than lucky, only if the target would still have been hit whatever other value the E variable had taken (provided it was in the limits of the gunman's adaptive powers). The E variable and the R variable are said to be directively correlated with respect to FC, when (a) they determine a hit at t$_2$, and (b) there is a range of values of the coenetic variable such that whichever value had occurred at t$_0$, it would have uniquely determined an alternative pair of values of E and R at t$_1$, and this pair would have led to a hit at t$_2$. An important condition, however, is that the E and R variables be 'epistemically independent'. That is, any combination (within limits) of values of E and R is possible as an initial state of the system.

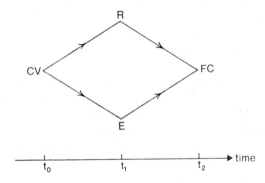

However, this model has certain parochial features which Sommerhoff eliminates by giving a more general account. First, the coenetic variable need not necessarily be an environmental variable. There is no need to distinguish R variables from E variables. If we think of the man-gun-target-environment complex as a closed deterministic system defined by a set of epistemically independent state-variables, the coenetic variable may be thought of as one or a set of these at t$_0$. Second, there may be any number of directively correlated variables. Third, the focal condition need not be the hitting of a target, but more generally the attainment or preservation of a certain relationship between the state-parameters. In 'The abstract characteristics of living systems' (abbreviated hereafter to *ACLS*), he makes a distinction between the goal event G and the focal condition FC. FC is the holding of a relationship that is necessary but not necessarily sufficient for G. This allows for the possibility that outside factors may prevent G from occurring, even though the system is directively correlated to G.

Nagel's theory of 'directive organisation'[3] is formally similar, though he uses a keeping paradigm instead of an aiming one. He takes the model of the temperature regulation mechanism in the human body. He thinks of the mechanism as a system defined by a set of parameters A, B, C, corresponding to the states of the causally relevant parts, such as the blood vessels, thyroid and adrenal glands. They vary in response to internal and external influences, such as changes in the muscular activity rate, or in the outside temperature. The whole system S is in a G-state when a relationship between the values either exists or is about to exist, such that their combined effect is to keep the body temperature within its normal limits. For the sake of simplicity, he considers only three state variables A_x, B_y and C_z, but the account can be generalised to cover any number. The system is so constituted that they can vary within the ranges K_A, K_B and K_C, respectively, without the system breaking down. Also, Nagel assumes to begin with that the environment stays constant in all relevant respects. Thus all influences potentially disruptive of homeostasis are located within the system's boundaries. At time t_0, S is in a G-state. At time t_1 the value of A_x changes to some other value within the subclass K_A'. Let this change be called a 'primary variation' in S. If it were the sole change, the system would be taken out of the G-state. However, the parts are so related that when A_x changes, an 'adaptive variation' takes place in B_y and C_z, in such a way that their values at t_1 fall into the subclasses K_B' and K_C' respectively. Again, if this change were the only change, the system would not be in a G-state at t_1. In fact, however, the elements of the class K_A' and the class K_{BC}' correspond to each other in a reciprocal manner so that their combined effect is to keep the system in a G-state. The system is said to be 'directively organised with respect to G'.

The primary and induced variations must be ones that would take the system out of a G-state if either occurred separately, otherwise the analysis is open to many counterexamples. Without this condition, a

[3] As expounded in *The Structure of Science*, ch. 12, pp. 406–21.

glass of water would count as a directively organised system. The tilt of the glass and the temperature of the water are independent variables, and the surface of the water remains horizontal in the fact of variations in tilt and temperature. But temperature is causally irrelevant to the achievement of this constancy.

Once the basic idea has been stated, Nagel can drop the assumption that the environmental factors stay constant.

> For suppose that there is some factor in E which is causally relevant to the occurrence of G in S, and whose state at any time can be specified by some determinate form of the state variable 'F_w'. Then the state of the enlarged system S' (consisting of S together with E) which is causally relevant to the occurrence of G in S is specified by some determinate form of the matrix '$(A_x B_y C_z F_w)$' and the discussion proceeds as before. (Nagel, 1961, p. 417).

The formal similarity between the two theories is clear. Just as Rt_1 varies concomitantly with variations in Et_1, thereby ensuring FCt_2, so B_y and C_z covary reciprocally with changes in A_x, thus keeping the system in a G-state. In Nagel's scheme, the 'coenetic variable' could be either that factor which causes the changes in A_x and B_y and C_z, or it could be equivalent to the primary variation in A_x. The 'directively correlated variables' would be A_x, B_y and C_z at a subsequent time. Because of the difference of models the time factor plays a slightly different role in the two expositions. Temperature regulation goes on continuously while primary variations occur, even if it takes time for B and C to react. The system can be said to be in a G-state at all times, so long as the adaptive variations occur. But within Sommerhoff's more general theory, this is merely a special case of directive correlation, where the adaptive responses are continuous. Directive correlation obtains, not just at time t_1, but at any time t, and the relevant value of the coenetic variable is that which obtains at time $(t - dt)$, where dt is the reaction-lag of the mechanism. So keeping turns out to be understandable in terms of Aiming. Searching is not separately considered, so I shall not investigate it further at this stage.

State-variables can be either continuous or of the Yes/No type. There can be more than one focal condition running concurrently, and each will have its own coenetic variable. The *degree* of directive correlation is measured by the size of the set of hypothetical alternatives to the actual value of a coenetic variable. A further measure that can vary is the *back-reference period* – that is, the time interval between the coenetic variable at t_0 and the adaptive response(s) at t_k. Nearly all animal movements are adapted to the environment in the short-term, in the sense that new stimuli can be reacted to quickly. Instinctive behaviour patterns and physiological mechanisms are also directively correlated towards survival in the long-term. The back-reference period extends across many generations to the time when the species first experienced pressure to evolve those characteristics. The term 'adaptation' enjoys its standard use here. Thirdly, there are medium-term adaptations, that is, directive correlations which take a chunk of the individual's life-span to become established. A rat, for example, might take three weeks to learn a maze. Here the focal condition is a state of affairs in which the rat's movements correspond to the correct pathway; the coenetic variable is the structure of the maze, first exposed to the rat at t_0; and its range equals the class of equally difficult alternative mazes which the rat could have learnt.

For any given animal, there will normally be many long, medium and short-term directive correlations going on simultaneously. With the aid of his central concept, Sommerhoff redescribes a variety of apparently purposive phenomena that are distinctive of living organisms. Physiological processes and motor behaviour are equally fertile areas in which to dig for directive correlations. Many examples are given in which sets of vital activities are synchronically co-ordinated, and where goal-directed sequences are diachronically integrated. Development is also an apparently purposeful process, but there the focal condition is not necessarily the attainment of a particular event, but rather the continuation of a direction of change – a 'chreod' in Waddington's terminology.[4] Even evolution as a whole is a directively correlated process, aiming at the 'continuous growth of the degrees and ranges of directive correlation in nature'. (*AB*, p. 186.)

One's initial reaction to Sommerhoff's theory might well be a suspicion that it is *too* comprehensive. It collects under one umbrella a number of phenomena which are normally kept separate. In particular, it covers both goal-directed activities of whole organisms *and* functional activities of parts. But the two concepts, goal and function, are surely quite different. There are many ways of dividing an organism's body into subsystems. Some, though not all, such subsystems will count as 'directively organised', and the activities of their components will count as 'directively correlated' with respect to some task which has a function for the organism. One example is the temperature-regulating

[4] For an explication of this term, see Waddington (1968) pp. 13–15.

mechanism which Nagel uses as his model. Another is the blood-sugar homeostat. But is it right to say that these internal mechanisms have goals of their own? They have functions, which license 'in order to' statements, but that is irrelevant. Plenty of other components have functions, e.g. bones, but they are not directively organised systems.

It is true that, if one of the organism's goals is to keep its own blood-sugar level well-adapted to prevailing conditions, then the blood-sugar mechanism contributes to this goal. But that is not enough to show that the mechanism has this as a goal of its own. Otherwise all the goals of the animal to which the regulator contributes, such as catching prey, would then be deemed goals of the regulator too. This is absurd. Clearly, we must keep track of which verbs go with which subjects. Just as there is a difference between 'activity of an organism' and 'activity of an organ', so there is a difference between 'goal of a system' and 'goal of a subsystem'.

Nagel's account is embedded in a chapter about organismic biology, and about the alleged peculiarities of biology as a science. Teleological explanations of the sort used in biology do not, he says, postulate conscious purposes or ends-in-view, but specify the *functions* which things or processes possess. He uses the words 'teleological' and 'functional' interchangeably, when they are followed by the words 'explanation' or 'analysis'. However, his conceptual analysis of teleological or functional analyses provokes him to ask why they are used in biology but not in physics. The difference lies in the nature of the subject-matter. Living things are 'directively organised', whereas inorganic systems in general are not. The elucidation of this idea is Nagel's analysis of the concept of a *teleological system*. A system is teleological in the sense of *'goal-directed'* when it consists of parts that are directively organised. Systems are not necessarily whole animals. The size of a system is relative to the placing of its boundaries, which are chosen with reference to the G-state that everything within the boundaries helps to maintain. G-states are the goals of the whole system, but the whole may be part of a wider whole, just as individuals are parts of ecosystems. It is at this point that my intuitions rebel, for I think that the thermo-regulatory system in the human body does not have a goal of its own, but only a function.

However, Sommerhoff would not agree that he has confused two quite distinct notions. He deliberately does not distinguish between goal-directedness and functionality, because he believes that he has found a general concept which helps to explicate both. For him, directive correlation is the objective kernel of teleology in all its manifestations, and the precise definition of it helps to untangle a skein of confusions. Arguments, not intuitions, will be required to prove that his analysis is on the wrong lines.

Nagel's views about functions will be considered more fully in Part Three. At present we are concerned just with goal-directed behaviour. It appears from the foregoing remarks, however, that the meaning of the term 'goal-directed' is not at all clear, given that people's intuitions differ about which systems are goal-directed. This makes it difficult to assess any analysis of that concept. The test is: does the analysis correctly capture the necessary and sufficient conditions for the application of the concept? But evidently people might disagree about the answer to this question.

Nevertheless, despite this vagueness, there is a broad measure of agreement about paradigm cases. Some systems clearly are goal-directed, on any plausible definition, and others clearly are not. So the method of counterexamples can still be used, if the counterexamples are clear cases.

Preliminary objections

Sommerhoff's diamond-shaped diagram is not like the lens-diagram that illustrated Braithwaite's theory, since in Sommerhoff's scheme the two causal chains occur together. In the lens-diagram, each line represents an *alternative* chain. But the parallelism between the two theories comes through clearly when the hypothetical alternative values

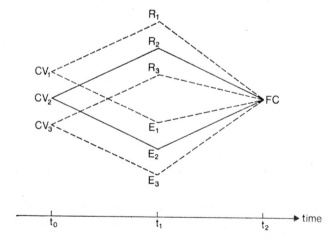

of the coenetic variable are illustrated (with dotted lines) so as to create a *fan* diagram (see p. 62).

Can this pattern be collapsed into a single line by the same trick that was played on Braithwaite? Since CV causes both E and R, and E and R jointly cause FC, it follows that CV causes FC. The range of CV's variation can then be concealed by a suitably generic description to yield a single causal 'law' true of automatic guns, to the effect that whenever a target appears within their range, it gets hit.

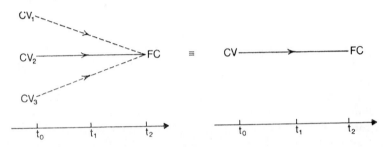

To do this would misrepresent the theory by obliterating an essential element: the synchronisation of two separate processes. The two causal chains interlock at start and finish, but their routes stray far apart in the interim. Sommerhoff's model possesses an extra bit of complexity that can give a reason for the apparent invariance of FC to changes in CV, despite the fact that FC depends on factors that are not invariant in respect of CV.

Does this really make much difference though? Surely it just means that we need to think of slightly more complex counterexamples. Instead of imagining one boulder rolling down a hill, we now imagine two. They start at the same time from different places near the summit, they travel by different routes, and they both end up in the valley. The coenetic variable is a variable that represents compendiously the positions of both boulders at t_0. Variables R and E represent their positions at t_1. The goal is the state of affairs such that both have arrived in the valley. This state obtains at and after t_2. R and E are clearly independent. There is a range of possible values of $CV t_0$, each of which determines a pair of values of R and E at t_1, and this pair jointly determines the goal at t_2. If either boulder stopped rolling, that is, if one state-variation occurred without the other, the goal of both getting to the bottom would not be achieved.

Of course there is a trick here. The coenetic variable is a measure constructed out of two distinct measures. Although its value at t_0 mathematically determines the values of R and E, given background information about the contours of the hill, etc., the formula is not a faithful reflection of the causal relations involved. The position of each boulder at t_1 depends upon where *it* was at t_0, not upon where both were. It is obvious that if we select artificial, compendious descriptions of the start and finish, such that two causal chains have the same start and finish under those descriptions, but have different intermediate stages, then we can discover diamond-patterns all over the place. Sommerhoff's formal definition is deliberately abstract, partly because to be abstract is a way of vindicating the claim that goal-directedness can be explicated without reference to underlying mechanisms. But it is precisely this abstraction which lays the theory open to formal trivialisation.

As it stands, the theory is also vulnerable to the difficulty of goal-failure, as state-variables are not directively correlated with respect to a goal unless they actually bring it about. Sommerhoff softens this requirement later. He says that the connection between firing and hitting the target could be probabilified, so as to take into account the possibility of external interference after t_1. Then again, he has at hand the distinction between the goal and the focal condition, defined as the relation between the target's flight and the bullet's flight which needs to obtain at t_1 if the goal is to follow at t_2, given the conditions prevailing at t_1. The holding of this relation is not causally sufficient for goal-attainment, since the conditions may change after t_1. However, he need not soften his theory in these ways if he is willing to incorporate excusing conditionals into the definition. He may then say that directive correlation with respect to G entails that G would be attained if nothing interfered and conditions did not change after t_1.

It is easy to miss a subtlety here, unless one distinguishes carefully between logically necessary conditions and causally necessary conditions. When Sommerhoff says that because goal-failure may occur, directive correlation is only a necessary condition, he could be taken to mean that directive correlation is necessary, but not sufficient, in order for a system to *count* as goal-directed. In other words, he could be taken to mean that he is providing only a partial analysis of the concept of goal-directedness. But this would belittle his theory, and would concede too much to the difficulty of goal-failure. It is not necessary for directive correlation to be causally sufficient for achieving the goal. Indeed it is necessary that it should not be, since goal-directedness is not causally sufficient either. A correct analysis provides logically necessary and sufficient conditions for a notion of goal-directedness which already allows for the possibility of goal-failure.

Let us turn to another objection. Every action that an animal performs fits into the grand sequence of its life-history. But the whole set can be divided up into countless subsequences. There are a number of ways of doing this, depending upon how we individuate subsequences. A set of actions can be unified by a single focus, or it may be more loosely strung together. Consider a sequence of three actions performed by a child: running, picking up a ball, throwing the ball. The child might perform each one entirely for its own sake. Or he may run in order to pick up the ball in order to throw it. Alternatively, he might run solely in order to pick up the ball, and then later, just before he picks it up, he might acquire the goal of throwing it. Other relations between the actions are possible too. Let us say that in the second case the agent performs an 'integrated sequence', meaning that each action is done ultimately for the sake of the last action in the sequence. It is left open whether the sequence can be further ordered by intermediate sub-goals. The third case is not an integrated sequence in this sense, because each action is done only for the sake of the *next* one. Sommerhoff's theory ignores this distinction, thereby exposing itself to Scheffler's difficulty of multiple-goals.

In *ACLS*, p. 188, he sets out the following 'Integration Theorem', which follows deductively from his definitions:

> If G_A is the goal event of a directive correlation A and if the occurrence of G_A is a necessary condition for the occurrence of the goal event G_B of a directive correlation B, then G_B is also a goal event of A.

From this he derives the concept of a hierarchy of directive correlations integrated by a single ultimate goal. His stipulation that G_B has its own set of directively correlated variables distinct from the set of variables that are directively correlated to G_A gives the theorem more content than the corresponding implication of Braithwaite's plasticity theory. In Braithwaite's account, any subsequent event for which G_A is a necessary condition would count as a goal G_B, simply in virtue of the fact that plasticity with respect to G_A would count also as plasticity with respect to G_B.

However, Sommerhoff's actual proof makes no mention of G_B's own set of variables. He writes

Let F_A (x, y, z) = O be the focal condition of the directive correlation A. Then according to our definition, F_A (x, y, z) = O is a necessary condition for the occurrence of G_A. *Ex hypothesi*, the occurrence of G_A is a necessary condition for the occurrence of G_B. It follows that F_A (x, y, z) = O is also a necessary condition for the occurrence of G_B.

No doubt he would not wish to say that x, y, z were directively correlated to G_B if G_B was not already known to be a goal on other grounds. But he is committed to it by this proof, since any subsequent event to which G_A's variables are directively correlated counts as an ulterior goal on those grounds alone.

Leaving this aside, I would maintain that even if G_B was a goal of some other action B, still the action A whose goal is a necessary condition of G_B is not *eo ipso* goal-directed to G_B. It might be so, but its being so does not follow logically. Sommerhoff welcomes the conclusion that every goal-directed action is directed to one or other of the ultimate goals of survival and reproduction. Indeed he thinks that the concept of a being whose parts and part-activities are integrated into an all-embracing hierarchy of directive correlations *is* the concept of a living being. It is in some ways an attractive picture. But it is a picture surely, of a hierarchy of functions, rather than a hierarchy of goals. The functions of bodily parts are relatively stable. They are organised into a dynamic hierarchy because they mirror the static hierarchy of organic structures. The concept of a hierarchy of goals is more complicated, since the majority of goals are transient or cyclic. Their ordering relations shift around as time passes. There are very few act-types of which we can say that type A standardly *is* the goal of type B, and B the goal of type C. Even if there were such types constantly related in these ways, it would not follow that A standardly is the goal of C. The reason is that this kind of transitivity may apply or not apply in a particular case, according to whether the sequence is being controlled by an overall plan or strategy. The relation 'being done for the sake of' is logically neither transitive nor intransitive. Furthermore, Sommerhoff's theory ascribes too many concurrent goals to the animal, even *after* what I call 'functions' are weeded out. Consider a rat running through an unfamiliar obstacle course to get a food reward. Each step it takes involves the co-ordination of several muscles. The muscles are said to be directively correlated with respect to the co-ordination (*AB*, p. 129). The rat's movements are adapted to bumps in the ground and obstacles in its path (*AB*, pp. 154–5). Also, the whole sequence is not only directed towards the food, but also to learning the obstacle course (*AB*, p. 155). Not counting internal processes that keep the rat alive throughout, there is at least one 'goal' per limb movement, at least one per orientation response, at least one for every stage in the maze, and at least two for the sequence as a whole (not counting long-term ends like survival). I do not deny it is possible to discover, with the aid of a theory, that animals have more goals than we originally thought. But this is going too far.

Epistemic independence and the question of objectivity

A distinctive feature of Sommerhoff's theory is the requirement that directively correlated variables must be epistemically independent, or 'orthogonal', as he later prefers to say. Systems which revert to a state of equilibrium after the balance of internal forces has been upset do not count as goal-directed, because, it is said, they do not meet this require-ment. But what exactly does epistemic independence amount to? Does it really provide an objective demarcation-line?

Let us agree, first, that Sommerhoff is quite right to want to dis-tinguish goals from states of equilibrium. First, it seems that we intuitively rely on some such distinction when we deny that pendulums swing *in order* to get back to the vertical. Second, it is possible to think of *any* stable physical system as preserving or tending towards some sort of equilibrium. For example, the volume of a fixed mass of gas at constant temperature varies inversely with pressure. This means that the product of quantitative measures of the volume and the pressure is a constant. Taking this measure to represent a parameter of the 'system', we can think of the gas as a system which acts in such a way as to keep one of its own parameters constant. According to Nagel, all quanti-tative laws can be formulated as 'extremal principles', which assert that 'the actual development of a system proceeds in such a manner as to minimize or maximize some magnitude which represents the possible configurations of the system' (Nagel, p. 407). Sometimes a law is formulated first as an extremal principle ('Light always takes the shortest path'), and later as a statement of functional dependence ('The angle of incidence èquals the angle of reflection'); but both describe the same phenomenon.[5]

[5] Wittgenstein makes this point in *Tractatus* 6·33–6·34.

So if goal-directed behaviour were simply equilibrium-restoring, every lawful variation could be regarded as goal-directed, which would again trivialise the notion. To think holistically is not necessarily to think teleologically. The former involves taking a thing or event as part of a wider whole or process, and describing in terms of the contribution it makes to the whole. To view it teleologically is to think of it occurring *in order to* make a contribution to the whole.

Nagel's opinions on this matter are slightly complicated by his double use of the word 'teleological'. He believes that minimax principles are, or 'have the appearance of' teleological *statements*, as they have a 'teleological form'. Since a balloon of gas does maintain PV constant, Nagel is reluctant to say that it is false to describe its behaviour teleologically. He says instead that it is misleading, because a balloon of gas is not a teleological *system*. It is inappropriate to explain behaviour teleologically if the system is not directively organised, although the TD does not assert that the system is directively organised. According to Nagel, when we say that behaviour is goal-directed, we presuppose that the system is of a certain restricted type, whereas according to Sommerhoff we assert that it is of that type in saying that its variables are directively correlated.

Both agree, however, that a precondition of its being of the right type is that the causally relevant variables be independent of each other.

Sommerhoff writes (*AB*, p. 86):

> A set of parameters of a physical system S is a set of *epistemically independent* parameters if the definition and imposed conditions of S, and the physical laws which are assumed to apply to it, admit arbitrary constellations of values of these parameters as possible initial states of S, and hence permit the *initial* values of these parameters to be treated as mutually independent variables.
>
> Since any point of time in the natural development of S may be selected as an initial point of time, it is evident that, according to this definition, a set of state parameters is epistemically independent if it is such that at any instant the value of no member of the set is determined by the value *at that instant* of one or more other members of the set by reason of the conditions imposed on the system *for that instant*, or of the laws held to apply to it.

This is obscure. In the mathematical sense, the value of one numerical variable 'determines' the value of another at the same instant, if given the one, the other can be derived from a formula of the form $x = F(y)$. All that is needed is that there should be some functional relation F that links them. But directive correlation is a functional relation. With discrete or 'singular' directive correlation, it is a relation that invariably holds between the values of the variables at a specific moment during any trial. With continuous correlation, it is a relation that holds at all times. For example, the direction of the barrel of the gun is invariably related to the position of the target *at the moment of firing*, provided all goes well. In Nagel's homeostat, whenever A varies as a result of a change in S, B and C vary by a corresponding amount in such a way as to keep the temperature constant; *therefore* A, B and C are not functionally independent. It goes without saying that the position of the target at t_1 does not *causally* determine the direction of the barrel at t_1. These are collateral effects of the position and velocity of the target at a previous time t_0. Nevertheless the value of the response variable R at t_1 is determined by, in the sense of 'calculable from', the value of E at t_1, provided they really are directively correlated at t_1.

However, there is supposed to be an epistemic sense in which state-variables that are directively correlated to each other are yet independent of each other. Sommerhoff's criterion is that arbitrary combinations of values are possible as initial states of the system. At the start of a trial the gun may be pointing away from the target, because the target has not yet been sighted, or because the mechanism has not had time to work. The value of R at t_0 is therefore independent of the value of E at t_0. But there is some terminological ambiguity here. Of course these values are unrelated at t_0: the two variables are not directively correlated at t_0. When he says that the direction of the gun and the target's position are directively correlated variables, he builds a time-reference into their identity as variables by calling them Rt_1 and Et_1. At the initial time t_0, the target variable is given a different *name*, to wit 'the coenetic variable CVt_0'. It is beside the point to remark that the direction of the gun at t_0 is independent of the position of the target at t_0. These are just not the relevant directively-correlated variables. Sommerhoff's claim is that the direction of the gun at t_1 is epistemically independent of the position of the target at t_1. We have still to work out what is meant by this.

He tells us that any point of time may be selected as an initial point of time. This implies that arbitrary constellations are possible at any point in time. He must be thinking here of continuous directive

correlation, since it is only here that we find variables that are directively correlated at all points of time. Now there are two kinds of
possibility that might be meant. It is *logically* possible for the parameters to vary in value independently provided only that they really
are distinct. Since the restoring force on a pendulum is distinct in this
sense from the extent of displacement, logical distinctness is not
enough.[6] It is *empirically* possible for values to vary independently
provided no laws of nature prevent a situation from arising in which
they would do so. The test of this would be either that they do vary
independently in the normal course of events (which is ruled out if
directive correlation is the normal state), or that they could be made
to do so. To get A, B and C out of step in Nagel's system, we have to
interfere with it; although this would temporarily destroy the directive
correlation, it would certainly show that they *could* vary independently.
I think epistemic independence means that independent variations are
not ruled out by any of the laws that are assumed. Furthermore, the
functional relation that holds between variables when they are directively correlated must not be taken as given, but as something the
system *brings about*. In the keeping paradigm we have to interfere with
the system to show that the variables are capable of assuming unrelated values, but once the external interference is taken away, the
variables become functionally related again. The general point,
applicable to both keeping and aiming paradigms, is that the system
brings about or maintains the desired correlation when given the
opportunity, but interferences can occur which deny it the opportunity.
A mass of gas at constant temperature, by contrast, cannot be prevented
from keeping its pressure in step with changes in volume.

However, there is a crucial weakness here. Before determining
whether it is epistemically possible for two system parameters to vary
independently, we must define the system and the environmental
conditions, and be clear about which laws are being assumed. For
instance, the pressure and volume of a gas could both rise together if
the gas were heated up or if Boyle's law ceased to hold. On either of
these assumptions, the pressure and volume are independent; but they
are not independent if we define the system to be a fixed mass of gas at
constant temperature, and assume a world subject to Boyle's law.
Similarly, if we specify that the heat regulation system is closed to
outside influences, it is impossible for A, B and C to assume arbitrary

[6] Nagel at one point writes as if 'independence' amounted to no more than
this. See *The Structure of Science*, p. 412.

constellations of values during the normal operation of the system. Their values are causally determined at all times by the prior state of the system. And the automatic gun, being a deterministic system, cannot help pointing at the target at t_1, provided nothing interferes either with it or the target. Sommerhoff himself points out (*AB*, p. 86) that

> the notion of epistemic independence formulated above is a contingent notion. It specifies a certain independence *only* in relation to a given set of fixed assumptions about the physical system concerned: it is contingent upon our definition of the system.

Suppose that we defined a gas-filled rubber balloon to be a system whose pressure and volume were independent state-variables. Arbitrary combinations of values are possible, because we assume that the temperature can fluctuate (within limits set by the melting point and elasticity of the rubber). Would P and V count as directively correlated with respect to any focal condition? If we define the focal condition to be the product of the P and V values, and let the coenetic variable be the atmospheric pressure, then the balloon counts as a directively organised system. PV stays constant in the face of atmospheric pressure changes, provided the temperature does not in fact fluctuate. If a change in temperature did occur, it would be treated as an interfering factor, external to the system. Similarly, the swinging pendulum can be made to count as directively organised with respect to the G-state of returning to rest. The magnitude of the restoring force would be epistemically independent of the deviation from the vertical, if we stopped assuming that the gravitational force acting on the bob stays constant throughout a trial. We could not calculate the value of the one at a given instant from the value of the other at the same instant, since we would not know the force of gravity at that instant. Any stable or dynamic equilibrium system can be converted into a directively organised system, simply by dropping one assumption.[7]

Now Sommerhoff is aware of this. He admits that the R and E variables would have dependent values at t_1 if we took it to be a law of nature that automatic guns point at their targets at the time of firing, provided nothing interferes. He argues, however, that laws of nature cannot be about automatic guns. But this is not the point. It could be replied that the E and R variables lack epistemic independence for us,

---

[7] Beckner makes a similar point in *The Biological Way of Thought*, pp. 137–9.

not because we think their covariation is a primitive law of nature, but because we know in detail how such a gun works. We can deduce that they will be functionally correlated from a set of known laws of nature conjoined with a full description of the gun's design, plus a description of the initial conditions.

The crucial objection is not concerned with whether laws can be about specific systems. It is that the concept of directive correlation is an intrinsically relativistic concept. There is no right answer to the question 'Are these variables really epistemically independent?' It depends on how the observer chooses to view them.

Perhaps Sommerhoff would deny that epistemic independence is a matter for individual decision. He would presumably prefer to talk about 'independence relative to our knowledge', i.e. relative to what is scientifically known. But the notion still remains relative to the state of science at a given stage in history. Imagine a primitive scientist for whom it is a basic law of nature that when a hungry lioness sees an antelope, she runs after it. The antelope's flight and the lioness's pursuit would not be independent for such a man, so it would be impossible for him to view the lioness as goal-directed. On the other hand, imagine Boyle, working at a time when 'PV = k at constant T' is not yet established as a law. Sommerhoff's relativism implies that Boyle was entitled to think that gas-filled balloons were goal-directed, but that we are not. In general, he would have to say that Leibniz, Maupertuis, and the other eminent scientists of that period who believed that least-action phenomena were intrinsically purposive, (assuming, for the sake of argument, that they did believe this, as well as believing that the phenomena were evidence of design), were actually quite right at the time, but that they would be wrong if they believed it now. This absurd consequence, reminiscent of the projectionist view of teleology, vitiates Sommerhoff's claim to have represented goal-directedness as being an *objective* system-property.

5

Charles Taylor's conception of teleology

We move on now to another theory, propounded by Charles Taylor in his book *The Explanation of Behaviour* (1964). Unfortunately for the reader, this means that yet another system of notation has to be introduced. This time, however, it is easier to master, and I stick to it throughout the rest of the book. Taylor's theory is second-order, rather than first-order like the previous ones. His object of study is the form of teleological explanations, and not primarily the objects or events so explained. But there is an obvious connection, since he regards a teleological system as precisely one whose behaviour is explainable teleologically. It is surprising, perhaps, in view of Taylor's aversion to behaviourist psychology, that his account turns out to be similar to the theories already considered. Given this fact, however, it is not surprising that it is vulnerable to similar objections.

Taylor's book attempts to establish two important theses. The first is that there is nothing intrinsically mysterious or unempirical about teleological explanations, and that they can be tested just as well as any other kind. He offers an analysis of the teleological form of explanation according to which it does not require hidden forces, entelechies, or causes operating backwards in time. Secondly, Taylor maintains that it is an empirical matter, one that behavioural scientists will eventually have to settle, whether animal behaviour is best explained causally or teleologically. Both types of explanation being logically sound, the issue is simply to discover which is more appropriate to the subject-matter. Taylor is not neutral on this issue, however. He believes that common-sense and experimental findings both favour the view that teleological explanations are more useful in this area. Part II of his book is a detailed critique of theories in psychology and ethology which avoid facing up to this.

The second thesis has aroused the most controversy, partly because of its deep scientific and metaphysical implications, but partly also because the precise status of Taylor's claim was obscure. It was soon recognised, not least by Taylor himself, that there were problems surrounding his notion of the 'basic level of explanation'. Some of his remarks on basicity were actually inconsistent with his second thesis. He appeared in some passages to be saying that teleological explanations were *necessarily more basic* than other kinds, since they presented their explananda as natural tendencies for which no further explanation could be given. Consequently, if scientists ever discovered a causal explanation with the same scope and explanatory power as an apparent teleological explanation, such that the apparent teleological explanation could no longer be regarded as more basic, then we should have to say that it was never a genuine teleological explanation at all. This is a way of saying that proper teleological explanations are incompatible with mechanistic explanations that have the same scope. Taylor holds, in fact, that 'our usual notion of purpose cannot properly be applied except in a metaphorical way to machines' (p. 21). A teleological and a causal explanation of a given piece of behaviour are compatible only so long as the teleological one is more basic than the causal one.

My aim in this chapter, however, is to examine the first thesis rather than the second. In particular, I shall argue that Taylor gives an incorrect characterisation of the form of a teleological explanation. There may exist useful explanations of the form he sets out, but they are certainly not teleological. If I am right about this, large chunks of the literature surrounding his second thesis are off the point as far as the question of compatibility is concerned. Taylor's T-laws are close to what Nagel calls 'extremal principles', which have nothing to do with teleology. I shall also show in passing that Taylor mischaracterises the relationship between causal laws and T-laws. In fact, explanations which rely on T-laws turn out to be a species of causal explanation, on the most natural interpretation of the term 'causal'. So his second thesis is invalidated on this score too. What Taylor is really arguing is that it is an empirical matter whether causal laws of a rather special type, in which the antecedent is described in terms of a certain relational property, are always replaceable by causal laws of equal or greater nomological force, in which the antecedent is described in terms of its intrinsic properties. This is an interesting question, but it has little to do with teleology.

Before we start the investigation, we need to be clear about a point of terminology. Taylor distinguishes between teleological explanation in general, which is marked off by its form, and purposive explanation, which is a particular type of teleological explanation that involves ascribing a mental state to the animal. The ascription of purposes or intentions requires also the ascription of other psychological states and capacities. For example, an animal behaving purposefully responds to his intentional environment, i.e. the environment as he sees it and interprets it, rather than to the environment *tout court*. Taylor believes that a great deal of animal behaviour is purposive as well as being teleological. Chapters 2 and 3 contain his arguments to this effect. But in chapter 1, he is not yet asserting this. His aim is to isolate that feature of purposive explanations which consists in their relying on laws of the teleological form, and to show that '*qua* teleological these laws will not be of the kind which makes behaviour a function of the state of some unobservable entity' (p. 9). My concern just now is solely with the general notion of teleology, hence I focus almost entirely on the first chapter of his book. It is only fair to add, also, that Taylor's views have changed somewhat since 1964, and that he would no longer hold all the opinions in that chapter.

With this distinction in mind, Taylor first defines a teleological explanation as one which accounts for some event or class of events 'by laws in terms of which an event's occurring is held to be dependent on that event's being required for some end'. To put it slightly differently, 'the condition of the event's occurring is that a state of affairs obtain such that it will bring about the end in question, or such that this event is required to bring about that end'. For instance, if an animal finds itself in a situation where fighting an intruder is required for territorial defence, and if the fact that this is so is a sufficient condition for the animal actually to start fighting the intruder, then that fighting can be teleologically explained by saying that it occurred for the sake of territorial defence. In Taylor's convenient notation: 'the condition of an event B occurring (the animal's actually fighting) is, then, . . . that the state of the system S (the animal) and the environment E be such that B is required for the end G (territorial defence); by which the system's purpose is defined'.

The last formulation may appear puzzling, because it seems to *take for granted* that the system does indeed have a purpose. (Nothing hangs on the mere word 'purpose' here; the word 'goal' would have done just as well, if not better.) The definition seems to require that we already know that territorial defence, in the example, is a goal of the animal, without offering any explanation of what this means. Instead of analysing what it is for G to be a goal, he gives an analysis of what makes the behaviour count as teleologically directed toward G. But perhaps this boils down in the end to an implicit definition of 'goal' in the manner of Braithwaite. Taylor may hold the view that to say that an end-state is a goal just is to say that the system does things for the sake of achieving it. If that can be independently understood, the definition is not circular. We can identify an animal's goals by discovering which values of G and B yield true laws of the suggested form.

However, this conception of teleological explanation is still rather obscure. According to Taylor,

> any given antecedent condition of B which fulfilled the conditions for the description 'requiring B for G' (let us call this T) would also fulfil some other 'intrinsic' description, E. But this is not to say that B's occurring is a function of E's occurring, i.e. that B depends on E. For it may be that in other circumstances a situation which fulfils the description E is not followed by B, the circumstances being precisely those in which the situation does not also fulfil the conditions for the description T; whereas all cases of T may be followed by B. (p. 13)

In reply to a query raised by Denis Noble, Taylor confirmed that he meant by 'E' the state of the environment plus the state of the system just prior to B.[1] If he had meant the state of the environment only, his point would have been correct but hardly worth making; any difference in reaction would be attributable to a difference in the state of S on the two occasions. Let us therefore substitute 'SE' for 'E'. Now the passage seems to assert that it is possible that two cases may obtain, in which the system and environment are in precisely the same state, intrinsically characterised, but in one the teleological description T holds, in the other it does not. In one, SE is followed by B, in the other not. The difference is due, so it is claimed, to the fact that in case (1), given SE, B was required for G; in case (2), B was not required for G. But surely it is obvious that in a pair of cases with identical antecedent conditions, if a response of type B is required for G in one, it must equally be required for G in the other. Whether B is required for G depends entirely on what *type* of situation obtains, and *ex hypothesi* the two initial situations are of the same type. It may, indeed, be conceivable that only in one of the two cases does an instance of B actually *occur*. But the reason why B occurred in that case could not be simply that the antecedent situation required B for G. That would have been a sufficient reason for B to have occurred in the other case too.

[1] D. Noble, 'Charles Taylor on teleological explanation', and Taylor, 'Teleological explanation' – a reply to Denis Noble', both in *Analysis*, 1967.

Noble makes this point neatly by using one of Taylor's own principles: that teleological explanations do not postulate the existence of properties which are undetectable apart from the events to which they give rise. He asks how we can know, given that the two SE situations are identical, whether the teleological description T applies to one of them. The only evidence that the T description was justified would be the occurrence of B, the event we seek to explain. Since this is ruled out by the principle just mentioned, in every case there must be some other way of telling whether the T description applies, and this must reveal itself as a difference in the 'intrinsic' descriptions of the two situations. 'We may conclude, therefore,' says Noble, 'that whenever a teleological explanation of the kind described by Taylor can be given, it is necessarily the case that a non-teleological (SE – B) account can also be given' (Noble, p. 103).

In Taylor's rejoinder, the scene switches. Taylor agrees that no such pair of cases could arise. The issue to be debated should deal, not in single SE – B and T – B connections, but in whole classes of such connections. The question is whether classes of connections between SE's and B's, or between T's and B's, generate laws, and if so, which laws are more *basic*, ones connecting behaviour with antecedent conditions intrinsically described, or ones connecting behaviour with the same conditions described in a way that links them to the goal. The teleological or T-descriptions will be instances of a general form of T-description, whereas the intrinsic descriptions may have nothing in common, hence there may be no law that links them. The general form of T-description is 'such that B is required for G'. Here 'B' is a *variable* ranging over responses that occur in different conditions, but 'G', as before, denotes a single type of end-state.

Taylor's point can be illustrated in concrete terms as follows: In experiment 1, a rat is placed on the bank of a moat. On the other side is food. Let us call this set-up, plus the hungry state of the rat, SE_1. The rat then swims across the moat (B_1) and eats the food (G). In experiment 2, the rat is on a suspended platform (SE_2), the food is on another within jumping (B_2)-distance. In set-up SE_3, the rat has to run across a bridge (B_3) for food. In all these cases, the rat does whatever is necessary to get to the food. In so far as the statement 'The rat does whatever is necessary to get to the food' is law-like, it can be 'extrapolated' to experiment 4, given certain provisos. Relevant factors like the rat's health and extent of food-deprivation must remain the same, and the required response must be within the rat's physical capabilities, and must not call for prior knowledge which the rat has not acquired. Given these conditions, as long as we can see from the experimental set-up what action the rat will have to perform to get the food, we can predict that it will perform an action of that type. For example, it may have to jump over a fence. But perhaps this action could not have been predicted from knowledge of the previous SE_x - B_x correlations, for perhaps they do not combine together to form a generalisation that can be extrapolated. Perhaps the only general description available is 'Whenever SE_1 or SE_2 or $SE_3 \ldots$, then B_1 or B_2 or $B_3 \ldots$ respectively'. But this disjunction of particular correlations is confined to situations in which the relevant behaviour has actually been observed; it cannot be extended to cover new situations as yet unobserved.

A specific SE – B correlation can be extrapolated to new cases of the same specific type. If we know that in situation SE_1 the rat always swims across the moat, then we can predict that in a new instance of SE_1 the rat will again swim across the moat. But it may be impossible to extrapolate to SE_4, where this is a new situation of a new type, since we may not know the general principle by which different types of SE count as members of the general class SE_x. Similarly, we may not know when a new type of response B_4 is of the right kind to figure in a general law, $SE_x - B_x$. But the T – B law does provide a general characterisation of the kind of behaviour and the kind of antecedent condition. Different types of response count as instances of the same teleological kind when they are each, in their separate contexts, required for the same G. Different antecedent conditions count as the same kind if they are such that, in them, a certain response B which the animal can perform is required to get to G. Thus the T – B law is extrapolable to hitherto unobserved cases. Furthermore, says Taylor (1967, p. 143), 'we shall be able to account for a correlation of the form $SE_x - B_x$ by means of the $B = f(T)$ law: we shall say that SE_1 gives rise to B_1 because the case where SE_1 holds is the case where T_1 holds; and we shall be able to predict what will happen when $(SE)_{n+1}$ occurs by seeing what it requires for G, that is, what its description is in T-terms'.

It goes without saying that we could not tell what form behaviour will take in a new case unless we knew enough about the structure of the situation to be able to see what behaviour would be needed in it in order to produce G. The T description goes through the SE description in each case. However, what is important is that the antecedent situation has a T description true of it, for it is the fact that the situation is of the T type which is responsible for its producing B. The justification for assigning the responsibility to that fact is the T – B generalisation, which has nomological force. Because explanation sentences are non-extensional, we may accept 'B occurred because a T-type situation obtained' while rejecting 'B occurred because an SE type situation obtained'.

It is not Taylor's intention to rule out *a priori* the possibility that a general SE description will be found which yields an SE – B law of equal explanatory power to the T – B law. If in a given case we have not yet found one, this may be due simply to inadequate knowledge about the state of the system and the environment, and these gaps may be filled by future research in psychology and physiology. However, he is sceptical of any such prospect. Animal behaviour probably just is the sort of phenomenon for which T-laws yield the best systematized account.

Before investigating Taylor's position more fully, let us note a couple of minor difficulties in his definition and suggest how it might be modified to get round them. His case is made less plausible than it could be through his excessively strict formulation. Firstly, a teleological explanation of a bit of behaviour surely does not assert that the behaviour is *required* for its goal, if this means 'necessary condition for achieving the goal'. Many writers would hold, on the contrary, that goal-directed systems can often adopt a variety of methods of getting to their goal, even in one and the same situation. Though no particular action out of the range of appropriate actions is necessary or required, we explain whichever one does occur by saying that it occurred for the sake of G.

Taylor does recognise the existence of this kind of plasticity, but he sticks to his view by saying on p. 9 of his book that 'if there are several possibilities, we cannot account for the selection between them unless we add another teleological principle, e.g. of least effort'. He is saying that since the selection of B_1 rather than B_2 or B_3 (where each will help S to get to G) is explained by a general principle, by presupposing the operation of this principle we can continue to regard B_1 as being necessary for G. B_1 was required, given the context in question, and given the truth of a general principle to the effect that nature always takes the shortest path. We need not pursue at this stage the question whether the least effort principle really is teleological. Taylor's idea is, I suppose, that if the selection-principle is teleological, then the teleological explanation of why B_1 occurred once selected is untainted by anything non-teleological in the background. In fact, the selection-principle does not need to be teleological itself; its role is merely to justify the claim that B_1 really is required for G. Any other principle of selection which favoured B_1 would do just as well.

It is not an adequate defence, however, since the principle of least effort would not decide between two equally economical ways of getting to G. Buridan's ass may hover between two equidistant bundles of hay, but if eventually he does go one way, it is still true that he goes in order to eat hay. Furthermore, Taylor admits that a system might achieve G without doing B at all, when he remarks on p. 16 that 'it is not necessarily a counterexample to a teleological correlation if the event first in time (the B-event) does not occur, while that second in time, G, does; that is, comes about by accident or through some cause outside the system'. Such an eventuality would be a counterexample to the claim that B was required for G, if this meant that B was strictly necessary. Let us, therefore, adopt a looser, more plausible interpretation, and say that the antecedent situation should be one in which B is a means to, or contributes to G.

A second defect in the definition is that it makes the teleological antecedent a sufficient condition of the occurrence of B. This again is too strict. Admittedly, when Taylor says that the $T - B$ connection holds invariably, he means by 'invariably' not necessarily every time, but such that exceptions can be cogently explained by interfering factors. However, certain other qualifications will have to be made too, e.g. that B is currently within S's power, and so on. A more realistic T-law might be: 'Whenever B is required for G, B occurs, provided the state of S permits it, and nothing interferes from outside'.

However, now that we have replaced 'B is required for G' by 'B is a means to G', there is an added complication. Now, one initial state of affairs may have two or more T descriptions. The situation in which Buridan's ass finds himself, for example, is both T_1 (i.e. such that going left (B_1) is a means of getting hay) and T_2 (i.e. such that going right (B_2) is a means of getting hay). If T_1 were sufficient for B_1 and T_2 sufficient for B_2, subject only to the above-mentioned provisos about ability and interference, the ass ought to go in both directions. Clearly another modification to the T-law is needed. We could leave it open which means-action occurs: 'Whenever B_1 and B_2 and B_3; ... are means to G, S does B_1 or B_2 or B_3 ..., subject to the other provisos'. Or we could make the generalisation less than universal: 'Very often when B is a means to G, then, subject to the other provisos, S does B',

This latter is perhaps more realistic. After S has done a specific action B, this generalisation provides some explanation of why S did it, although it would not have enabled us to predict with certainty in advance that S was going to do it. But this surely is the normal position we find ourselves in when giving explanations, including straightforward causal ones.

In view of these modifications to the T-law, teleological explanations will not be so simple as Taylor's original deductive-nomological schema:

Whenever B is required for G, B occurs.
B is required for G in this situation.
_____
Therefore, B occurs in this situation.

There will be a number of other minor premisses like 'S has the power to do B', and 'Nothing prevents B from occurring in this situation'; and the inference will become inductive rather than deductive, since the law is not universal. But these complications do not detract from Taylor's main idea, that to explain B teleologically is to assert, relying on the support of a law-like generalisation, that B occurred *because it was a means to G*. In asserting this, one need not deny that the occurrence of B was contingent upon a number of other factors as well.

What sort of an explanation is this? What is the force of the explanatory 'because'? It depends on what sort of a generalisation the T-law is. One possibility is that it is simply a classificatory generalisation of the same type as 'Nearly all swans are white'. Teleological explanation would then be like 'This bird is white because it is a swan'. But this clearly is not what Taylor has in mind, for he regards teleological explanations as explanations of what *made* S do B. The teleological antecedent, the situation in which B is required for G, is supposed to *bring about* B; it is efficacious in *producing* B, given the relevant standing conditions. Taylor would certainly wish to say, too, that the T-law licenses counterfactuals of the form 'If this situation had been T, S would have done B'. Quite clearly, then, the T-law is a kind of causal generalisation, and teleological explanation as Taylor defines it turns out to be a kind of causal explanation. What makes it teleological is that the causal antecedent is described in a way that links it to the goal, rather than being described in terms of its intrinsic properties. Thus the difference between a teleological and a simple causal explanation of the same phenomenon lies in the way the cause is *described*. *Qua* teleological, the antecedent is described in T terms, *qua* simple-causal, it is described in SE terms. But the antecedent is the same in both cases. The T description and the SE description have the same reference, namely the state of the system and environment just prior to the action. This state is the cause of the action, however it may be described; Taylor's point is that the T-description presents it under a more fruitful aspect.

It is perhaps ironic, in the light of Taylor's strictures against 'conceptual reductionism', that we are forced to construe his theory in this way. More important, though, is the question whether it is correct as an analysis. In a recent paper, Larry Wright (1972) argues that it is fundamentally correct, though the definition is over-rigid. Wright offers the following modified formula, which is close to my version as suggested above:

'S does B for the sake of G' means
    (i) B tends to bring about G, and
    (ii) B occurs because (i.e. is brought about by the fact that) it tends to bring about G.

More simply, 'behaviour is teleological if it is being brought about by its tendency to produce a certain result'. My only complaint about this formula is that Wright does not emphasise that this rather peculiar locution, in which the cause of B is said to be 'the fact that B tends to produce G', or 'B's tendency to produce G', are merely ways of describing the prior state of the system-plus-environment. It is *this* that causes the particular occurrence of B, under the aspect of being so structured as to confer this tendency upon B. There is a danger that the formula might be read as asserting that the fact or the tendency are themselves entities that can figure as terms in a causal relationship, independent of the concrete objects and events which go to make them up. But such a construal is unnecessary. When we distinguish aspects of a cause by using 'the fact that' locutions, (e.g. 'The cause of the bridge's collapse was the fact that the wind was force 8, not the fact that it was blowing in a north-easterly direction'), we are gesturing towards the law under which the sequence falls by describing the antecedent as an event or state with a certain property. We are not saying that the property was itself the cause, independent of its concrete instantiation prior to the effect.

Before turning to criticism of this analysis, let us note one further point of interpretation. I take it that it does *not* mean 'S does B now because B has led to G in the past'. Taylor, certainly, would not wish to claim that B must have led to G in the past if B occurs for the sake of

G now. His T – B law is supposed to be extrapolable to new cases in which the response required for G may never have led to G in other situations in the past, and indeed may never have occurred before at all. All that is claimed is that B's occurrence must be *dependent upon* the present situation's being one in which a B-type response would contribute to G. To *establish* this dependency and to rule out coincidence, we could repeat the experiment under various conditions or call upon inductive evidence from similar situations in the past. We might well have evidence that B had led to G in the past. But teleological explanation is not *restricted* to cases where the animal has past experience of B-type actions leading to G-type consequences.

Objections to the analysis

Unquestionably, Taylor's account makes teleological explanations empirically testable, and shows how they might be useful. But is it *correct* as an analysis? Does it provide necessary and sufficient conditions for the truth of 'S does B in order to do G'? I think not.

There are many kinds of phenomena that can be explained in a way that conforms to the Taylorian formula, yet which are not goal-directed. For example, when a free pendulum is displaced from the vertical, it oscillates in the way that it does because the initial conditions are such that this kind of oscillation tends to restore equilibrium. When water is poured down one arm of a U-shaped tube, the level of water in the other arm goes up, because that keeps the level equal in both arms. Many thermodynamic phenomena can be explained by Maupertuis's principle of least action. They occur because they are the most economical way of bringing about a state of equilibrium characteristic of the system. In all these cases, the cause of the phenomenon is the prior state of the system and environment. But they satisfy the formula, since the cause can be described in relation to a future state of equilibrium, and furthermore the phenomena can be subsumed under laws in which those very descriptions appear. Nevertheless, the fact that an event occurs because it restores a balance of forces is not enough to establish that it occurs *in order to* restore the balance.

This argument rests on counterexamples. But there is another completely general argument, which I shall call the 'double-edge' objection. Since Noble has proved that every instance of a Taylorian T – B connection must have an SE – B counterpart, it is equally true, given the nature of his proof, that every simple causal connection has a teleological counterpart, provided only that there is a description of the antecedent which makes reference to some future state of affairs. But there always is such a description. Every event brought about in a lawful way occurs because by doing so it accords with the law. That is to say, by occurring, the event brings about a situation which consists of the law's having been confirmed. Therefore, on Taylor's definition, it occurs for the sake of according with the law.

Timothy L. S. Sprigge was the first person to use this argument, in his paper 'Final Causes', (1971). He did not, however, point out that we have here a *reductio ad absurdum* of the Taylorian analysis, since it is absurd to suppose that an analysis which has this consequence could be correct. Wright's formula, like Taylor's original, allows any law instantiating behaviour to count as teleological, so long as the cause is described relationally with respect to a future state of affairs. If behaviour B is caused by antecedent A, then it occurs because it tends to achieve G, where G is the generic state of affairs described by the law A – B.

The double-edge objection and the counterexample objection each prove that the analysans is no sufficient condition of goal-directedness. Is it a necessary condition though? Wright's formula is looser than Taylor's original, hence easier to satisfy, hence more likely to be a necessary condition. Whether it is so depends on whether determinism is assumed. The previous paragraph invoked Sprigge's argument that any event will satisfy the formula provided it is brought about in accordance with a law. On the assumption that all events are caused, no event can fail to satisfy the formula provided it falls under a law, and so the formula is a trivially necessary condition. All events, not only events that we intuitively call goal-directed, have to satisfy it. To defend his formula as a non-trivial necessary condition. Wright would have to deny that causal connections are always lawful, or show that Sprigge's argument is invalid.

If, on the other hand, there are some uncaused events, the question is: Could any of them be goal-directed? According to Wright, a necessary condition of an event's being goal-directed is that it be caused by a certain fact or state of affairs. Thus his formula entails that no goal-directed events are uncaused. Wright does say that when there is a set of alternative responses appropriate to G, the teleological explanation of the member of the set that actually occurs is compatible with a degree of indeterminacy among the factors responsible for the selection of that member. So he leaves open the possibility that the event might have no completely determining cause, while closing the possibility that it might be totally unconstrained.

In my view, the failure of Taylor's theory to yield a sufficient condition can be traced to a general defect in any behaviourist theory of teleology. The general criticism of these theories is that they require us to assume that whatever 'G' stands for is a goal, without providing any independent non-behavioural criterion of goalhood. We are supposed to infer that an event is a goal by observing the directedness of movements towards it; that is, we are to refine our hypotheses about goals by the method of successive approximation. However, the mere systematicity of a pattern of movements with respect to some object or parameter G is not enough to prove that the movements are goal-directed to G, since G may not be a goal. Although the use of the letter 'G' may mislead us, G could, on the evidence, be no more than the *de facto* terminus of movements going in that direction. It is true, of course, that convergence upon a certain state can provide good evidence of goalhood. The point is, an analysis is required to state what goalhood *consists in*, i.e. what 'goal' *means*. This general defect is present in Braithwaite, Sommerhoff, and Nagel, as well as in Charles Taylor. For this reason, the early Taylor belongs on the same side of the fence as the so-called 'behaviouristic reductionists'.

Although the counterexamples seem conclusive, doubt may be cast on the double-edge objection. It could be urged that the pseudo-teleological laws which Sprigge says can always be constructed out of causal laws are not really of the same form as Taylorian T – B laws. Here is an illustration of the objection at work:

'We can just see that what is required of a stone, if the "goal" of obeying the law of gravity is to be achieved, is to fall when dropped. We test the stone by dropping it, in a number of trials with initial conditions varied, and we find that it always does what is required to achieve this "goal". We conclude, therefore, coincidence having been ruled out, that its behaviour is causally dependent on the fact that such behaviour is appropriate. Thus, according to the analysis, the stone is goal-directed towards satisfying the law of gravity. But this is false, *ergo* the analysis is wrong.'

Note that the 'goal', in the double-edge argument is described as 'to satisfy the law of gravity'. For the 'counterexample' argument, the 'goal' of a boulder rolling downhill (the whole scene being conceptualised as a system tending towards equilibrium) is not to satisfy the law of gravity, but to get to the bottom. To put it more generally, the 'goal' of a system in static or dynamic equilibrium is to restore the balance whenever external forces upset it.

A Taylorian T – B law says that T, i.e. the state of affairs in which B leads to G, causes B. Sprigge postulates a novel value for G, namely the holding of the law 'Whenever A, then B'. Thus we get a T – B law of anything caused by any antecedent A: 'The state of affairs in which B leads to the truth of "Whenever A, then B" causes B'. But doubt may be cast on the propriety of this so-called law; e.g. John Watling (1972) has claimed that the falling of a stone does not lead to conformity to the law of gravity, but *entails* it. In general, B must cause G, not entail G. This is a doubt about the first conjunct of Wright's analysans ('B tends to produce G'). When 'G' means 'The holding of the A – B law', it is wrong to say that B's occurring (as a result of A) *produces* G.

What does it mean to say that the falling of a stone *entails* conformity to the law of gravity? It seems to me that there are two interpretations, corresponding to two conceptions of 'law'. On the first, the law is simply a summary of what happens when stones and other things are dropped. If the stone, when dropped on a particular occasion, had gone into orbit, the law would not have been falsified, but rather the statement of it would have been revised so as to take account of this case. Thus B, whatever it is, cannot fail to conform to the A – B law, simply in virtue of the fact that it is analytic that B conforms to the A – B law. But this conception of law is not what is intended by the strong thesis.

On the second, the A – B law has a nomological force which goes beyond a mere summary of the A – B connections that have occurred so far. The law as stated claims to be true in advance of the occurrence of this particular B. If it is a true law, then whatever happens on a particular occasion conforms to it in the sense of 'obeys it'. When a stone falls, it is a contingent fact that it obeys the law of gravity, since the law of gravity as stated could conceivably have been false. However, Watling's point would presumably be that it is still misleading to say that B helps to produce the truth of the statement 'Whenever A, then B', or even to say that B tends to bring about a situation described by the law. Rather the occurrence of B in those circumstances *constitutes* a situation described by the law. The case envisaged by Wright and Taylor is one where the state of affairs described as the goal is brought about after B and as a result of B.

Sprigge might reply here that Wright and Taylor ought not to have limited their formulae to cases of this kind, since it is not true that the goals of behaviour must always come after the behaviour. Some actions are performed for their own sakes, others are performed because they are the right thing to do. They are performed in order to do something that satisfies a certain description. The case being discussed is exactly parallel to the case of a man who bows to a lady in order to pay respect. B occurs because it is the right thing to occur according to the A – B law. The phrase 'B leads to G' ought, on quite independent grounds, to be construed widely so as to include the case where the occurrence of B in the circumstances *amounts to* a situation in which a G-description is fulfilled.

Wright might concede this point, yet still see a problem for the double-edge argument regarding the second conjunct of his formula: 'The fact that B leads to G *causes B to occur*'. For it is surely misleading to say that the cause of B is the fact that a law said that B must occur. To say this would suggest that the law itself was a cause. On the supposition that it is a law that fire causes smoke, the cause of a particular bit of smoke is a particular fire, not a particular fire plus the fact that fire causes smoke. When a causal explanation is set out as a syllogism, both the major and the minor premisses are needed to derive the conclusion, but only the minor premiss refers to the cause of the effect referred to in the conclusion.

In reply to this objection, we need only observe that the double-edge argument no more confuses causation with causal explanation than Wright does. For the second part of his analysans to work, a law has to be built in to the description of the causal antecedent in any case. This is allowable insofar as the antecedent is not the law itself, but the state of affairs in which the law holds. The law in question is 'B in SE leads to G'. It is true that on Sprigge's novel interpretation of G, this law has yet another law embedded in it. The law 'B in SE leads to G' comes out as 'B in SE leads to the state of affairs described by the law "A leads to B"'. But this is surely unexceptionable, since the holding of a law, or the state of affairs such that a law holds, is agreed by all parties to be capable of being a term in a causal relation, either as cause or as effect.

It is also true that the evidence, obtained from a number of trials, which might support the hypothesis that the cause of B is the fact that B leads to the holding of the law A – B, is equally evidence in favour of the simpler hypothesis that the cause of B is A. But the simplicity of the A – B law as compared to the T – B law is irrelevant. In a

Laplacean closed deterministic universe, where A is always followed by B and B is always followed by C, the evidence that A causes B is necessarily evidence that a state of affairs in which B leads to C causes B. For all we know, our world might be like this. We find Taylorian T-laws useful in the present state of ignorance, but all the evidence in favour of them might, for all we know, be evidence for much simpler laws with intrinsically characterised antecedents. In the deterministic system, the 'goal' C really does come after B, whereas in the pseudo T-laws the 'goal' is the law obeyed by B. But this is not a relevant difference. What Taylor would need to show is that the trivialising T – B law is *inapplicable* to the case of the falling stone. The relation between the contorted T – B law and the matching A – B law is identical with the relation between any Taylorian T – B law and its known or unknown SE – B counterpart.

The double-edge argument, that all phenomena can be subsumed under T – B laws, entails that there are counter-examples, i.e. that *some* non-teleological phenomena can be so subsumed. But the form of T – B law required by the double-edge argument may be felt to be objectionable. It is important, therefore, not to forget the argument from counter-examples, based on the existence of equilibrium systems. This argument does not equate the goal G with the holding of the A – B law, but takes G to be the state of equilibrium brought about by B. Thus the T – B laws applicable to such systems are not distorted rewritings of simple A – B laws, but are genuinely different. They are the sort of T-laws that Taylor meant, yet not all the systems to which they apply are teleological.

The central failing of Taylor's theory is, in my view, the idea that behaviour which is goal-directed is so only in so far as it is *described* in a certain way. The phenomena themselves are neither teleological nor non-teleological until they become characterised and subsumed under a generalisation of the prescribed form. Teleological explanation is not 'explanation of that which is independently and objectively teleological'; rather it is explanation, in a 'teleological form' or mode which *we* adopt and find convenient, of that which is objectively neutral. Teleology, on Taylor's definition, becomes a purely epistemological notion.[2]

[2] For later developments of his views, see Taylor (1970).

6

General assessment of behaviourist theories

The theories that have been considered so far took their object of analysis to be a general notion of goal-directedness. They all claimed that it was in virtue of a pattern exhibited by a range of behaviour that a particular action included in that range counted as goal-directed. No mention of any internal state was made, nor were such states covertly assumed. Nagel is no exception, despite the fact that he posits state variables associated with internal parts of the directively organised system. In order to accommodate overt goal-seeking behaviour within the paradigm of homeostasis, Nagel simply extends the boundaries of the system so as to include environmental variables within it. His 'state-variables' of the whole system then comprise stimulus conditions and overt responses.

It is not fantastic to countenance goal-directed behaviour that is not consciously purposive. We think that many lowly organisms behave in a goal-directed way; and we have learnt to describe certain self-correcting mechanisms as goal-directed. So without necessarily having any philosophical bias in favour of behaviourism, we might well think that a behaviouristic analysis was possible in this area.

However, none of the theories provides a satisfactory characterisation of the concept. In spite of their differences of approach and paradigm, they seem to be susceptible to certain common objections. It will be useful to state in general terms the basic flaws endemic to theories of this type. Then it will be easier to decide which directions look promising for further investigation.

Braithwaite, Sommerhoff and Nagel aim to give an abstract account of what goal-directedness really is. They look first at behaviour, either single responses or sequences unfolding through time, and find that the goal-directed kind is distinguished by the fact that it has a special effect or terminus. The main feature of the terminus is that it can be reached from a variety of different routes. Whichever route is followed, the end-point is reached despite changes in the circumstances that are met along the way. By observing an organism's behaviour in different situations, we build up a picture of its repertoire. Then on a particular occasion, when the organism exhibits only one or a few responses before reaching such an end-point, we draw upon the inductive knowledge to justify a belief that if the conditions had been different in certain ways, the organism would have responded differently, and that these different responses would normally have brought the organism to the same terminus. If this belief is true, the organism is goal-directed.

Taylor's aim in his first chapter is to analyse the meaning of 'S does B for the sake of G'. He claims that the teleological description explains *why* S does B. Its explanatory validity depends on there being a kind of law stating that, within a certain range of circumstances, S does whatever is required for G, together with the fact that on the occasion in question the circumstances fell within the range, and that the response which happened to be required was B. The evidence that backs up the 'teleological law' is the same sort of behavioural pattern which the other philosophers take as constitutive of goal-directedness: B_1 occurs when B_1 happens to be the response that leads to G; B_2 occurs when B_2 leads to G, and so on. The justification for saying of any item of behaviour in the range that it occurs *because* it leads to G is that the fact that a response within the range leads to G seems to be a sufficient condition for the occurrence of that response. So all the theories exploit the pattern of behavioural convergence, as illustrated in the fan-diagram or the lens-diagram.

Taylor differs from the others in not assuming that the system is deterministic. He regards teleological explanation as autonomous of causal explanation in virtue of its *form*; and that living systems may turn out to be not causally deterministic. This is really a secondary issue for us, although it is a central theme of Taylor's book. Our primary concern is to understand what 'goal-directed' *means*. As we have seen, Taylor was confused about the status of his own analysis, since the T-law is, in fact, a kind of causal generalisation. It is consistent with all four theories to view Taylor's 'T-law' as a kind of emergent super-law that rides on top of a network of converging causal connections.

Many of the connections between types of field-conditions and types of responses may have been observed to hold in the past, but others may be inferred indirectly. Past observations may provide the outline of a convergence-pattern that contains a number of gaps. On a particular occasion, all that is actually observed may be B itself, and perhaps the subsequent occurrence of G. What is *meant* by saying that B occurs for the sake of G, according to these theories, is roughly that B is the kind of response that leads to G, B occurs, and that there exists a range of hypothetical alternatives which would occur instead of B if the circumstances were different, and which would lead to G in those new circumstances. Goal-directedness is not a simple *observable* property of the behaviour that occurs, but is a property of that behaviour in virtue of a truth about hypothetical alternatives.

There is no doubt that plasticity and persistence are highly relevant evidence of teleology. But as analyses of the *meaning* of 'S does B in order to do G', these theories provide neither sufficient nor necessary conditions. They are not sufficient, because too many things display the plasticity pattern. The central problem is to formulate a general criterion for ruling out objects which tend naturally toward a state of stability or quiescence in the face of changes in their surroundings, such as snowballs rolling downhill, pendulums, and other equilibrium systems. It is natural to suppose that there exists some additional property possessed by genuine teleological systems. But such a property is peculiarly elusive.

Sommerhoff and Nagel suggest that the difference lies not in the phenomena themselves, but in our assumptions. They attempt to pin it down by means of the notion of epistemic independence. But the notion is incapable of bearing such weight. Even if it could provide a principle of demarcation, the dividing line would be relative to background assumptions, and would constantly shift as science advanced. It is tempting, though, to consider seriously the possibility that the dividing-line is not wholly objective, for this would explain their failure to provide a sufficient condition. I pointed out that Braithwaite's idea of 'variancy in field-conditions' could be loosely interpreted so that every object exhibited plasticity in some situations. Similarly, Sprigge's argument, if sound, proves that *any* law-governed transaction could be regarded as subject to a T-law.

It is a more complicated question whether the theories give a necessary condition. One thing at least has been established beyond doubt; no teleological description of an action entails straightforwardly that the goal of the action will be achieved. Consequently I built a 'goal-failure toleration' clause into the theories that needed it. But it has not yet been decided whether a teleological description entails the conditional prediction that S will get to G provided no obstacle interferes.

Nor has it been decided whether a TD entails that if the conditions were different, S would still get to G provided no obstacle interfered. If anything, the discussion has treated plasticity and persistence as if they were necessary features, but ones which are difficult to characterise precisely. It remains to be considered whether they are necessary, without being *trivially* necessary. The objection that they are necessary merely because all stable processes necessarily have them is just a version of the argument that they are not sufficient. I shall now consider in more detail whether a TD entails any conditional statements asserting plasticity or persistence.

Conditionals that might be entailed by TDs

Entailment is a relation between propositions, so we need to have the propositions explicitly formulated. It is also a relation that holds in virtue of their meanings, not in virtue of the evidence for them. So we need to keep meaning and evidence separate. This is not easy to do when dealing with conditionals. What precisely are the conditional statements we have to deal with? How specific are they, and what factors are mentioned in their antecedents? Let us picture a scene of the sort that gives rise to teleological judgments. A man is standing on a river bank watching a rat swim across to the far side. On the ground beyond, there is some food. The rat is steadily swimming towards that part of the bank which is nearest to the food. The man frames the judgment that the rat is swimming across the river in order to get the food. For the man, this teleological judgment is a hypothesis. The reasons he has for entertaining it may be good or bad. But these are of no concern to us. Our sole task is to work out what the teleological description entails.

The man is not judging that the rat will get the food, or even that it will reach the river bank. Another rat might eat the food first, or the swimming rat may drown. An indefinite number of things might happen which would be immediately recognisable as obstacles that the rat could not surmount or prevent. So if any prediction is entailed by the TD, it is one with an escape clause that sums up the indefinite range of obstacles: 'The rat will get the food provided that no obstacles prevent it'. A prediction that the rat will get the food is equally a prediction that the rat will have done other things as well, namely all the steps that will have been necessary for getting the food. What these steps are exactly depends on the layout of the scene. No specific intermediate step is entailed by the prediction, or by the TD. What the man can see about the layout equips him with the material for making more specific predictions, but he is not actually making them by uttering the TD.

In addition to the information about the present scene provided by his senses, the man has a stock of general knowledge about the capacities and habits of rats. This background knowledge enables him to construct in his mind a series of pictures, like fragments of a documentary film about rats. If the scene he is now witnessing develops in ways different from the way he expects it to develop, his general knowledge about rats will equip him with new sets of expectations about what the rat will subsequently do. But he is likely to continue to expect that the rat will get the food, so long as the changes in circumstances are not ones that count as obstacles. His state of mind may be summed up as follows: he has a background of general knowledge, a foreground of perceptual knowledge, a set of beliefs about what the rat will do, and a capacity for imagining alternative possible situations. On top of the foreground and the beliefs about what the rat will do, his imagination superimposes a set of conditional beliefs, constructed out of the background, about what the rat will do in different circumstances. Their combined content may be summed up by a general plasticity-asserting-conditional: 'If the conditions change in certain ways, the rat will still get the food'.

We now have examples of the two kinds of conditionals that were first distinguished in chapter 3. The changes in conditions that count as obstacles are not specified, and nor are the imagined changes in conditions that do not count as obstacles specified. But the man can recognise a range of possible changes that do not count as obstacles.

In setting the scene in this way, I have introduced a conceptualising observer whose suppositions and consequent beliefs provide the material for constructing conditionals. Once I have identified the sorts of conditionals that are appropriate to a given scene and a given goal-hypothesis, I can dispense with the observer and concentrate on the meanings of the conditional statements. It is useful, however, to bring him in, since it helps to clarify the temporal relationships. Conditionals may vary in mood and tense, depending on what the speaker knows and on the time of utterance. These two factors interact with each other. If he talks about a possible *future* state of affairs, the conditionals do not need to be subjunctive, since the supposition in the antecedent is not contrary to an already established fact, nor is it necessary for him to signal grammatically that the supposition is doubtful. Since the TD is assumed to be uttered at the time at which B occurs, the conditionals are also uttered at that time. I am able, there- fore, to make them both indicative, and hence directly falsifiable. I can set up a direct test of entailment: Would the TD be falsified necessarily if the conditionals turned out to be false?

Actually, neither of these conditionals can possibly be entailed. The TD 'S does B in order to do G' claims to be true of B at the time when it is done. But it may take time for S to pass from B to G. At any time in the interval between doing B and the time by which S may reason- ably be expected to have done G, if it is going to do G, S may *cease to be goal-directed to G*. If this happens, the conditional prediction 'S will do G provided no obstacle prevents it' will almost certainly not be fulfilled; but its falsehood does not entail that the original TD was false. Similarly, 'If the conditions change in certain ways, S will still do G' will almost certainly be false, but will not necessarily block the truth of the TD.

When S stops having the goal G at some time during the trial, a highly material chance occurs. But it is not a change in external circumstances. The plasticity theorist is obliged to account for a change of this kind somehow. It is no use adding another clause to the con- ditional, 'provided S continues to be goal-directed to G'. Nor is it possible to think of such a change as an obstacle already taken care of by the clause providing for goal-failure. The primary task is to explain what is meant by saying that S is goal-directed to G at a particular time t_1, when B is performed. Since the theorist aims to analyse the concept of having a goal' by means of conditionals, he naturally wishes to explain the concept of 'ceasing to have a goal' out of the materials provided by this analysis. But he has to provide these materials first.

If the TD entails any conditionals, and the TD is true at t_1, the conditionals must also be true at t_1. These two types of conditionals fail because something that happens later than t_1 can affect the truth of their consequents without undermining their antecedents, and without affecting the truth of the TD. According to the conditional analyses proposed so far, being goal-directed to G at t_1 is partly a dispositional property, manifested by behaviour *subsequent* to t_1. But the time-lag is fatal. S might cease to have the disposition in the interval. Indeed, this problem arises with all dispositional properties. A strip of rubber may be elastic at t_1, yet fail to stretch at t_2 because at t_2 its temperature is close to absolute zero. Consequently, any conditional analysis of a dispositional property assigned at t_1 has to employ *subjunctive* conditionals whose consequents pertain to the same occasion.

This point is clearly brought out by Mackie (1973, pp. 123–7), and by Goldman (1970, pp. 197–207). Mackie, however, gives reasons, in chapter 3 of his book, for thinking that subjunctive conditionals are not capable of being simply true or false. They ought rather to be assessed as reasonable or unreasonable in the light of the available evidence, which may be drawn from parallel cases. In Mackie's terms, our question is not whether the TD *entails* subjunctive conditionals, but whether it *sustains* them. Would a reason for thinking a conditional unjustified in a particular case automatically be a reason for withdrawing the TD? This question, which may be called the 'contrapositive test', is still the right one to ask, whether we take it as a test of entailment or sustainment.

Two types of 'simultaneous' subjunctive conditionals are suggested by the theories we are considering. The first is a *plasticity-conditional* which says that if the circumstances were different at t_1, the behaviour at t_1 would be different. To refer back to our scene, the man would perhaps want to assert 'If the food were further to the left, the rat would be swimming further to the left', 'If the food were not on the far side of the river, the rat would not be swimming across it', and a host of others, more or less specific, affirmative or negative. These are all too specific to be entailed by the TD alone, because they draw upon knowledge of the layout of the scene. A general form of plasticity conditional would present behaviour and conditions as determinables taking a certain range of determinate values in the particular case.

The second type of subjunctive conditional says that if the circumstances were different at t_1, the behaviour would be the same. Reading this as being compatible with the first type, I take it as saying that the same *type* of behaviour would persist. However, such a conditional would clearly not be entailed by a TD, *unless the type of behaviour was already teleologically characterised.* The different responses in different circumstances count as being of the same type, only in virtue of the fact that they all aim at G. What persists, then, is the directiveness to G. Unless the persistence-conditional is understood as a mere re-phrasal of the plasticity-conditional, there is no point in thinking of it as an analysis. Moreover, persistence is primarily a feature of behaviour *over* time, not *at* a time. The concept of diachronic persistence, like the concept of having a goal for a period of time, has to be constructed out of a series of synchronic plasticity-conditionals.

For every moment t, throughout a trial lasting from t_1 to t_n, there is a separate set of synchronic plasticity-conditionals: 'If the circumstances were C_1 at t, S would do B_1', 'If the circumstances were C_2 at t, S would do B_2' and so on, where B_1, B_2, etc., are actions that are appropriate to G in C_1, C_2, etc., respectively. The set may be summed up elliptically by a Taylorian T-law with a time reference added: 'S does at t whatever is appropriate to G at t'. One T-law representing an indefinite set of conditionals is entailed by 'S is goal-directed to G at time t_1', another T-law is entailed by 'S is goal-directed to G at time t_2', and so on. On an ideal trial in which S gets to G at or by t_n, every relevant moment, or nearly every moment, between B and G is one at which S is doing something appropriate to G. Also, if the circumstances had been different at any moment, S would then have done something else which would have been appropriate to G. If a trial is unsuccessful because S ceases to be goal-directed to G at some time t, this can be explained by reference to the fact that the plasticity conditionals pertaining to t and after were not true or sustained.

It is impossible to obtain direct evidence sustaining each member of a synchronous set of conditionals. Only one of them can have its antecedent fulfilled; the rest are supported by evidence from other occasions. But as time goes on during the trial, and as each set has one of its members confirmed, the evidence mounts up in favour of the hypothesis that S is goal-directed throughout the whole period. In this way, evidence about the whole sequence lends support to hypotheses pertaining to particular times. It is logically possible, however, that S be goal-directed at t_1, t_3, t_5 . . . for example, yet not goal-directed at t_2, t_4, t_6 . . . At time t_2, S might do something appropriate to G by accident. At time t_4, S might not do anything that is appropriate. At t_6, S might do something inappropriate. However, if the general trend of S's behaviour is towards G, an observer will probably stick to the hypothesis that S is directed to G throughout. In fact, he will be wrong, but the available evidence is not enough to show that he is wrong. That is the reason why it is important for the plasticity theorist to observe the separation between evidence and meaning, and to insist that the meaning of the TD is given by conditionals that pertain to the relevant moment, not by ones that have to wait until a later moment to acquire a truth value.

Braithwaite occasionally speaks of plasticity as the capacity to perform in one and the same situation a number of different, equally appropriate actions as means to G. Plasticity, so construed, *could not* be a necessary condition, since, as S gets nearer to G, there must come a time when only one pathway to G remains. The scope for plasticity goes down to zero as the sequence approaches consummation. However, no such objection holds against the sort of synchronic plasticity being considered here. Even at time t_m, just prior to goal-attainment, there is a set of alternative responses that would be performed if the circumstances were different. For instance, if the goal object were further to the left at t_m, the animal would move further to the left. It is possible that from some vantage points, the animal could get to G by a variety of different routes, even if the situation does not change. But the only sense in which the analysis *requires* that S be able to get to G by a variety of different routes is that S could get to G by different routes in a variety of changed situations – each route being laid out for it by each respective situation.

It is not easy to sum up in one idiomatic sentence the set of conditionals that define synchronic plasticity. Taylor's T-law is an attempt, but it is vague. It fails to convey the information that for each member of the set of alternative situations there corresponds a response which is appropriate to G relative to that situation, and it is *that* response which would occur. Let us employ the variables 'B_i' and 'C_i', where C_i is i-th member of the set of alternative circumstances, C_1, C_2, C_3, ... C_n that might have obtained at a given time t, and where B_i is the i-th member of a set of alternative responses B_1, B_2, B_3 ... B_n such that B_i is the (or a) response that is appropriate to G in C_i. The plasticity theory claims that 'S was goal-directed to G at t' entails 'For any C_i if C_i had obtained at t, S would have done B_i at t.'[1]

This still isn't quite accurate; it takes the 'no obstacles' clause for granted. A restriction must be placed either on the range of circumstances or on the range of responses. A proposition like 'The rat had the goal of getting the food' would not be expected to imply 'If there had been a 20-foot high wall between the rat and the food, the rat would

[1] It is interesting to note that if no single, implicitly general conditional of this type existed, the plasticity theorist who was a phenomenalist about dispositions could not regard goal-directedness as a single disposition at all. As Mackie remarks (1973, p. 146): 'If a disposition consists just in the holding of a conditional, there should be just as many dispositions as there are conditionals, that is, as there are manifestations,'

have jumped over the wall'. To be fully explicit, we should add another condition: 'provided B_i was within S's power at t'. The procedure for interpreting and testing the conditional is: (i) Imagine an alternative situation to the actual one. (ii) Calculate what behaviour is required for G in that situation. (iii) Check that that behaviour is within S's power. Only if this condition is satisfied can one sensibly ask (iv) Would S have done it?

An equivalent but different procedure would be: (i) Imagine an altered circumstance. (ii) Restrict oneself to considering responses that are within S's power at the time. (iii) Calculate which response within S's power is appropriate for getting to G in that circumstance. There may be none. If so the situation is not included in the range of admissible alternatives, because it contains an insurmountable obstacle. The idea here is that the total range of possible alternative circumstances $C_1 - C_n$ comprises two subclasses, one being the class of circumstances that contain obstacles, the other being the class of circumstances in which the appropriate response is within S's power.

These two subclasses are relative to each other in size. The bigger the class of obstacle-containing situations, the smaller the class of situations in which an appropriate response is within S's power. The question arises, therefore, what we are to say about a case where every conceivable situation apart from the actual one contains an obstacle for S. Is the plasticity-conditional false in such a case? The theory says that a TD entails a conditional of the form 'In alternative circumstances S would if S could'. The conditional is false if its antecedent is true and its consequent false. But in a case where S could not behave appropriately in alternative circumstances, the antecedent is unfulfilled. It is impossible to give a yes/no answer to the question 'Would S behave appropriately in alternative circumstances?' In order for it to be empirically decidable whether S is plastic or not, it must be possible to establish independently, with respect to every appropriate action, whether S *could* do it, without prejudging the issue of whether S would do it on a test occasion. There must be a distinction between excusable failures to respond appropriately, and failures which falsify the conditional. We must admit the logical possibility of falsifying the conditional, otherwise the claim that it is entailed by the TD would be vacuous. Both I and the plasticity theorist have an interest in insisting that the conditional is not trivial.

It seems to me that the theory is wrong, because the conditional might be false when a TD is true. Indeed, in the case of human beings, it is a familiar fact that goal-directed behaviour is not always plastic. Sometimes a man won't act unless the conditions are exactly right. The same goes for animals. It makes sense to suppose that although S is goal-directed to G and responds appropriately at t, nevertheless in other circumstances S would not have made an appropriate response at t even though he could have done. In other circumstances S would have refrained from acting on that goal at t. The circumstances would not count as obstacle-containing ones. *Ex hypothesi*, they are ones where it is within S's capabilities to respond appropriately. Rather they are circumstances in which something inhibits S from aiming at G at that moment without destroying S's disposition to do so. It is natural, in view of this, to think of S's *having goal G* as an internal state or intervening variable which mediates causally between the external stimulus and the overt response. Its effect on behaviour seems to be conditional upon other internal states which interact with it and sometimes inhibit it. The state of having a goal, like the state of desiring, can obtain at t yet be 'unengaged' (a term used by Pears (1973)).

One common reason why S would refrain from doing any B_i other than B_1, even though he could do it, is that to do it would conflict with some other goal that he has. The internal state of having one goal is disengaged by the internal state of having another goal. Suppose that S did B_1 in C_1 in order to get to G_x, but that S also had goal G_y at the same time. What would have happened if the circumstances had been C_2? The plasticity theorist says that 'S had goal G_x' entails 'If the circumstances had been C_2, S would have done B_2', where B_2 is appropriate for G_x in C_2. The truth is, however, that what S would have done depends on which goal would have taken precedence in that changed situation. S might have refrained from doing B_2 because B_2 would have lowered the chances of getting to G_y later. S might have engaged G_y, and done B_{99}, where B_{99} is appropriate for G_y in C_2. S might, because he got confused, have done something that is inappropriate both to G_x and to G_y. Similar uncertainty attaches to what S would have done in C_3, C_4, and so on. There may be no other situations apart from C_1 in which S would have done an action appropriate to G_x.

Nor is it possible to counter this point by incorporating within the conditional an extra condition ruling out competing goals. The plasticity theorist might suggest that 'S had goal G_x' entails 'Provided S had no other goal G_y, then if C_i had obtained, S would have done B_i

(the response appropriate to G_x)'. But he then faces the problem of explaining what is *meant* by 'Provided S had not had goal G_y'. Having goal G_y clearly cannot be a matter of being plastic with respect to G_y; this very case is proof of that. He has to say that 'S had goal G_y' means or entails 'If S had had no other goal G_x, then if C_i had obtained, S would have done Bj (where Bj is the response appropriate to G_y in C_i)'. What now is meant by 'If S had no other goal G_x'? We are back to the original problem. The two conditionals together are locked in a vicious spiral. Neither succeeds in analysing out the term 'goal'. The fact is, it is impossible for S to be plastic with respect to G_x and to G_y simultaneously, though S can *have* both goals simultaneously.

Even if we ignore the possibility that S might have two or more competing goals, or try to evade the problem by stipulating that our analysis is concerned with the concept of a predominating goal, i.e. a goal which takes precedence over all others at a given time whatever the circumstances, it still seems to me that the generalised conditional is not entailed. It might be the case that in all other circumstances apart from C_1, some *other* internal necessary conditions for doing the appropriate action would be absent. S might, for instance, be too scared at that time to do anything in other situations, even though *capable* of doing B_2 in C_2, B_3 in C_3, and so on.

It is important to be clear about what my argument does *not* prove. At first sight, it might seem that the fact that S can have an unengaged goal at t indicates that the concept of having a goal cannot be analysed dispositionally at all. Unlike the earlier problem about time-references, (i.e. When does a temporary disposition start and stop?), this problem, of a disposition being present yet being unengaged at certain times, is not usually raised in connection with dispositional properties of inanimate objects. A permanently fragile vase cannot temporarily be in a state in which it would refrain from breaking if struck. If it is struck sufficiently hard at t-dt and fails to shatter at t (dt being the time-lag between triggering cause and manifestation), it is deemed not fragile at t, even though it may be known to have been fragile prior to t. But the phenomenon *does* arise with inanimate objects of a certain complexity. If the object can exist in several internal states, it might have a dispositional property whose manifestations are either issued or held back depending on the internal state obtaining at the time. We might call dispositions of this sort 'conditional'.[2] They are manifested if certain external conditions hold, on condition that a certain internal

[2] They are discussed by D. F. Pears in 'Ifs and cans' (1971–2).

condition holds. The peculiar feature is that on occasions when the internal condition is not holding, we still say that the object has the disposition, instead of saying that it has temporarily lost it. For example, a machine might be said to be lethal, on the grounds that if anyone were to touch it he would get an electric shock. It is presupposed that this test applies only when the machine is switched on. But it is still a lethal machine, even when not switched on. Similarly, a rat might be said to have an aggressive character, meaning that the rat is aggressive by nature and not merely aggressive at certain times, on the grounds that it tends to attack other rats if they get near it. Though there may be times when it is too tired to attack if other rats get near it, it is still an aggressive rat at those times. There would be nothing wrong with saying that S is generally disposed to behave in ways that lead to G, even though there are times when S would not behave appropriately for G. The plasticity theorist can perfectly well acknowledge that goal-directed behaviour is not manifested unless certain internal necessary conditions hold. Like Taylor, he accepts Noble's point that if there are two situations, identical as far as the environmental circumstances are concerned, in one of which S does B and in the other of which S does not do B, the difference must be accounted for by a difference in the state of S. He can also allow, if he is a realist about dispositions, that having a goal is itself an internal state, logically distinct from, and causally necessary for, the behaviour by which it is identified.

The crucial difficulty for the plasticity theorist is that his conditional has to be both general and *synchronic*, for reasons mentioned earlier. Its generality comes not from an implicit quantification over times, but from a quantification over hypothetical alternatives at a time. For him, having goal G at t is a polymorphous or multi-track disposition identified as such by reference to the *range* of possible responses at t. If all the *internal* necessary conditions for manifesting the disposition hold at t— as they must do if S does B_1 at t for the sake of G— then all the *internal* necessary conditions hold for any one of a multiplicity of manifestations. It is incoherent to suppose that the multi-track disposition might be partially unengaged and partially engaged, such that it would be manifested in one possible environmental situation at t but not in the rest. If a disposition would be manifested in only one set of circumstances, it is not multi-track.

So my argument does not prove that having a goal is not a disposition (though it does suggest that it will be difficult if not impossible to give a general specification in terms of behavioural manifestations). It proves simply that if having a goal is a disposition, it is not necessarily multi-track. I do not deny that evidence, drawn from a variety of occasions, which supports the proposition that S's behaviour is plastic with respect to G is also excellent prima facie evidence for the proposition that S is goal-directed to G. But I insist that plasticity is merely *evidence* of goal-directedness, not constitutive of it.

Although the argument proves conclusively that plasticity-conditionals are not correct as analyses of TDs universally, a dogged plasticity theorist could argue that there is a *basic* concept of goal-directedness which essentially involves the notion of a range of alternatives, and that situations, however common, in which there is only one response are, from a conceptual point of view, limiting cases, which we can only understand by reference to central cases where there is a range. He recognises that goal-directedness is sometimes, perhaps often, a single-track disposition, but maintains that the concept of single-track goal-directedness develops or has to be theoretically constructed out of the concept of multi-track goal-directedness. When there are two or more goals competing, the behavioural rigidity has to be thought of as the net outcome of an interaction between several antagonistic multi-track dispositions. In calling it goal-directed, we are *logically* committed to thinking of the action as the animal's unique solution to a time-sharing problem, as opposed to, say, McFarland's view that the action is, as a matter of fact, a solution to such a problem (see McFarland and Sibly, 1972).

He might explain the possibility of cases where an animal with only one goal fails to exhibit plasticity by saying that the individual has been deprived of the normal plasticity possessed by other animals of the same kind when they have that goal, but is being understood on analogy with a normal member of the species. His account would be bolstered by a story purporting to show, by citing events in the individual's life history, that S started out with a potential for plastic action which became whittled away by psychological traumas. His claim is not that there is in fact usually some such developmental explanation available, but that it is *built into our concept* of single-track goal-directedness that there must be some explanation linking it historically to the multi-track kind. I cannot prove *a priori* that in the basic case plasticity is not entailed, for the simple reason that the theorist stipulates that a case does not count as basic unless plasticity is present.

Two directions for further development

The problem of analysing TDs proves to have as its core the problem of determining what goalhood is, or what it is for a system to have a goal. Instead of 'S has goal G', we could say 'G is the goal of S's behaviour.' The two are equivalent, but have different emphases. The former lends itself more readily to the view that having a goal is being in some sort of internal state. But the mere form of words does not commit one to that view, which is unclear in any case pending clarification of the concept of an internal state. The plasticity theory tries to give a multi-track dispositional account without committing itself one way or the other as regards the ontological status of the disposition. Even if it had to have a material basis, an analysis would not characterise that basis, but would simply assert its existence. Although I have proved that the conditionals I consider are not entailed by a schematic TD, a determined plasticity theorist could continue to claim that goal-directedness of a special *basic* kind involves a disposition to behave plasticly.

However, I have established that such a disposition would not be sufficient. There are many end-states which possess the relational property of being converged upon, but which are not goals. Until an additional element is found, we do not fully understand what it is for an end-state to be a goal. Consequently, the conditionals are useless as criteria for goal-directedness, unless there is some reason for thinking that the focal point is a goal rather than a state of physical equilibrium. The main task outstanding is to identify this extra element.

It is obvious that we often have preconceptions about an animal's goal on a particular occasion, before we observe what it does. The relevant conditionals, whether synchronic or diachronic, cannot be formulated until a goal has been hypothesised, and the observer has calculated what is required for that goal in such and such circumstances. This, in itself, is not damaging to the plasticity theory. That so and so is the animal's goal is only a hypothesis, which subsequent events may lead us to retract. More damaging, however, is the fact that the observed behaviour, however complex, is always consonant with an indefinite number of goal-hypotheses. Thus plasticity by itself cannot determine exactly which goal is the operative one, although a number of wrong goal-hypotheses can be ruled out.

Two completely divergent pathways for further research open up at this stage. The first takes 'S has goal G' as its banner and its object of analysis. The second takes 'G is the goal of S's behaviour'. According to the first, having a goal is predicated primarily of the system itself, not of its behaviour. The job is to characterise the state of S more fully. Perhaps it is partly dispositional, but it is also more than that. The extra element might help to reveal indirectly what an end-state needs to be like in order to be a goal. The second pathway sticks to the idea that a goal is an end-state of S's behaviour, but it proposes that a goal is an end-state of a certain *kind*. The task is to discover the extra property which all goals have in common, but which is not possessed by *de facto* termini. It may well be a further relational property. It, plus the property of being a focus of convergent behaviour, might define the concept of goal completely.

Both pathways are worth exploring. I shall follow the second one in chapter 9, so far as it proves negotiable, and then return to the first path in chapters 10 and 11. Before trying the second one, it will be necessary to introduce a completely new topic, that of functions. The analysis of the concept of function eventually crystallises out something that might be the crucial additional goal-property. To understand this property we have to see how it stems from a completely different kind of teleology. When it has been fully discussed, we shall be able to apply it back to the problem of goals. If it proves to be the missing ingredient, the whole exercise will have an unexpected spin-off; it will effect a synthesis between the concept of function and the concept of goal, linking the two types of teleology into one.

In what sense are the two pathways utterly divergent? I have already said that the two formulations of the core proposition are equivalent, differing only in emphasis. But the emphases are symptomatic of a divergence of opinion about the way teleological descriptions *explain*. A philosopher who sets himself to discover more about the internal state of having a goal is almost certain to be a realist about it. Although he may believe that having a goal is a disposition, and although this does not by itself commit him to realism, he must also believe that there is more to having a goal than its dispositional aspect. For him, having a goal is not a logical fiction constructed out of behaviour, but is an internal state defined partly by the behaviour for which it is responsible and partly by something else. A philosopher who follows the 'internalist, path will mean by 'teleological explanation of B' an explanation saying that B occurs *because S has a goal*. The relationship marked by 'because' is presumably causal. So goal-explanations turn out to be a special kind of causal explanation, distinguished from other causal explanations solely by the special nature of the cause. Behaviour, being an effect of the internal state, is evidence for goal-directedness but not constitutive of it. The term 'goal-directed' connotes two components: the idea of movement towards a goal (like 'homeward-bound'), plus, more importantly, the idea of propulsion caused by the having of a goal.

The second pathway leads to quite a different conclusion about the way TDs explain. A philosopher who accepts behavioural plasticity as partly constitutive of goal-directedness, not just a sign or effect of it, sees a teleological explanation as fitting the explanation into a pattern of convergent behaviour. It characterises the action as an event of a certain *type*, that is, as a member of a class of events possessing a special kind of effect. He still has the job of defining the special nature of the effect, and until he has succeeded in this, he will not have a complete picture of the way in which it is explanatory to cite such an effect. It is plain, though, that teleological explanations are not causal. They are more like interpretations, which explain by redescribing in an illuminating, relating way. Because they classify the action on the basis of its expected outcome, they presuppose the causal laws that make it legitimate to expect that behaviour of that kind will have that outcome. But the kind of explanation they provide is supervenient upon the causal network, and perhaps *sui generis*.

Since the factors that make G a goal are outside S, we may call the second pathway 'externalist'. Its strongest argument against the first pathway is the claim that internalism postulates hidden internal states in the same cavalier way that Driesch postulated Entelechies.[3] Not only were Entelechies in principle unobservable, hence useless for science, they failed to do the job for which they were invented. They were supposed to answer the question, 'Why are these organic activities integrated in this way?' But, according to the externalist, to cite Entelechies as an answer betrays misunderstanding: what is wanted is not a causal antecedent, but a consequent, the purpose which the integration serves. The teleological question still awaits an answer, even after a causal explanation has been given. On the other hand, a great difficulty for externalism is to account for the phenomena of operativeness and disengagement of goals. It has to confront the difficulty of multiple goals, and the fact that an animal can have a goal yet not be acting on it.

[3] This notion is discussed in L. Von Bertalanffy, *Modern Theories of Development*, p. 37.

Both approaches account satisfactorily for the fact that we think we can *see* teleology in the behaviour. For example, we can just see straight off that the lion is trying to catch the antelope. The internalist explains this by showing how relative is the distinction between observation and theory. We say that we see electrons when we observe their traces on a screen. Similarly, we interpret the lion's movements in the light of the hypothesis that it has a goal, we describe them as 'trying to get', and hence we see them as trying to get. The externalist's position is not really very different. The total plasticity pattern cannot be observed on a particular occasion, since only one behaviour sequence actually occurs. The single sequence has to be interpreted against the background of hypothetical alternatives. For both theories, to 'see' teleology is to see behaviour as teleological, which involves interpreting it. And the interpretation can be objectively true.

Theories of teleology are often classified as reductionist or non-reductionist. But there are many different kinds of reduction. As a theory of teleological explanation, internalism denies it autonomy of form, but accords it a special type of causal antecedent. This is what is meant, presumably, by a 'reduction of teleological explanation to causal explanation'. However, from the internalist point of view, externalism is reductionist in a more traditional philosophical sense, since it tries to bring down the meaning of TDs as near as possible to the behavioural evidence. To compare the two theories along a single dimension of reductionism would be a sign of confusion. Nothing but muddle can come from equating the 'reduction' of teleological to causal explanation with the reduction of one theory to another, or with the reduction of one category of entity to another.

PART THREE

FUNCTIONS

7

Functions and ends

One of the basic rules of lexicography is: pitch the definition on the right level. Don't make the definiens technical or subtle if the definiendum is not technical or subtle. Subtlety comes in in choosing a suitable definiens. If the term being defined is vague or open-ended, then a definition will be exact only if it too is vague or open-ended. This commonsense rule is perhaps implicit in the substitutivity test for synonymy. When a word has several related senses, however, the rule does not tell us whether to separate the senses first and then find separate synonyms, or to find a single synonym that matches the ambiguity of the original word. Nor does the rule help to decide *when* a word has several senses.

> Kindred senses may be so interwoven, that the perplexity cannot be disentangled, nor any reason assigned why one should be ranged before the other. When the radical idea branches out into parallel ramifications, how can a consecutive series be formed of senses in their own nature collateral? The shades of meaning sometimes pass imperceptibly into each other; so that though on one side they apparently differ, yet it is impossible to make the point of contact.[1]

Methodological problems of this sort affect philosophers too. In recent years, a number of attempts have been made to analyse the concept of function. While it is true that some genuine philosophical disagreements exist, many of the discrepancies between these analysis are due to differences of philosophical method. There are several reasons for this. Firstly, the sorts of things which are said to have functions belong to an enormous variety of categories: ships, sealing wax and artefacts in general, parts of artefacts, properties of artefacts, activities of artefacts; parts of organisms, properties and activities of parts of organisms; characteristics, including behavioural characteristics, of

---

[1] Dr Johnson (1755), *Dictionary of the English Language*, Preface, 5th page.

whole organisms; social institutions, events and relations, individuals and groups in the context of wider groups, and so on. Disagreement occurs over the extent to which the differences between categories of items correspond to different senses of 'function'. Secondly, discourse about functions often demands a complex 'stage-setting'. Questions of the form: 'What is X for?' standardly expect functional answers; but the degree of detail and explicitness in an answer varies according to how much the speaker and hearer know, and take each other to know, about the situation. Philosophers differ over how much information should be packed into a paraphrase, and how much should be left contextually understood. Thirdly, they may differ about the aim of the analysis, whether it should faithfully reflect actual usage or reconstruct a purer concept. My general position is to seek as much economy and continuity of senses as the semantic facts permit, to build into the analysans no more than the analysandum strictly asserts, and to find a theory which *both* harmonises with linguistic intuitions *and* provides deeper insight. General principles do not always lay down one and only one pathway for an analysis; philosophers who agree about method on a general level may yet differ over particulars. But a great deal of unnecessary conflict in this field would be avoided if more attention were paid to method.

My aim in this chapter and the next is to build up a satisfactory overall account of functional teleology by arguing for certain paraphrases. The main philosophical puzzles to be solved are:

(1) Hempel's problem. Why is it that only some of an item's activities are functions, and the others accidental?

(2) Nagel's problem. Why is it that we ascribe functions to the parts of some systems (like organisms) but not to the parts of others (like the solar system)?

(3) The problem of functional explanation. How can it be explanatory of an item to cite one of its effects?

There is also the general 'taxonomic' problem: what are the differences and similarities between functions, ends and goals, and why are they all called 'teleological' notions?

My first step is to impose some initial order on the multiplicity of sentences associated with ascribing functions. I distinguish between *function-statements* (e.g. 'The/A function of the heart is to circulate the blood'; 'Keeping order is one of the functions of the police'; 'Bottles have the function of holding liquids', etc.) and *functional TDs* (e.g.

'The heart beats in order to circulate the blood'; 'The police exist in order to keep order'; 'Bottles are the way they are in order that they may hold liquids', etc.). In a functional TD the word 'function' does not occur. The activity mentioned last is asserted to be a function of the item or activity mentioned first in virtue of the meaning of the teleological connectives 'in order to' or 'in order that'. In a function-statement, the word 'function', in the positions or roles illustrated, does occur. This verbal distinction corresponds to a distinction which is sometimes made between a functional *analysis* and a functional *explanation*. The former simply specifies a function of an item. It answers the question: 'What function(s), if any, does X have?'. The latter explains the existence or presence of an item by reference to a function that it has. It answers the questions: 'What is X there for?', 'Why does X exist?' or 'Why does X do so and so?'. In some cases, both types of locution seem equally acceptable as answers to a teleological 'Why?' question, but this is not always the case. When it is the case, the illusion of equivalence seems to be due to contextual features supplied or taken for granted by the speaker and hearer.

In the well-known 'Hawthorne Experiment', the fact that the workers in a factory were being studied led unexpectedly to a rise in productivity. Merton calls this effect a 'latent function' of the experiment. Yet it is not the case that the study occurred in order that there should be increased productivity.[2] Again, it is certainly not true that rain falls in order to water the crops; but to say that rain performs the function of watering the crops seems to me not *false*, but misleading. I agree with Wimsatt (1972, p. 68) that 'a function can be attributed to an entity in situations where that function is not responsible for the existence and form of that entity'. Admittedly, the question 'Why does the heart beat?' *could* be answered merely by specifying the function which the beating heart performs for the organism, but this is because the speaker and hearer take it for granted, in this biological case, that the function of the heart-beat happens to be its *raison d'être*, rather than because the function-statement is *intrinsically* explanatory. This thesis is diametrically opposed, therefore, to Larry Wright's view (1973) that merely to specify the function of a thing *is* to explain why the thing is there. Cohen in his paper drew an illuminating parallel: To assert 'Event E' brought about Event E' is to venture a causal explanation of E in

[2] R. K. Merton (1949), pp. 120–1. This example was used to make the same point – that functional ascriptions are not necessarily functionally explanatory – by G. A. Cohen (1974).

virtue of the meaning of 'brought about'. To assert 'Event E' preceded Event E' *may* be to offer an explanation of E in certain circumstances, not because of what is strictly said, but because of what is conversationally implied.

Quite apart from these reasons for distinguishing function-statements from functional TDs, there are other purely grammatical reasons why they cannot be given the same kind of paraphrase. Functional TDs contain two verbs, the main verb plus either an infinitive or a verb in a 'that' clause. But the typical schema of a function-statement, 'A/The function of X is to do F' is superficially of the subject-predicate form. The typical schematic TD has three terms: 'X performs activity A in order to do F' ('in order that F may be done'); the two-termed TD, 'X exists/is there in order to do F' can be easily assimilated to it. But function-statements typically have two terms. Three-termed function-statements have to be assimilated to *them*, as, 'A function of X's doing A/having property A is to do F'. A further reason for recognising two distinct forms of statement, which will come clearer in due course, is that the blank in the sentence, 'The function of X is – ', must be filled by expressions that denote functions; whereas the blank in the functional TD, 'X does A in order – ', can be filled by expressions that denote functions and expressions that denote *ends*.

In the present chapter I explain what it means to ascribe a function F to an item X, first where X is an artefact, then where X is a part of a biological system. Ascriptions of functions to the activities and properties of such items, and to the behaviour-patterns of whole organisms, and to social institutions and groups, are treated as natural extensions of the primary patterns. The main finding is that functions are *relative to ends*. So the next task is to examine the various different concepts of end. The thorniest problems concern biological ends, like survival and reproduction, which underpin natural functions. Is the concept of a natural, biological end logically dependent upon the concept of a goal? This question is important in the light of our previous discussion at the end of Part Two. The externalist, having failed to provide a satisfactory account of goal-directedness in purely behavioural terms, hopes to bolster his theory with the aid of functional notions. If biological functions themselves had to be analysed in a way that relied on a prior understanding of goals, his hopes would be shattered. But if, on the other hand, natural functions can be explicated autonomously, the way is clear for an attempt to establish a conceptual dependence going in the other direction. Perhaps the concept of a goal can be analysed in terms of the antecedently understood concept of a natural function. This issue carries over into chapter 8, where I defend the view that a biological end of an organism is essentially a state or activity that is intrinsically good for the organism. The concluding section of chapter 8 sets out a theory of functional explanations that hinges upon the analyses of functional TDs.

Simple ascriptions of functions

(a) *Artificial functions*

The reason why little has been written about the functions of artefacts is, presumably, that the notion is felt to be reasonably clear. An artificial function is simply 'the special kind of activity proper to anything, the mode of action by which it fulfils its purpose' (*Oxford English Dictionary*). To settle what the purpose of an artefact is one must refer to the purpose of the designer or maker in designing or making it, or of the user(s) in using it. Their intentions and expectations determine which activity is proper to it. A particular object may take on a function through being assigned one individually, or through being an exemplar of a kind of artefact which already has a standard function. In the latter case, an individual item counts as good of its kind if it does well the activity proper to things of its kind.

Many artefacts, though not all, are *type-identified* by reference to their functions; e.g. an object counts as a tea-strainer if its proper activity is to strain tea. Thus it might be thought that the statement 'The function of a tea-strainer is to strain tea' is analytic; indeed that any function-statement of the form 'The function of X is to do F' is analytic provided that the term for which 'X' holds a place is derived in an appropriate way from the verb for which 'F' holds a place. But this is not so. The function-statement says more than that a doer of F does F. It provides the extra information that doing F is a *function*, i.e. an activity which serves a purpose. Also, if the term for which 'X' holds a place is a referring term, then the statement entails that there exists something whose proper activity is to do F. These are both synthetic claims.

Given this general framework provided by the *O.E.D.* definition, two main points about artificial functions need to be clarified. The first concerns the identity of the being(s) whose purpose is served. Let us call whoever it is 'S'. Is S the designer, maker, user, or the community of users, or any member of a social group containing some users? Artificial functions cannot always be traced back to a designer's or a maker's intentions. Non-artefacts, like pebbles, which do not have functions initially, may acquire artificial functions by being taken from the beach and used as ashtrays or doorstops. Sometimes objects that are designed to serve a certain function are later used to serve a different function which the maker never intended. Items are occasionally created unintentionally, as by-products, for which a use is found later. So it is too restrictive to say that F is an artificial function of X only if a designer or manufacturer intended X to do F. Nevertheless, a designer's intention that something he creates should do F does seem to be sufficient, in certain circumstances, for F to be a function. The inventor of a gadget may stipulate: 'The function of that component is to vibrate the spindles'. It is irrelevant that other people may never use the gadget.

The issues can get extremely involved as we pile on more and more layers of intentionality. One man can design a product with the intention that it should serve some other man's purpose. A commercial manufacturer's intention is not merely that his product should do F, where F serves some common human purpose, but that it should actually be used, or at least bought, by people to do F. The actual creation of an item might be contingent upon the maker's expectation that the envisaged users will recognise his primary intention that it should do F.[3]

Since there are so many alternative possibilities, it is better not to specify who S is, but to say rather that the S or Ss whose end is served by F is/are the same as the S or Ss, whoever they are, for whom F is functional. That is, one may regard the schematic function-statement itself as being elliptical for a fuller statement that relativises the function to some S or set of Ss.

The second point is that F may be the proper activity of X even though X never actually does F. If a safety device buzzes only when the machine gets too hot, and the machine never gets too hot, there is no time at which the device buzzes. This is not an important matter, though, for we may say the device *does* buzz, in a dispositional sense. Also, when an item fails to perform its function because of a defect, we may say that it has a function in so far as it is of a certain kind, and

[3] There are many points of analogy between the way artefact functionality gets culturally transmitted and the way in which utterances acquire conventional meaning. Compare H. P. Grice (1968), pp. 1–18.

non-defective specimens of that kind do F. The most important case, however, is where the item does not do F, but is *believed* to do F (e.g. 'In such and such a tribe, coconut shells hung up outside the hut have the function of warding off evil spirits'). The example emphasises again the intentionality implicit in ascriptions of cultural functions. A tribesman would say that the coconut shells have a function because they do ward off evil spirits. But the philosophical analyst has to stand outside the tribe's framework of beliefs. If it is true that coconut shells have that function for the tribe, then cultural functionality must be relativised to the tribal beliefs. It would seem, then, that 'X has the artificial function F for S' means, roughly, 'Within S's framework of beliefs, X does F and F serves some end'.

(b) *Natural functions*

To say that some part X of a biological system S has the function of doing F is to say more than that X does F, or that F is an effect of S, or that X is a necessary condition of F. But some philosophers argue that the extra elements are not conveyed by the *meaning* of the original function-sentence, but are the results of contextual presuppositions. E. Nagel (1953, p. 541) asserts that: 'The function of chlorophyll in plants is to enable plants to perform photosynthesis' *means* no more than: 'A necessary condition for the occurrence of photosynthesis in plants is the presence of chlorophyll', but he maintains that this function-sentence would not be applicable if plants were not directively-organised systems. Similarly, R. Gruner (1966) holds that: 'B serves a function A' means just 'B has an effect A', but he stipulates that B must be part of a system, and A must contribute to the maintenance of the system. Scheffler (1963), pointing out that 'necessary condition' in Nagel's account should be construed as 'nonsubsequent necessary condition', also observes that functions contribute to the welfare of the organism (1963, Part I, section 5.)

However, function-statements must mean more than 'F is an effect of X', since not every effect of X is a function of X. To use Hempel's now-standard example, the heart makes beating sounds, but the production of beating sounds is not a function of the heart. If it is the case that only activities or processes that contribute to the survival or welfare of organisms *count* as functions, surely one would be asserting this when one called an activity or process a function. It would determine the kinds of effects that could meaningfully be said to be functions, and should be built into the paraphrase.

Several analyses have been put forward which acknowledge this. They consist of two parts, and they allude explicitly to survival, maintenance or adaptation in the second part.

John Canfield, for instance, suggested in 1963 that: 'A function of I (item) in S (system) is to do C' means 'I does C, and C is useful, in the sense that if, *ceteris paribus*, C were not done in S, then the probability of that S surviving and having descendants would be smaller than the probability of an S in which C is done surviving or having descendants,[4]

These analyses claim to capture the meaning of 'function' as it is used in biology, though Hempel's paper goes on to deal with the use of the term in sociology, which he thinks is borrowed from its use in biology. Each one assumes that the item said to have a function is either a part of an organism or something happening inside an organism. They all take it for granted that an organism is a self-maintaining system. Canfield and Lehman begin with 'A function of –' rather than 'The function of –', so as to cater for items having more than one function.

As far as the first conjunct of the analysis is concerned, I, like Canfield, see no reason to opt for anything more complicated or precise than 'X does F' (in my standardised notation). To assert that X must be a necessary condition of F is to commit oneself quite unnecessarily to the position that nothing other than X could perform the function that X performs. Not only is it possible to conceive of an item that would be functionally equivalent to X in the context; there are in fact many examples of functional equivalents in physiology. Thus it is not necessary that X should be necessary.

Given that a living body is very complicated, and that each process depends on many other conditions being satisfied, there would be no point in saying that X should be sufficient for F. Nor is there good reason to stipulate, as Lehman does, that an item having a function must never do anything that conduces to the malfunctioning of the organism. A good kidney may cause damage to a blocked bladder simply by functioning properly. Function-statements are loose in the same way as ordinary causal statements, with respect to whether X is sufficient, or necessary, or sufficient and necessary, for F. For this reason, one cannot really improve on 'X causes F' or 'F is an effect of X' or 'X does F', as the first step in the analysis.

A minor complication arises over the possibility that a particular item might have a function but might never actually perform it.

---

[4] Canfield (1963). Other papers offering similar analyses are: Carl Hempel (1959); Hugh Lehman (1965); and Michael Ruse (1971).

However, in biological contexts, the fact that a particular item might be defective in individual cases is offset by the fact that other members of the same species have non-defective items of the same type. Other instances of the same type of organ provide the evidence that the organ does F. Also, it is not necessary to convert 'does' into 'would do if the opportunity or appropriate circumstances arose', since we can take that proviso to be built in already.

Turning now to the second part of the analyses referred to, one finds a variety of formulations with a common underlying thought: functions contribute to the survival and maintenance of the whole organism. According to Darwin, the criterion of an animal's fitness is its ability to survive and leave behind fertile descendants. The idea suggests itself that a function is an activity or process which contributes to the survival of the individual, or to the survival of the species via the reproductive success of individuals. The questions that remain to be answered then group themselves under three headings: (i) how to interpret 'contributes to'; (ii) how to deal with cases where survival-functions and reproductive-functions seem to be antagonistic, or have different weights; (iii) whether the two biological ends of survival and reproduction, or some amalgamation of the two, are enough. The philosophers listed disagree over minutiae, but they agree on the general form that the analysis should take. In general, the analysandum contains two terms, 'X' and 'F', whereas the analysans contains three. The extra term, which we may call 'E', stands for a specific biological end, like survival, or a set of ends. The general form of analysans is 'X' does F, and F contributes to E', which explicitly asserts what was covert in the analysandum.

Regarding question (i), the arguments against unpacking 'F contributes to E' into 'F is a necessary condition of E' run parallel to the arguments against paraphrasing 'X does F' as 'X is a necessary condition of F'. It is true, given what we know about vertebrates, that blood circulation is indispensable for survival. But it seems conceivable that vertebrates might evolve which have a different mechanism for carrying nutrients and oxygen to the cells. So even a vital function like blood circulation need not be necessary for all vertebrates for all time. The notion of 'contributing to' as a causal relation is familiar, even if the philosophy of causation is controversial. To attempt to replace it by something more technical would be to go beyond the level of precision that the analysandum demands.

Question (ii) arises because the two biological ends of survival and reproduction sometimes compete. For example, the function of the red belly in male sticklebacks is to attract a mate, but it may also attract predators; giving birth puts the mother's life at risk. In contemporary treatments of the concept of adaptation, it is customary to reject a disjunction of ends in favour of the single end of species-survival. Thus Frankfurt and Poole (1966) criticise Canfield for giving a quasi-biological analysis of 'useful' that fails to conform to this current biological practice. Adopting the single end facilitates the systematisation of adaptive features within the theory of evolution. Darwinian fitness is defined in terms of differential reproductive success instead of differential survival rates (see F. J. Ayala, 1970).

This manoeuvre has the added advantage of incorporating functions which do not strictly come under the heading 'reproductive', such as the nutritive function of mother's milk, and other features adapted to the rearing of offspring. Indeed, as Ruse remarks (1971), the beneficiaries need not be just offspring. Any conspecific can benefit from, say, warning-calls. When the lemming population is overcrowded, the 'suicide' of some is functional for the rest.

There are a number of difficulties of detail in the programme of reducing all functions to species-survival functions. Many of them are best left to evolutionary biologists. If, for example, mutant animals possess a feature which other members of the species do not possess, and this feature favours its possessors, is the feature functional for the possessors only, or for the species as a whole? The answer depends on the evolutionary fortunes of the descendants, and will vary for each particular case (cf. Dobzhansky, 1969, pp. 172–3). Another question is: if 'survival' can be predicated of whole species, why can't it be predicated of units bigger than species? The alarm signals of birds can alert animals of other species as well as their own to the predator's approach, so why not say, as Aristotle might have done, that such sounds have this as their function? *De Partibus Animalium* 696b 27 cites a similar case. It would dilute the concept of function dangerously; there would be no end to the proliferation of functions, once we conceived of whole ecosystems as living units whose parts, animal and plant populations, had survival value for the whole. But from an evolutionary point of view there is very little reason for not allowing this. Each member of a symbiotic pair has a function for the other, hence for the pair. From a systems-theoretical perspective, an ecosystem is no less of a self-maintaining whole than an organism. I think it would be stretching the concept, however, to say that within a certain ecosystem a function of cats is to promote the fertilisation of red clover, even though Darwin observed that cats keep down the fieldmice that destroy the nests and combs of the humble-bee, which alone has a long enough proboscis to reach the nectar of the clover (1859, p. 125).

Then again, some functions do not appear to contribute to the survival of the species. The function of the mule's eye is to see, but mules are infertile, hence do not form a species. Ruse attempts to deal with such cases by appealing to the analogy between mules and the donkeys and horses that produce them. Actually, the difficulty can be generalised to cover any animal that has passed the age of reproduction, whatever its species. Ruse's tactic would presumably be to say that their organs still have functions, because what they do is the same as what they used to do earlier, and what they did then contributed to reproductive success. Alternatively, old members may confer benefits on the species in some other way than by breeding. Their presence may increase the survival-chances of the young ones that already exist.

Question (iii) asks whether these two biological ends are enough to collect all functions together. If there are other functions that do not fit into a hierarchy of functions with either individual or species-survival at the apex, there must be more than two biological ends. Of course, different people may formulate their lists of ends differently. E. S. Russell (1945), for instance, describes the main biological ends as 'maintenance, development and reproduction', but it may be that everything he includes under 'maintenance and development' could equally well appear under the heading 'survival'.

Richard Sorabji (1964) has invented a hypothetical example to show that logically there could be functions which had no survival or reproductive value. He imagined an animal having a mechanism inside it which comes into operation only when some lethal damage has occurred, like a major heart-attack. The mechanism has the effect of shutting off pain from the damaged area. Unlike the ordinary mechanism of sensory adaptation, it does not promote the survival either of the individual or the species. But it would surely be correct to say that shutting off pain was the function of the mechanism. Therefore, survival and reproduction are not the only possible ends. There are other ends over and above mere life, such as health, pleasure and the absence of pain. Sorabji then cites some of Aristotle's examples of 'luxury functions', i.e functions which are not essential for survival, but which do the organism good in some way.

It is probable that no examples of luxury functions actually *exist* in nature, since natural selection does not favour features that confer no adaptive advantage. But this is merely a contingent matter. So long as it makes sense to think that animals could have good done to them in other ways, it is conceivable that they might have had parts which did them good in these other ways. For one who wishes to understand the meaning, the conceptual boundaries, of the term 'function', it would be a mistake to consider only those features that happen to exist in nature. It would be irrelevant, if true, that no mechanism of the sort Sorabji hypothesised could actually be produced by the evolutionary process. The importance of hypothetical cases is to sharpen our awareness of what is essential to the concept. Perhaps organs or behaviour-patterns which have luxury functions cannot evolve unless they have survival-value as well, or are genetically linked to other features that have survival value. But the question still remains: what does it *mean* to say 'A function of X is to do F' when F *is* a luxury-function? To think that evolutionary theory can explicate the *meaning* of 'function' is to get things back to front. The word 'function' was in common use long before Darwin, and Darwin himself used it in the accepted sense. His theory of natural selection explained how organic features came to be present by exploiting the fact that they had functions which contributed to reproductive success. He did not claim that to ascribe a function to a feature just *is* to assert that the feature contributes to reproductive success. Sorabji's hypothetical case is important, because it shows that the sense of the word 'function' is independent of Darwin's great discovery that many or all natural functions yield to systematisation within evolutionary biology. Indeed, insistence upon this point is essential in order to defend Darwin against the criticism that his 'natural selection' hypothesis was a mere tautology.

If this point is correct, then the programme for analysis, as conceived by the philosophers whose accounts I listed, would presumably be to specify an exhaustive list of ends which includes all possible ones. I suggest that we ought to modify our idea of what the analysis should look like, in such a way that the question of how many ends to specify does not arise.

Suppose, for the sake of argument, that functions do not all fit into a hierarchical system with a single master-end at the apex, and that biologists have to rest content with a variety of mutually irreducible ends $E_1, E_2, E_3, \ldots E_n$. Would it be correct to say that 'The function of X is to do F' means 'X does F, and F contributes to E_1 or E_2 or E_3 or $\ldots E_n$'? I think such an analysis would not be satisfactory. Surely a deeper understanding would have enabled us to reveal a common feature of the Es, the feature in virtue of which they all count as ends. So, supposing now that biologists do succeed in assimilating all the other apparent ends to species-survival, would it be correct to offer 'X does F, and F contributes to species-survival' as an exhaustive paraphrase of 'The function of X is to do F'?

I think it would be wrong, because it is essential for an analysis of 'function' that the end or ends remain *unspecified*. As soon as it specifies a certain E, or a set of Es, it claims that these are all the ends there are, in so far as it claims that the meaning of the function-sentence is exhausted by such a list. But this is a mistake, since all one asserts when one calls an activity a function is that the activity contributes to *some end or other*. Whatever views one holds about the meaning of 'end', the possibility that the Es mentioned on a given list might not be all the ends there are should be left open. It is an advantage to insure the analysis against the possibility that the extension of 'function' might have been different in the past, or might change in the future. If prevailing views on the identity of ends should change or be enlarged, the range of functions would change or be enlarged too; but *nothing in the concept of function would have changed*.

In view of this, we can improve on all the analyses so far offered by substituting the indefinite expression 'some end' for the expression naming specific ends. This yields as the analysis of 'A function of X is to do F': 'X does F, and F contributes to some end'.

We have now reached what appears to be a unified general analysis of function-statements. It may well seem extravagant now to postulate one sense of 'function' in biology, one in sociology, one for artefacts, etc. The paraphrase is the same whatever the subject-matter; category-differences are marked, not within the analysans, but outside it, by the different restrictions on substitutions for the letter X. The differences between substituends for letter F appropriate to the X in question reflect the fact that different categories of thing do different things, and serve different ends. In order to decide whether an item is functional we need to know what the relevant end is. But a general analysis of the meaning, expressed in terms of schematic letters, should not *specify* any ends, because to mention a specific end would make the analysis parochial. What the end *is* which a certain item serves cannot be settled by reflecting upon the analysis.

There is, indeed, the point that an intensional operator needs to be present in the analysis of artificial or cultural function-statements. But

perhaps this phenomenon, where a word is used with implicit intensional 'bracketing', is widespread, and subject to systematic rules. It
might be better, from a theoretical semanticist's point of view, to treat
this as a feature of the use of the word rather than as an ambiguity in
the meaning. Alternatively, we could pay respect to the two uses in the
single analysans 'X does (or is supposed to do) F, and F serves (or is
supposed to serve) some end'.

Nevertheless, this is not a satisfactory overall position. The fact
that a general definition can be formulated with built-in relativity
to ends does not prove that the word 'function' is univocal. It could be
ambiguous in a way that exactly mirrored some ambiguity in the word
'end'. That is, it might be agreed (a) that activities count as functions
only in relation to ends, and (b) that the end served by a particular
function should not be specified in a general analysis, yet it might still
be objected that there are two senses of the word 'end', and hence that
there are two different concepts of function which it is the business of
an analysis to keep separate.

Furthermore, it is obvious that our theory is not complete without
an analysis of 'end', for we have not solved the three basic puzzles.
Why, for example, is it incorrect to say: 'The function of the heart is
to make beating noises, relative to the end of making the world
noisier'? Hempel's problem arises anew, now that we have omitted
specific reference to survival or reproduction. Secondly, why can't we
regard the solar system as having an end, and say that the function
of the sun, relative to that end, is to stay at the centre of it? Since the
relevant causal conditions are satisfied in both examples, the answers
must be that making the world noisier is not an end of an organism,
and that the solar system is not the sort of system that can have an end.
But we need to explain why not. Finally, the theory has not yet
provided any insight into functional *explanation*.

Strategies for dealing with ends

Artefacts and artificially created social institutions have artificial
functions for mankind in so far as they serve the purpose of their users,
designers or participants. Although no conclusion has yet been
reached about the true *analysis* of goals and purposes, it is clear that
when we talk of the ends served by artificial functions we use the word
'end' in the sense of 'goal' or 'purpose'. But it is not clear that biological

ends which relate to *natural* functionality are ends in the same sense.[5] There are several possible ways of construing natural functions on the 'artefact-model', but none is particularly plausible. One way is to regard a biological end as a purpose of God. But prima facie, ascriptions of function in biology are not committed to the existence of God. Many biologists accept that organs have functions, who do not believe in God. Another way is to take a projectionist line and say, for example, that it is *as if* a god wanted the animal to survive, and so designed the kidney to excrete waste fluids. But equally, one could say, it is *as if* a god wanted the heart to make a noise, and so designed it to beat. Alternatively, one could regard a biological end as a goal of the owner of the organs in question. But it is surely strained to say that the animal *uses* his (internal) organs to further his goals. If there is anything in this idea, it had better be dissociated from the artefact-model at least.

In fact, there are two plausible theories about biological ends. Both regard ends as immanent, i.e. possessed by the organism in question; and both can fairly claim to offer solutions to the three puzzles. Theory One links the concept of end directly to the concept of goal, but without asserting that S uses its organs as instruments to further its goals. The link is that physiological functions contribute to goals on a sub-molar level, without passing through any perceptual processing on S's part. A biological end just is a goal of the system to which contributions are standardly made by the parts. Theory Two, on the other hand, equates the natural ends of an organism with those states, activities and processes which are intrinsically good for it. Bodily functions are activities that normally do the system good by characteristically contributing to things which are intrinsically good for S.

I shall briefly sketch here some of the points in favour of Theory Two. It is suitably non-technical, and fits in well with my account of natural functions. Circulating the blood is a function because it contributes to survival, and survival is, for a living being, a paradigmatic natural good. Producing heart sounds is not a function, because it does not contribute to anything good for S. We could imagine types of life in which the noises did characteristically have some beneficial consequence for S, and in such circumstances, consequently, they would be functional. As there may be several goods that organisms can enjoy,

[5] L. J. Cohen argues that there is no philosophically important connection between biological function-statements and statements of purpose (1950, pp. 269–79).

there is no logical need for all functions to be fitted into a mono-lithic hierarchy. Physiological mechanisms with no survival-functions, if they existed, might nevertheless have luxury-functions.

Intuitively, it seems right to link the notion of function to other semi-evaluative notions, like flourishing, welcoming, enjoyment and fulfilment; it is natural to describe the beings served by functions as 'beneficiaries'. Reproductive functions may be regarded as beneficial either to the parents, who stand to gain offspring, or to the offspring, who are given the benefit of life, or to the species.

Theory Two explains why inorganic natural objects, like stones and mountains, do not have functions for the earth or the solar system. The earth and the solar system are not thought to have immanent ends, since we regard it as inappropriate to say that good can be done to them. The class of entities susceptible of being benefited comprises only living things. Plants are included: they can flourish, be healthy, and they have needs just as animals do.

Another feature of the theory is its Aristotelian spirit. It acknow-ledges the continuity between our present concept of function and the concept from which it presumably developed. For Aristotle, the concepts of *ergon* (normally translated as 'function') and *good* are inter-connected. In the Nicomachean Ethics 1. 1097ᵇ, for example, his method for determining the supreme good for man is to ask what is man's *ergon*. Unlike us, Aristotle believed that the world as a whole had an *ergon* and a *telos*, but that was because he believed it was a living thing. It is a great virtue of Theory Two that it can explain why the class of things that are deemed to have ends has become more restricted than it used to be, without maintaining that the Greeks had a totally different concept of function from ours. The change in extension is the result of a changed cosmological theory, not a changed intension. Theory Two not only solves Nagel's puzzle, but also explains why Aristotle's cut-off point was different.

In the sociological literature on functionalism, the point is often made that ascriptions of social functions are evaluative. Defenders of functionalism usually try to argue that the concept of function is *not* evaluative, despite appearances. If it were evaluative, doubts would be raised about the objectivity of function statements, and hence about their scientific respectability. The question whether function-state-ments are ever objectively true certainly arises if we accept Theory Two. For Theory One, however, such a problem would not arise. Indeed, the main motive of philosophers who have proposed theories like Theory One has been to neutralise the evaluative element in the concept of function by relating it to the concept of goal. The concept of goal has an evaluative aspect too, goals being valued by the organism in so far as it pursues them; but this notion of 'valued by' can perhaps be handled scientifically, whereas the notion of 'valuable for' seems intractable. We must examine Theory One further, therefore, to see whether the value element can be successfully 'carried over' in this way like a transferable commodity.

8

Ends and functional explanations

The theory that biological ends are goals (Theory One)

According to Nagel, 'The function of X is to do F' means simply 'X is a necessary condition of F', but the function-statement presupposes that X is part of a *goal-directed system*. This qualification explains why natural functions are not ascribed to the parts or the behaviour of 'inanimate bodies that have not been deliberately constructed to achieve certain effects' (Nagel, 1956, p. 248). In his 1953 article, he writes:

> It is because living things exhibit in varying degrees adaptive or regulative structures and activities, while the systems studied in the physical sciences do not – so it is frequently claimed – that teleological explanations are peculiarly appropriate for the former but not for the latter (p. 544).

His account of functions thus passes rapidly into an account of goal-directed systems, which we considered in chapter 4. We have loosened his analysis by changing 'X is a necessary condition of F' into 'X does F'; and we assume that the letter X stands for a part of a system S. If we incorporate Nagel's 'presupposition' into the analysans, we get 'X does F in S, and S is a goal-directed system'. But since Hempel's 'heartbeat' counter-example is still effective against this, a tighter connection must be forged between F and the goal-directedness of S. There are various ways this could be done, but the way which best reflects the spirit of Nagel's approach is to write 'X does F and F contributes to a goal of S'. Statements of this form presuppose that X is part of S, that S is goal-directed, and that 'does' and 'contributes' are in the 'habitual present' tense, implicitly qualified by the adverbs 'normally', 'characteristically' or 'for the most part'. The basic idea of Theory One, then, is that a biological end just is a goal of the system.

Whereas our previous analysis was right as far as it went – a natural function is an activity which contributes to a natural end of the system – Theory One modifies it by replacing 'end' by 'goal'. It thereby brings out a conceptual connection between functionality and goal-directedness. 'The deeper formula shows how the teleology of organs is borrowed from the teleology of organisms: hearts have a function only because their owners have goals.

Let us illustrate how the theory works. Why does the excretion of wastes count as a function of the kidneys? One answer is that the excretion of waste-products helps S to survive, and survival is a goal or G-state of S. Another possible answer is that although survival might not be a goal in its own right, the excretion of wastes does contribute to other goals. Indeed it contributes to any goal that S might have, *via the contribution it makes to survival*. Being alive is a causally necessary condition of behaving, and S has to behave if it is to achieve any goal.

If an organ gave rise to pleasure but had no other function, Theory One could maintain either that pleasure is itself a goal of S's, or that the organ contributes to other goals by giving rise to pleasure. Perhaps it encourages more *enthusiastic* goal-seeking. Since the theory does not specify any particular goal, it is compatible with our view that there could be such things as luxury functions.

So far we have concentrated upon internal organs associated with the autonomic nervous system. The heart, liver and kidneys perform their functions continuously, regardless of what S may be doing. But the theory copes equally with the functions of limbs and sense-organs, and with reflexes and behaviour-patterns. Behavioural functions fit the schema very naturally. For example, 'The function of head-flagging in gulls is to appease conspecifics' means 'Head-flagging appeases conspecifics, and this contributes to a goal of the gulls'. In this case, the goal would no doubt be survival, ultimately, but it might also be some intermediate goal. Limbs and sense-organs are slightly different. A general description of their function will be a description of a behavioural or perceptual capacity, exercised in a variety of different situations. According to Theory One, seeing is the function of the eye because seeing is something that S often needs to do if S is to achieve a goal. In fact, this theory is more at home with external parts whose movements are under S's control than with internal parts, since the events in a causal chain leading from a limb-movement to a goal are all describable on the same level. Our description of the chain will not need to mention the internal conditions which make the limb-movement possible.

How is one to evaluate this theory? It, or a close relative, has been fairly influential. Many philosophers have accepted that functional analysis has something to do with goal-directed systems (including Woodfield, 1973). But I now think it is wrong.

It might seem that the theory is immediately refuted by the case of plants and vegetables. Apple-trees are not goal-directed systems, yet their roots have a function – to absorb liquids from the soil. It cannot, therefore, be necessary for a natural function to contribute to a goal of the system. However, this quick argument is not available in the present context. According to Nagel, plants *are* goal-directed, since they satisfy his criteria for directively organised systems. In Chapter 4, I argued indeed that directive organization is not the same as goal-directedness. But I have not yet reached any firm conclusion about what goal-directedness *is*. In particular, I have not proved that plants are *not* goal-directed. So my tactic in this section is to argue as follows: although we haven't analysed the concept of goal yet, we know enough about goals to know that it is not they which underpin the ascription of functions.

There are two ways of taking the sentence 'X does F and F contributes to a goal'. On one reading, the phrase 'a goal' means *any* goal; on the other, it means a certain goal. It is important to distinguish these, given that Theory One offers this schema as an improvement upon the old agreed schema 'X does F and F contributes to an end'. It is clear that the phrase 'an end' means any end. So on the first reading, the theory claims that all goals are biological ends; on the second, it claims that only some goals are. We need to examine each version.

Is it logically necessary or sufficient, in order for F to count as a function, that F contribute to some goal or other, no matter which? Imagine a case where a certain dog's kidneys, by excreting waste products between t_1 and t_2, contribute to the dog's survival during that period, and thus contribute indirectly to the attainment of a goal at t_2, say, burying a bone. Survival is not the end of a chain, but a mere staging-post that the chain goes through towards the goal. Is the excretion of wastes a function because it contributes to the burying of a bone? Surely not. The kidneys would have had that function even if the dog had never had that goal. The only relevant aspect of the case is that waste-excretion contributes to survival. There is no need to trace causal chains to further goals beyond that.

Conversely, suppose that the dog's stomach rumbled, thereby helping the dog to achieve some goal it happened to have, like frightening away a cat. Rumbling would not count as a function of the stomach on the strength of that. We may say, for physiological functions generally, that it is not necessary that they contribute to any behavioural goal at all, provided they contribute to survival. (But there remains the thesis that survival is itself a goal.) Furthermore, the fact that an activity contributes to some goal or other is not sufficient to make it a function.

It is pretty obvious, in these examples of internal organs, that survival is the operative factor underpinning the functional ascription. For behavioural functions the picture is somewhat more complicated. When a functional behaviour-pattern contributes to a goal, it very often does so directly, rather than by contributing to survival first. What is the operative factor that confers functionality upon a behaviour-pattern? One point, made by Beckner (1959, pp. 146–7), is that when a response has both a function and a goal, the goal is not necessarily identical with the function. Another point, made by Beckner (1969) and by Wright (1973) is that reflex movements like shivering and blinking have functions, yet are not goal-directed. However, Theory One does not make the mistake of claiming that a functional response must be *directed* to a goal. It says that a response has a function F only if F *contributes* to a goal. Nor does it claim that F is itself a goal, although it allows that F *might* be one.

Still, it is clear that the formula fails to provide a sufficient condition of functionality. Heroin addicts habitually apply tourniquets to their arms. This makes the veins stand out, and helps them achieve the goal of injecting heroin into the bloodstream. But making the veins stand out in this way is not biologically useful. Indeed, if the formula were true, all goal-contributing behaviour, however maladaptive the goal, would have a function.

One may doubt, moreover, whether the formula states a necessary condition. It could be argued that some functional responses do not contribute to any goal at all. Shivering, for example, is a reflex whose function is to maintain the body temperature. It is possible that certain animals have goals which are furthered by shivering (e.g. the goal of informing other members of the species that they are cold); but shivering would have a function, even if they did not have such goals. But there is a complication here. It could be argued on the other side that maintaining body-temperature is itself a goal of all animals that shiver; or, at least, that survival is a goal, and is furthered by temperature-maintenance. The issue then returns to the question of what it is to be a goal, and whether survival is one. However, the *unrestricted* version of the theory has been proved untenable, since evidently not *any old goal* will do.

That there exists some restriction upon permissible goals seems actually to be implicit in the formula. Given that the verb 'contributes' is in the habitual present tense, it is not enough that F contributes to a goal on one or a few occasions only. F is a type of activity which is supposed to contribute to a goal characteristically and normally. This means there is a further quantificational ambiguity in the theory, in addition to the ambiguity over 'any goal' v. 'a certain goal'. The former reading can be taken in two ways: either as 'F characteristically contributes to some goal or other (perhaps a different one each time)'; or as 'F characteristically contributes to some goal or other (but the same one each time)'. On the latter interpretation, the goal in question can be of any kind: but it must be one that S characteristically *has*. If it were a fleeting goal, present on only a few occasions on which F occurs, F could not possibly contribute to it characteristically and normally. Thus there is an implicit restriction to goals that are *stable* in the context of S's life. We must therefore investigate whether this restriction saves Theory One from counterexamples like the above, or whether further restrictions on the kind of goal need to be made.

It is easy to see that further restrictions are required. If an activity can be a function without ever contributing to any goal, then a *fortiori* it can be a function without contributing to a stable goal. So we need not trouble further over the 'necessary condition' claim. The claim is still in play, of course. One can still argue that maintaining body temperature would not count as a function of shivering unless survival were a goal. But the ground of the claim is that shivering serves a specific goal that happens to be stable, not that it serves any old goal that is stable. To use this as a ground is already to commit oneself to the stricter version of the theory.

Nor does Theory One, interpreted in terms of stable goals, provide a sufficient condition. Counterexamples relying on addictive goals still apply; taking heroin already is a stable goal in the life of a heroin-addict, and the act of making his veins stand out contributes to it characteristically. Nor does it avail the theory to appeal to yet another dimension of generality in the formula: an implicit quantification over all members of a given species. For it is quite possible for all the members of a species to be drug addicts. To rule this out would be to place some further restriction on stable goals (e.g. that they be innate rather than acquired). One seems forced to abandon the idea that the concept of a biological end just *is* the concept of a goal. But the restricted version is much more plausible. It says there is a certain limited class of stable goals, possessed by all or most organisms of a given species, which define the biological ends of the species. The criteria in virtue of which these states and activities count as goals are independent of the criteria of functionality, so no questions are begged.

How wide might this class of special goals be? No doubt it depends a lot upon the species in question. Plants presumably have the goals of growing and multiplying; but sentient creatures have additional goals like pleasure and the avoidance of pain. But how wide can the class be, within a given species? Let us suppose that appeasing aggressors is standardly a goal of black-headed gulls in situations that elicit the head-flagging response. Should it be included in the class of special goals? Surely we do not wish to regard it as a biological end? Ethologists would say that appeasing aggressors in such situations is itself a function, because it contributes to species-survival. This ultimately is the operative factor which makes the head-flagging response functional, not the fact that appeasement is a goal. Behaviour-functions can be strung together in chains just like organ-functions. Only the termini of such chains warrant the title 'biological ends'. So the only goals that should figure in the special class are the high-level ones, i.e. the ones that are termini of such chains. These goals confer functionality upon activities which contribute to them, but they must not be functions themselves, on pain of a regress in the theory.

We have now stated the conditions which a goal must satisfy to be included in the class. It must be stable (cyclical or permanent), shared by most members of the species, and sought for its own sake. It must be, in other words, an *ultimate* goal of S's. According to Theory One, the class will include survival, reproduction (where S is any organism), and pleasure and avoidance of pain (where S is an animal) – that is, the things that one would intuitively count as *natural ends* of S. The theory thus tallies with our intuitions about what counts as a function and what does not. I do not think, however, that it explicates the *concept* of function correctly. Since the three conditions for being an ultimate goal are empirical ones, identifying the ultimate goals for a given species is a matter for empirical inquiry. One has to observe the behaviour of the species over a sufficiently long period to discover what the members' goals are, and then arrange them in order of importance. It is quite conceivable that the lists of ultimate goals might turn out to be totally different for different species. Indeed it is logically possible, though empirically unlikely, that the members of a hitherto unstudied species might have extraordinary ultimate goals, like running round in circles, or gnawing their own limbs. It seems clear that such goals would not be capable, *in themselves*, of justifying the ascription of biological functions to mechanisms that further their pursuit.

Suppose a tribe of men was discovered in the Amazon jungle, whose main aim upon reaching adulthood was to die of influenza. Suppose also that they have a gene which lowers their resistance to the germ. Would we say that the function of the gene was to help the men catch 'flu? If not, then contributing to an ultimate goal is not a logically sufficient condition of being a function. And if, as I assume, the hearts, livers and kidneys of these tribesmen still have survival-functions even though the men have no desire to survive, then contributing to an ultimate goal is not a necessary condition of being a function (unless the theorist maintained, sophistically, that these organs contribute to the men's ultimate goal indirectly, by enabling them to stay alive until they catch 'flu).

A final point worth mentioning is that many philosophers would question whether pleasure, and perhaps survival and reproduction too, were properly termed 'goals', in the sense of 'things aimed at'. Bishop Butler, for example, maintained that: 'All particular appetites and passions are towards *external things themselves*, distinct from the pleasure arising from them' (*Sermon XI*, para. 229).

Usually it is only in situations of great danger that animals and people do things purely for the sake of staying alive. And animals normally mate because they have an urge to copulate, not because they want offspring. But I shan't pursue this line of thought. My argument against Theory One does not depend upon any special views about goals. I am quite willing to accept that survival and other biological ends *are* goals; I argue only that 'being an end' does not mean the same as 'being a goal'.

The theory of ends as goods (Theory Two)

The crucial feature of organic functions is that they do the organism good. This vague idea is made more precise by Theory Two: S's bodily functions do S good by promoting S's natural ends, where 'ends' means states or processes or activities that are intrinsically good for S. Now there are two sorts of questions that might be raised about this. First, there are questions concerning its correctness as an analysis of what is ordinarily meant. Second, on the assumption that it gives a correct analysis, there are questions about the status and justification of function-statements.

I think this theory is roughly correct as an analysis. People do use function-statements evaluatively; many sociologists regard functional analyses as scientifically disreputable for precisely that reason. If Theory Two is correct, the objectivity of function-statements is cast into doubt. For it may be doubted whether there are objective natural goods. If people can have different subjective opinions about what is good for animals, and if there were no question of some people being right, others wrong, then there could be non-empirical disagreements about the functions of animal parts. Two people might agree that X does F and F contributes to survival, but not agree that survival is an end. One of them might hold that survival was a bad thing. Puritans might hold similar views about pleasure. Some people might be of the opinion that death was a good thing for animals.

Before confronting this problem, let us note that the theory does impose *some* objective restrictions on what can count as a validator of functionality. Even if a sceptical attitude is possible concerning natural goods, the subjectivist certainly does not have *carte blanche* to regard anything he likes as a biological end. It is by no means obvious that death, for instance, could count as an end (although every life ends in death). Functions are characteristic, normal activities. To establish that death could be an end of an organism, one needs to show that the normal activities of its parts do contribute to death. But on our present notion of what is a normal activity, this is not so. When an organ stops contributing to survival, it often starts contributing to death. It does so by *not* doing what it normally does. In some cases, an organ contributes to death by doing what it normally does, provided there is a breakdown elsewhere. The hypothesis requires, however, that the activities which all or most of the organs *normally* perform should contribute to death, which is just false. Death occurs in the long run, sure enough; but it would catch up sooner if the organs did not do the things they normally do. Thus it seems impossible both to think of death as an ultimate end, and to take over intact the system of inter-locking functions that followed from thinking of survival as an end. The sceptic must contrive to view as normal those activities we now view as abnormal, and vice versa. To do this involves an unfeasibly radical restructuring of the concepts we employ to describe animal physiology. If we are to reconceptualise the heart as an organ whose proper function is to fail to beat, each individual heart can perform its function successfully only once. In order to construe heart-failure as normal activity and death as the normal state, we should need to think of live animals against the background of their dead ancestors. Life must be made to appear as a state of transitory irritability suffered by entities that are normally quiescent. If corpses were animals in their normal state, our concept of an animal would have to change. Physiology would have to be renamed 'pathology'. The whole point of functional talk, as a vehicle for making fine discriminations between parts, would be lost, since not all organs would have their own characteristic way of contributing to death.

These considerations are sufficient to show that death could not be a biological end. The experiment has been undermined solely by appealing to the normality requirement. There was no need to prove that death is not a good. However, we have not fully met the sceptical challenge. We have shown only that there exist *some* objective constraints on what counts as a function. Certain bodily activities, like the production of heart sounds, satisfy the 'normality' condition, yet still fail to count as functions. If Theory Two is right, the reason is that heart sounds do not do the animal any good. But isn't this a matter of opinion? There might be people who thought that making noises was a good in itself.

It is tempting to appeal here to the systematising role of functional hypotheses in biology. One might try to argue that the production of heart sounds fails to be a function on the grounds that it cannot be integrated with other functions. It is an irrelevant side-effect of the heart's pumping. If bodily functions are pictured on a diagram showing how they fit together into an immensely complex, yet unified system, the production of heart-sounds would figure as a dangling appendage. Functions, it might be argued, are not just normal activities; they must also co-ordinate together into a systematic whole.

But this is not necessarily true, on my analysis. Given that F is a function, anything which regularly contributes to F, however remotely, has that as one of its functions. Backward systematisation, where we start from something that it is agreed to be a function and work backwards along causal chains leading to it, is generated automatically, as a necessary consequence of the transitivity of the relation 'contributes to'. Thus even the production of heart sounds fits into some hierarchy, namely the hierarchy of which it is the apex. The important question concerns *forward* systematisation. I have argued that it is not essential to the concept of function that all functions should be fittable into a single hierarchy. If that can be done, it is a bonus. But if survival, reproduction, pleasure and the absence of pain are not interreducible, then it can't be done. The most we can say is that survival, or perhaps species-survival, yields the highest degree of backward systematisation, and this no doubt gives it a privileged position among the apexes. They may not form a fraternity of equals, but each one is autonomous within the republic. If Theory Two is a correct analysis, all such attempts to suppress the embarrassing evaluative element are in vain. We may push it to the periphery, but we cannot get rid of it completely.

Given that all organisms have evolved, it is probable that all the functional components of existing organisms contribute to species-survival. That species-survival should be privileged in this way is explained by the theory of natural selection. Anatomists often use evolutionary theory as a guide when they classify organic structures. The idea that all organs have adaptive significance is used as a regulative principle which helps them to decide what to count as a significant part in the structure. Thus it would be no coincidence if a complete description of the system of bodily functions were isomorphic with a description of all the parts. Our concept of function, according to which species-survival is accounted a biological end, has yielded a system of anatomical knowledge with great power and comprehensiveness. Does this furnish a kind of external justification for employing a semi-evaluative concept? Not a bit. The whole system of functions could equally well be described as a system of effects that are systematisable, without mentioning that they are good effects. One cannot justify a belief in natural goods by pointing to the heuristic or systematising advantage of holding such a belief. In any case, now that anatomy and physiology are well-established, the systematisation so far achieved will remain even if the evaluative language of functions is purged from science.

Another way of combating the spectre of subjectivism is to claim that the things we regard as biological ends are good by definition. On this view, it is a necessary truth that life is good for anything that can have it, but it so happens that only animals, plants and other organisms have it. If the solar system were alive, it too would have a good. Reproducing, enjoying pleasure, and being free from pain are also good by definition for anything capable of doing or undergoing such things.

Since pleasure and pain require sentience, and sentience and reproduction require life, it so happens that only animals enjoy pleasure and
freedom from pain, and only living things reproduce. There are many
goods that animals can enjoy, and different species may enjoy different
goods, but there are certain goods that all animals enjoy, life being
among them. Furthermore, animals must be alive if they are to enjoy
any of the others. This provides another sense in which life is a
privileged member of the class of biological ends. The others do not
causally contribute to it; they are manners, modes or enhancements of
it.

To say that life, reproduction, pleasure and freedom from pain are
good by definition is a last resort in the face of the sceptic's challenge.
But it is unlikely to convince him. The sceptic who has been doubting
that survival and the other ends are good for organisms will not agree
that they are good by definition. He might argue that it is difficult to
establish the correct definitions of ordinary words; or that definitions
which make the terms partly evaluative ought to be discarded from
science. If one tries to subvert scepticism by appealing to definitions,
all one succeeds in doing is shift the locus of disagreement. It is far
better to realise from the start that a sceptical position *is* logically
tenable in these matters.

The aim of an analytical theory is to make explicit all the elements
that go to make up a concept. At some stage, the analysis has to stop.
It crystallises out elements which are regarded as basic enough for the
purposes in hand. Once that stage is reached, questions about the
empirical application and justification of the concept can be investi-
gated with fresh clarity. Our analysis has shown that ascriptions of
natural functions presuppose that living things have natural goods. In
so far as we regard functions as objective, we must regard the good of an
organism as objective; but equally, if we are subjectivists about goods,
we must be at least *partially* subjectivist about functions. I do not
propose to analyse the concept of a natural good, nor do I uphold any
particular view about its epistemological status. I have registered some
of the difficulties for an objectivist, but I leave it open whether he can
solve them.

Nevertheless, I should like to reach a decision about the objectivity
of functional 'in order to' statements. Is it possible for functional TDs
to be wholly objective, even though their corresponding function-
statements might not be? The third puzzle which must now be solved is
how functional explanations work.

Functional explanations and functional TDs

Several philosophers have doubted that function-statements are explanatory just on their own. Canfield, whose analysis is similar to mine, says that they are not scientifically explanatory, though they have heuristic value. They generate new ways of seeing things; they also invite the questions: 'How does X do F?', 'In what way is F useful to S?', which open up new avenues for research. Other philosophers have suggested that insofar as the functions of parts can be shown to fit together into a harmonious whole, function-statements do have some explanatory value, because to show how something fits into a system is a way of making it more intelligible. T. L. S. Sprigge offers an interesting suggestion in his paper 'Final causes'. Subscribing to the traditional view that teleological explanations of a certain kind are bound up with the notion of Good, he writes: 'To ask what a thing exists for the sake of is here the same as to ask what it is good for. A satisfying answer is like an explanation for the thing's existence inasmuch as it stops us worrying about it' (p. 170). Justifying the existence of a thing is like explaining it, because the two operations have similar illocutionary effects.

But *why* does the citing of a beneficial effect stop us worrying? I think it is because the mention of good consequences leads us to imagine the item as having figured in a process of practical reasoning. A child asks 'What's that for?', pointing to a scarecrow. He has no clear opinion about whether it is an artefact or a natural object – indeed he may not have these concepts yet. His parents tell him that the scarecrow is there because it stops birds eating the crops; they add, or leave it to be understood, that this is a good thing from someone's point of view. The child is now in a position to reason: 'Someone thought it would be a good thing to stop birds eating the crops, and he thought a scarecrow would stop them, so he made a scarecrow and put it over there.' The child then naturally extends this basic thought-process to other cases. He asks: 'Why do those butterflies have wings that look like a big pair of eyes?'. His parents tell him it is because the wing-pattern scares away birds who eat butterflies. The child is led to think, on analogy with the previous case, that some unspecified agent put the design on the wings because he thought it would do some good. The child need not have a clear idea of who or what this agent is in order to find this answer satisfying.

On this picture, to understand the meaning of 'What for?' questions, one must recognise that their primary application is to artefacts. Correspondingly, to understand the meaning of 'in order to' answers, one has to see how they involve getting inside a hypothetical agent's mind and reconstructing his process of practical reasoning. They say: 'The thing is there because of what some agent thought, and, as a result, did.'

This is a plausible psychological account of why the citing of natural functions is felt to be explanatory. But it entails that it is not really explanatory. Although I accept that mere statements of natural function are not explanatory, I believe that natural functional TDs really are. These, too, may have developed out of artificial functional TDs; but offspring can become logically independent of their parents. There are other ways of interpreting them in addition to the anthropomorphic way. The story of the imaginary agent does, however, introduce a crucial new element into the analysis, which I shall exploit henceforth. Functional explanations, even of artefacts, do not say merely 'This does some good'; they say 'This is here *because* it does some good'. Functional TDs specify a function and assert that the function is a reason for the item's being there. Since a functional TD is an intrinsically explanatory statement, the word 'because' should figure in its analysis.

I suggest that the schema for natural functional TDs, 'X does A in S in order to do F/in order that F be done', should be analysed as 'X does A in S because A contributes to (or level-generates) F and F is good for S'. A brief elucidation of this formula is required before I show how the explanation works. Function-statements contain one verb, functional TDs contain two. But F in the former may correspond to A in the latter. For instance, 'A function of the heart is to beat' may be compared with 'The heart beats in order to circulate the blood'. In a functional TD, activity A is said to be a function of item X in virtue of the contribution it makes to something further. This further thing may itself be a function of X, and there will be another TD in which A stands for *that* activity (e.g. circulating the blood), and F stands for something else. The verbs for which A and F hold places get shunted along to the left. The shunting process has to stop when F stands for an end, like survival. However, since the end is S's survival rather than X's, the schema appropriate to this limiting case is 'X does A in order that F may obtain'.

F can also be an activity of X's specified by reference to an end, as, e.g. 'contributing to S's survival'. Thus, 'The heart circulates the blood in order to contribute to survival' is a valid substitution-instance of the schema 'X does A in order to do F'. This presents a notational problem,[1] since in the analysans, the clause 'A contributes to F' would then have as a substitution-instance 'Circulating the blood contributes to contributing to survival'. To avoid this, I invoke Goldman's notion of level-generation (Goldman, 1970 ch. 2. See below, page 168). Roughly speaking, act A *level-generates* act A' when the agent does A' *by* or *in* doing act A. The heart, by circulating the blood, contributes to survival; so X's activity of contributing to survival is generated by an activity of X's which contributes to survival. From now on, I shall abbreviate this clause to 'A ⇒ F'.

In the analysans, the clause 'F is good for S' covers *both* the case where F is extrinsically good for S because it contributes to an end, *and* the case where F is intrinsically good for S because F *is* an end. It also covers the case where F is good because it is specified as a contribution to an end. Given Theory Two, this clause captures all that was meant previously, in the function-statement schema, by 'F contributes to some end'.

This is the schema for functional explanations of organs. A different schema is needed when the item with the function is a behaviour-pattern. I take my standard form here to be 'S does B in order to do F' and analyse it as 'S does B because B ⇒ F and F is good for S'. Thus the *form* of the analyses of all natural functional TDs is the same, though the schematic letters reflect category differences.

How, finally, are the analyses to be interpreted? I take them to be explanation-sketches in Hempel's sense, which need to be supplemented by extra premises. There are several different methods of turning them into formally satisfactory explanations, but only two of these have empirical application. The functional TD is not referring to any particular heart, but to hearts in general, or to the heart, *qua type* of organ. Consequently, it is not about any particular occasion of beating, but about heart-beating in general. It asserts 'Hearts in general beat because beating (characteristically) contributes to blood circulation, and blood circulation is good for the organism'. The question arises, which organisms are benefited by which hearts? This vague generalisation quantifies loosely over not only hearts and heart-beats, but also over the owners of the hearts. There are two ways of unpacking it. Nearly every heart that ever beats is present in its owner's

---

[1] L. Nissen encountered the same problem in Nissen (1971).

body because other hearts, present in other bodies, have beaten in the past. By so doing, they have contributed to the survival of their owners, who were the ancestors of this organism. If it hadn't been for the ancestral hearts, this heart would never have come into existence. Thus it would be true of any heart (except a mythical 'first-generation heart') that it beats because heart-beating has contributed to the preservation of the species of which this heart-owner is a member, even if this particular heart happened not to be beneficial to its owner. By construing 'S' as the name of a type of organism rather than as the name of an individual, we may slur over the detailed evolutionary story and say simply that blood circulation is good for S.

This is the 'phylogenetic' interpretation. But the TD can be given an 'ontogenetic' interpretation, where 'S' stands for an individual. Every beating heart does, in fact, benefit its owner under normal circumstances. At any time t in the life of an individual with a heart, except perhaps for the first few moments after birth, it is true to say that his heart has contributed to his surviving up until t by circulating his blood. If the heart had not beaten prior to t, the owner would not be alive at t. Therefore, every heart beats because its own earlier beating has helped its owner not to die. In virtue of this general truth I can say that my heart is beating now because it circulates my blood and contributes to my survival. But when I say this I do *not* mean that my heart is beating now because it will circulate my blood in the future. Admittedly, functional explanations convey the *impression* that later events are influencing earlier ones, but this is an illusion based on the fact that they fudge tense-differences. The explanans is 'Because beating contributes to circulation, which is good' – a tenseless general statement about event-types. It refrains from giving any information about the temporal ordering of particular events of those types. The explanandum is not about any particular event either. One would not normally ask for a *functional* explanation of why a particular heart emitted a beat at a particular time t. The reason for this is that if we make the time references and the quantifications precise, the functional TD loses that ambiguous generality which alone invests it with explanatory power.

Phylogenetic and ontogenetic interpretations can be given for behaviour-functions too. Head-flagging occurs in gulls because head-flagging has survival value, and so the precursors of the existing gull population were naturally selected partly because they did it. Also very often an individual gull that emits the response owes its continued life to the fact that it has done so before, under the appropriate stimulus conditions, and has thereby appeased aggressors who would otherwise have killed it.

Both of these interpretations rely on the fact that the activity A or B does S some *good* by contributing to F. If F were not good for S, then the fact that A or B has contributed to F in the past would not explain, in the same way, why A or B persists or occurs now. So the evaluative element does play a role in the explanation, but it does so only by hinting at the relevant causal pathway. In these examples, the good in question is either species-survival or individual-survival; the explanations would have worked in just the same way if survival had been mentioned explicitly. The role of the possibly non-objective term 'good for S' is to indicate that the causal chain goes through an end of the system. The class of ends is demarcated by an evaluative criterion, but once the relevant end has been *identified* in a given case, then the evaluative description of it can be replaced by a non-evaluative description. The causal connections between the events and processes themselves are always objective, even though the descriptions which identify them may contain evaluative terms. There is a sense, then, in which natural functional TDs are objectively explanatory, even though their analysis contains an evaluative term. In fact, only two biological ends, survival and reproduction, will support the interpretations I have given. It would be false to say of Sorabji's mechanism that it exists *because* it shuts off pain, and this is good for S. The fact that mechanisms of that type shut off pain plays no causal role in the genesis of any particular mechanism of that type. So if it were claimed that the mechanism existed in order to shut off pain, I should first construe this as an artefact-function TD, i.e. as saying that some unspecified agent put the mechanism there because he *thought* it would be good to fit S with a mechanism that shuts off pain. If this is not the intended interpretation, I should argue that the TD is false. I accept that the mechanism has the function of shutting off pain, designer or no; but I would deny that the mechanism is there *because* it performs that function.

Nevertheless, there are other ways of supplementing a natural functional explanation-sketch which might have had, but do not in fact have, empirical application. When one is considering an imaginary mechanism, one invents an imaginary world to put it in. If Lamarck's hypothesis had been right, offspring could have inherited features from their parents which the parents had developed during their lifetimes. Suppose it were possible to develop, by practice, super-sensitive taste-buds which increase the pleasures of eating. In a Lamarckian world, offspring would be born with super-sensitive taste-buds because such taste-buds have (i.e. have had) the beneficial effect of increasing pleasure. Alternatively, in an optimific world governed by laws of the form 'Whenever an item X would, by doing A, have a beneficial consequence F, X does A', a particular explanandum could be functionally explained by subsuming it directly under this functional law. But in our world, there is no inheritance of acquired characters, and there are no true 'functional laws' of this form.

In social science, functional explanations of all the types so far admitted can be found. Although the 'artefact-model' and the 'natural-function model' of functional explanation have a totally different logic, the tendency to confuse them often proves impossible to resist when the explanandum is a social phenomenon.

Imagine again the tribe in which there exists a custom of hanging coconut shells outside one's hut. If this custom has a function in virtue of the fact that the tribesmen believe, rightly or wrongly, that it has a certain beneficial effect, say the effect of warding off evil spirits, then a functional explanation on the artefact-model can be given. But it may be possible also to give a natural-functional explanation. The natural function may be quite different from the one the participants ascribe. For example, an anthropologist might hypothesise that coconut shells are hung outside the huts in order to strengthen social cohesion. The custom persists because it has helped the tribe to survive as a social unit. Alternatively, the natural function may be identical with the function that the participants ascribe. They may themselves view it as a natural function, and explain it on the phylogenetic or ontogenetic interpretations. Or they may regard it as an artificial function. If a social custom has a natural function which is identical with its artificial function, then the difference between a natural and an artificial functional explanation of it lies only in this: that the mechanism by which the anthropologist believes the social function to operate is different from the way the participants believe it to operate. In such cases it is impossible to guess from the words that are used in the functional TD which explanatory pattern is meant. The logic of an artificial functional explanation is the same as that of a purposive explanation. But the way in which a purposive explanation works has not yet been settled. It depends on the meaning of purposive TDs, to which we must return.

PART FOUR

GOALS

9

An externalist theory of goals

I now return to the topic of goal-directed behaviour, and investigate the second of the two pathways that were distinguished at the end of Chapter 6. I gave the name 'internalism' to the view that the goal-directed character of an action consists in its being caused by the agent's having a goal, which is an internal state. Externalism, on the other hand, regards the postulation of internal states as unnecessary. It is claimed that we sometimes ascribe goals to animals without ascribing minds to them, and certainly without necessarily knowing any physiology. Internalism 'reduces' teleological explanation to a kind of causal explanation. But, according to externalism, this is to fail to appreciate the force of the teleological 'why?', which is *sui generis*. If a satisfactory version of externalism applies to animal goals of the most primitive kind then perhaps it could be elaborated to cope with more sophisticated ones later.

I shall try in this chapter to concoct a plausible version of externalism by using the notion of plasticity and adding something extra. In Chapter 6, I argued that plasticity was not a necessary condition of goal-directedness. But I left a loophole when I admitted that there might be such a thing as a basic or primitive case which did involve plasticity. Externalism exploits this concession, and asserts that plasticity is necessary in central cases, where there is no conflict of goals, no deprivation and no abnormality.

The primary task for externalism is to say what it is for an action to be a goal. Braithwaite wrote (1953 p. 329):

It seems impossible to find any characteristic of the final state by itself of a teleological causal chain which is general enough to cover all the goals of goal-directed actions and yet specific enough to differentiate such actions from other repeated cycles of behaviour.

His notion of plasticity is not a complete answer, however, because behaviour can be plastic with respect to end states that are not goals. According to externalism, we need to keep looking for that additional characteristic which Braithwaite thought could not be found.

Many goals, especially the most primitive and basic ones, are biologically adaptive. This is surely no coincidence. But is it a contingent fact, or does it reflect a necessary truth? In the previous chapter, I argued that it was impossible to build a bridge from the concept of goal to the concept of end. The concept of an end as something good for the organism seemed to be autonomous and primary. But externalism proposes that we try to build a bridge in the other direction. Taking the concepts of end and function as given, we can try to understand what *kinds* of things goals are in terms of biological functions, and then we construct the concept of an actual goal out of that, plus plasticity. If it succeeds, the theory will be non-vitalist, and non-mentalist.

Exposition

We have already noted that characteristic actions of the whole organism can be functions, if they contribute to a biological end, just as the activities of organs can be. Some such actions have beneficial consequences that are not themselves actions. Either they contribute directly to an end, or they facilitate physiological processes which in turn contribute to an end. Let us call these actions 'ultimate behaviour-functions'. They are ultimate because there is nothing further the animal as a whole can do which ensures their contribution to an end. Some actions contribute to or facilitate further actions which have beneficial consequences. Let us call these actions, which contribute to ends via intermediary actions, 'subordinate behaviour-functions'. Eating and drinking are paradigms of ultimate behaviour-functions. They are functions because they regularly contribute to survival: and once the animal has eaten or drunk, there is nothing further it can do to ensure its own survival by those channels. Hoarding food is a typical subordinate behaviour-function. Two important characteristics of behaviour-functions are that they are *kinds* of action that animals of the species characteristically perform, and that performance of them *regularly* and *normally* leads to beneficial consequences for the individual or species.

All normal members of a species perform the same behaviour-functions. This is so because a function is a characteristic action of the type of thing that performs it, and the type of thing that performs a behaviour-function is a normal member of a species. But it is characteristic of the animal in a different sense from the sense in which an organ's function is characteristic of the organ. An organ usually has only one characteristic activity, which it does all the time or periodically. By contrast, a whole organism may perform many different types of activities, some of which it does regularly, others irregularly. Regularity of performance is not a necessary feature of behaviour-functions. Mating, for instance, occurs at most once in the lifetime of animals of some species. What is important is that all normal members of the species do it if the opportunity arises.

Organ functions can be arranged in a hierarchy that mirrors the interlocking organisation of the separate organs. Different organs perform their different ground level functions, which co-operate and give rise to higher level functions. Behaviour-functions on the other hand, are all performed by the same item – the whole organism. Consequently they can only be arranged in order of importance on a set of lines. Each line comes eventually to an ultimate behaviour-function, and only then may they converge upon a common end. But some lines may not converge at all, since there may be several different ends.

Whenever a behaviour-function contributes to an end, it occurs in order to bring about the end, in the functional sense of 'in order to'. Eating and drinking occur in order that the animal may stay alive. But this does not mean they are goal-directed to survival. Actually they cannot have survival as a goal, according to the theory under construction. Although the word 'goal' is often used loosely, covering actions, events, states of affairs and objects indifferently, externalism restricts the term to actions.

Whenever a subordinate behaviour-function like a courtship dance contributes to an ultimate behaviour-function like mating, it occurs in order that the ultimate behaviour may occur. Here again, this is the functional sense of 'in order that'. It gains a purchase here because the subordinate behaviour-function, by contributing to an ultimate behaviour-function, contributes indirectly to an end. Since it is important not to confuse the two types of 'in order to' or 'in order that', which have separate criteria of application, I shall write 'in order$_F$ to' for the functional sense, and 'in order$_G$ to' for the goal sense. The aim of externalism is to construct the meanings of 'in order$_G$ to' and 'in order$_G$ that' out of the foundation laid so far.

It is far more difficult to classify actions into kinds about which generalisations can be made than it is to classify objects. Animals live in a constantly changing environment. Two tokens of the same movement type, if performed in different environments, may have very different causal consequences. In order to classify action-types according to their functions, we have to abstract from the different contexts and talk on a general level. An action which contributes to an end on a particular occasion does not automatically have a function because of that. The beneficial outcome may have been fortuitous. The logical primacy of types in functional talk imposes stringent conditions and has the effect of freezing the temporal dimension of behaviour. The model treats behavioural functions as a relatively permanent framework, analogous to the material structure of the organism, which remains stable beneath the flux of transitory stimuli and responses.

There is a need for an additional method of classifying actions, which accommodates the fact that different tokens of the same act-type may have different consequences, in different environments, yet which recognises that these differing consequences are not necessarily accidental. It is here that *goals* enter the picture. The same action can be goal-directed to G_1 on one occasion, G_2 on another; it can be directed to a goal even when not of a kind that *normally* leads to a behaviour function. What makes a particular action goal-directed in something about *it*, not about its type.

Let us introduce the concept of a *basic goal*. The first condition on a basic goal is that it be an action of a certain *kind*, namely a behaviour-function. Ultimate basic goals are ultimate behaviour-functions, subordinate basic goals are subordinate behaviour-functions. The second condition is that it be an action with respect to which the animal's behaviour is plastic at t. This is a relational property which an action has or lacks depending on the circumstances, rather than on the kind of action it is. Only actions that are behaviour-functions *can be* basic goals, but to say that they *are* goals is also to say something about the role they are playing at the time. A particular action B may contribute to a behaviour-function on a particular occasion, without occurring in order$_G$ that the behaviour-function should occur.

How is it possible to distinguish cases where an action accidentally contributes to a behaviour-function from cases where it is goal-directed to a behaviour-function, given that the dependability of the connection between types is lacking? In the one-shot goal-directed

case, accident is ruled out by the plasticity and persistence requirement. We invoke hypothetical variations in circumstances, and ask
whether the behaviour-function would still be achieved despite such
variation. Plasticity necessarily comes into the picture to supply the
element of nomologicality that functions already have, but goal-
directed actions lack. Instead of saying that B is timelessly of a certain
kind, we assert that B is a member of a certain transient class at t.
The class is defined relative to a class of alternative circumstances
which might have obtained at t. For each alternative circumstance in
the class, there is an action appropriate to the same beneficial consequence that B facilitates, which would have occurred at t if the circumstance had obtained.

Things that have functions, and functions themselves, are types.
However, things that have goals are primarily particular actions or
sequences, not types. If it were true that whenever an action of a certain
type is performed, each performance is goal-directed to a goal G, then
it would be true that that type of action had that goal. But it is hard to
think of an action-type whose tokens are always done for the same
purpose. Less spectacular regularities do occur, however, in the goal-
directed behaviour of individuals and species. When an individual is
behaving plasticly with respect to goal G, it has goal G at that time. If
the times when it has goal G are frequent, we may say, loosely, without
limiting ourselves to a particular time, that the animal is such that it
has goal G. Extending this further, when most members of a species
have goal G, we may say that the species has goal G. The important
point to remember is that these locutions are built upon the primary
locution, 'G is a goal of the behaviour of an individual at a time',
which is in turn built upon the general statement 'G is a behaviour-
function of the species'.

In view of this it may appear paradoxical that goals themselves are
action-types, not tokens. Yet this is indeed so, according to externalism. It must be so, since, if S does B in order$_G$ to do G, G is the goal
of B irrespective of whether a token of G actually occurs. First, G may
be prevented from occurring by an obstacle. Second, B has a goal,
hence there *is* a goal which B has, at the time when B is performed. So
even if an instance of G does occur, the goal exists prior to the instantiation. It follows from the definition of synchronic plasticity in terms of
hypotheticals (i.e. 'If the situation were such that a B-type action would
lead to a G-type action, then S would do B (provided nothing interfered)') that the sort of thing with respect to which behaviour is plastic

must be a *type* of event. Thus goal-directedness, construed as a relation, holds between an action-particular and an action-type. Furthermore, the relation holds from the moment that the action-particular B occurs. It can be seen that the concept of a basic goal is more complex than the concept of a behaviour-function. An action-type counts as a basic goal at t both in virtue of being of the right kind to be a behaviour-function and in virtue of being a focus of plastic behaviour at t. A teleological description conveys both of these pieces of information through the meaning of 'in order$_G$ to'. Externalism supplements a pure plasticity theory by holding that goals are essentially *behavioural foci of beneficial kinds*.[1]

The most immediate advantage of this theory is to rule out the plethora of non-biological counterexamples like the rolling boulder and the magnet. It also rules out guided missiles, which many people might think ought to be kept in. Still, perhaps the ascription of goals to such machines is a metaphorical extension from the animal paradigms, provoked by their extraordinary powers of plasticity. Another consequence is that it allows for the possibility of ascribing goals to plants. This might be thought extravagant. However, perhaps plants do not have the behavioural repertoire necessary for satisfying the plasticity requirement. When Francis Darwin ascribed mind to plants (1908), an externalist would say that he made two mistakes; first, plants are probably not adaptable enough to be said to strive after their biological ends; second, even if they were goal-directed, this would not imply they had minds. Russell was perhaps reacting against this kind of anthromorphising when he proposed his behaviourist theory of animal desire.[2]

The real test of the theory, however, is not whether it correctly identifies the class of things capable of having goals, but whether it shows how to identify their goals correctly. Imagine a sequence of actions – say the actions performed by a dog during the course of one day. As Kenny rightly remarks (1964, pp. 108–9), 'we need some criterion for deciding where one behaviour-pattern begins and another ends'. Externalism approaches this problem in a way that Kenny recommends. It agrees with him that 'such a criterion is provided, in

[1] Compare D. M. MacKay's insistence on the difference between 'adaptive' and 'variational' criteria, in MacKay (1972). Externalism tries to combine the two criteria.

[2] 'This detour through the animal's supposed mind is wholly unnecessary' Russell (1921, ch. 3, p. 62).

the case of animals, by their needs'. By insisting that only behaviour-functions can be basic goals, it makes it *impossible* for a bird to have the basic goal, in flying from A to B, of making its shadow move from A′ to B′.

But this is not the whole story. We do not simply split up the sequence of the dog's behaviour into autonomous stages, each ending in the fulfilment of a need. We also divide the stages into nested sections and subsections. How do we decide where to draw the boundaries, given that there may be no apparent breaks in continuity? As ethologists are well aware, the description of animal behaviour poses difficult taxonomic problems. The task is to divide the behaviour into units that lend themselves to systematisation within an overall theory of the organism. Externalism, which is a philosophical theory about the concept of goal, tries to provide a rationale for ethological theories which use this concept in their attempt to construct taxonomies.

The initial problem is to decide which types of events in the life of the organism are behaviour-functions. Often, a behaviour-function is a necessary condition of survival. But not all actions necessary for survival are behaviour-functions. First, it goes without saying that a behaviour-function must be of a kind that is beneficial for most members of the species. Needs that are peculiar to individual circumstances are disqualified. Second, our desire to systematise as economically as possible imposes constraints even on action-types that are not peculiar to the individual case. If eating food is a necessary condition of survival, then, quite generally, getting to within an inch of food, two inches of food, three, four etc. are necessary too. We do not want to say that these are also behaviour-functions.

Suppose that every type of action that we now think of as a behaviour-function were regularly preceded by and causally depended upon another type of action, which we could call 'a shadow behaviour-function'. As far as the generality requirement for functions is concerned, shadows are on a par with the real ones. Why not include them in the class? The list would become twice as long, but why should this matter? Even conceding the desirability of parsimony, there remains the fact that the list of 'real' behaviour-functions alone is no shorter than the list of shadows alone. Why do we prefer the former list to the latter? One cannot choose between them purely on grounds of system, since the overall *structure* of the system of shadow behaviour-functions is identical.

The problem of identifying the main behaviour-functions is highly complex. Ethologists often disagree among themselves about the best way to classify and count them. But certain general principles are agreed on. The whole system is grounded upon ultimate behaviour-functions, which are defined as actions of the whole animal whose contribution to an end is not mediated by any further action. So they can agree on how to anchor the system even if they disagree on the number of points of anchorage. Shadow behaviour-functions cannot possibly infiltrate the class of ultimate functions.

Next, they can agree that redundancy is undesirable in the list of subordinate behaviour-functions. An action is redundant in the list if the fact that it is a necessary condition of an end can be inferred immediately from the presence of another action in the list. If a certain action is such that another action must necessarily precede it, then no more information about the organism is added by including that other action in the list. Most shadows would be excluded by this test, if the list already included the actions they foreshadowed.

Next, the descriptions of subordinate behaviour functions should impart the maximum amount of information. In choosing between two equally economical lists, one should opt for the list that implies more. Given that many shadows would be described in a way that anticipated their sequels, a list of these would be entailed by, but would not entail a corresponding list of sequels.

Finally, there are a number of other factors that play a part in determining the natural breaks in a behaviour sequence, such as pauses, and radical physical changes in the environment (or in the organism) brought about by the action. The behaviour systematist also has his eye on opportunities for generalising across species, so he prefers descriptions that lend themselves to this. However, it must be admitted that there is still ample scope for multiplying subordinate behaviour-functions, and consequently ample scope for multiplying the range of things that can be subordinate basic goals.

We now examine how these considerations affect the identification of basic goals. Let us assume that an experimenter has established that a rat is behaving plasticly. He believes that it is goal-directed, but needs to determine exactly what its goal is. On the first trial, it ran two yards, reached the north west corner of the room, and ate the food that was there. On the second trial, everything was the same, except that the rat had to run four yards, having started from a different position. The event which happened at the end of a trial is a focus of convergence, but this leaves a lot of leeway, since many different types of action are exemplified by what the rat does at the end of a trial. There are at least three possible hypotheses consonant with the observed plasticity: (1) that the rat's goal on the first trial was to run two yards, (2) that its goal on both trials was to reach the north west corner, (3) that its goal was to eat the food.

One way to decide between (2) and (3) is to test the rat again, under different circumstances. If the food were placed in the south east corner, would its behaviour still be plastic with respect to reaching the north west? We may discard goal-hypotheses of lesser scope. However, the great defect of this method is that it relies on a possibly unwarranted assumption, that the rat has the same goal on each trial. If we have no reason to assume this, then we cannot even rule out hypothesis (1). The evidence of a third experiment, where the food is placed in the south east corner three yards away from the rat, will be compatible with the hypothesis that its goal is to run three yards on that occasion.

No doubt anyone presented with a choice between (1) and (3) would prefer (3). It is not plausible that a rat should have the goals put forward in (1). But is it theoretically possible that a rat might have those goals? According to externalism it is not possible, if the goals are basic goals. Hypothesis (1) and hypothesis (2) are both ruled out flatly by the requirement that a basic goal be a beneficial *kind* of action. It is not necessary to test further in order to know that the rat's goal was to get the food. Our background knowledge about the needs of rats, or indeed of animals in general, tells us that only one of the kinds of action mentioned *can* be the rat's basic goal.

It is a central tenet of the theory that a goal-directed organism does not necessarily act intentionally, or see its goal as anything. This implies that once the identity of the goal has been fixed, the organism can be said to aim at it under any of its descriptions. Nevertheless, one must guard against misinterpretation here. A goal is not a particular. A goal-description is not a singular term that refers to a concrete occurrence. Goals are action-types; the identity of the action-type which the goal *is* is heavily dependent upon the actual description chosen. If it were possible to have two or more descriptions of the same action-type, then the theory would agree that they were inter-substitutable *salva veritate* in a teleological sentence. But no two predicates ever do introduce the same action-type, except if they are synonymous or theoretically interreducible.

It might be objected at this point that the theory fails to determine uniquely the identity of the goal in cases where a number of action-types are candidates, and that in this example there are several candidates. This is not a question of having several descriptions of the same action-type whose identity is unproblematic, and of being unable to choose between them. The theory admits that it is indifferent as regards which one we choose. It is a question of having several possible goals amongst which we cannot choose. For example, it might be said that in the first two trials, the circumstances were such that getting to the north west corner was beneficial, since that was where the food happened to be. It is quite true, therefore, that on those occasions the rat was trying to reach the north west corner.

The theory has two restrictions on the proliferation of goals: the plasticity test and the 'biological end' test. If goals were allowed to be too relative to individual circumstances, the desired results could not be obtained from plasticity tests. These tests prove goal-directedness by showing that the end-point remains the same despite changes in the circumstances. The identity of the end point must, therefore, remain constant throughout all tests intended to show that *that* end-point is a goal. Our third trial, when the food was placed in the south east corner disconfirmed the hypothesis that the rat's goal throughout the three trials was to reach the north west corner.

Let us suppose, however, that plasticity has already been established on the first two trials. Then the evidence of plasticity does not determine a unique goal. In general, however many trials are run, there will always be more than one goal-hypothesis that abstracts sufficiently from the changes in circumstances during the trials to remain compatible with the plasticity data. If we are to decide between 'getting to the north west corner' and 'eating the food', we are forced to do so on the basis of biological significance. The question boils down to this: can biological significance be relative to individual circumstances? Clearly the answer, in the basic case, must be No. The property of being end-furthering belongs to types of action performed by types of organism. If the conceptual link between goals and functions were severed, externalism would collapse.

Still, some concessions must be made here in view of the plausibility of the objection. Instead of saying that eating the food and reaching the north west corner are rival goal-candidates in the first two trials, but that the latter is completely ruled out by failing the 'biological end' test, one might well say that the rat's main goal is to eat the food, but that in the circumstances it also has the subsidiary goal of reaching the north west corner, this being the means by which it gets the food. In the third trial, the rat has the subsidiary goal of reaching the south east corner. If we wish to amalgamate a set of trials in order to prove plasticity, it is essential to assume the same goal throughout. This goal is, for the purposes of that block of tests, a main goal. But once goal-directedness has been established, there is no harm in allocating subsidiary goals as well. There is a limit to this, of course. We must not count as a subsidiary goal any action-type whose usefulness was so relative to its circumstances that there does not exist a range of hypo-thetical alternatives sufficiently large to prove the plasticity of other actions with respect to it. The lower limit of segmentation into sub-goals is thus set by the plasticity test. The upper limit is set by the condition that the main goal of a segment be of a biologically beneficial kind.

In this way we erect a framework of ultimate and basic goals, then we fit subsidiary goals into the interstices. These are circumstance-relative foci of plasticity, possessing basic goals as their own foci. The notion of a subsidiary goal is not alien to the theory: subordinate goals are subsidiary to ultimate goals. It is a natural extension of the theory to acknowledge a class of subsidiary goals that are sensitive to circumstances.

This, then, is a sketch of externalism. It is only a beginning. If the theory is to be realistic, it must be able to account for the fact that organisms sometimes have ultimate goals that are not biologically adaptive. Human beings, for instance, can reach states where they strive after money for its own sake, or in which their main aim is to commit suicide. To cope with these sophistications, the theory intro-duces the concept of a derived goal. The organism starts life with an infrastructure of basic goals. As it gets older, it learns to adopt strategies for attaining basic goals by means of subsidiary goals which are relative to circumstances. Certain types of circumstances may frequently recur in its life, and these instil the habit of aiming at certain subsidiary goals. After a point, the habit becomes engrained. The subsidiary goals become autonomous, in the sense that the organism strives after them even in circumstances in which they are no longer means to basic goals. Goals like this are derived goals. To call an action a derived goal is to allude to its past history. Once an action-type acquires this status, it can function just like a basic goal; that is, it can be ultimate, or subor-dinate, and other goals can be subsidiary to it. Unlike basic goals, derived goals are characteristic of the individual, since they result from his own, possibly unique, development. But they must be understood as superstructures built upon the foundations of basic goals. To say that making money or taking drugs are derived goals of an individual implies, in virtue of the meaning of 'derived goal', that they are action-types with respect to which the behaviour is plastic, and which are foci because they used to be subsidiary to basic goals.

A next step might be to construct the concept of a displacement goal, along the lines of the ethological concept of displacement activity. An individual may find himself in a conflict situation, where each dis-position to behave plasticly is thwarted by others. The interaction between goals produces a conflict, whose net result is that he becomes plastic with respect to something which contributes neither to a basic goal nor to a derived goal. The goal of committing suicide may come into this category. Alternatively, suicide might be explained as a sub-sidiary goal aimed at a basic goal like alleviating pain.

The externalist will probably introduce conscious goals at this point. Conscious thought involves the capacity to represent the outside world symbolically. Organisms with this capacity are complex information-processing systems, able to calculate plans of action, defer goals, stack them, persist for long periods, overcome obstacles by subtle methods, and so on. Their subsidiary goals are sometimes determined by reasoning. It is often not apparent to an outside observer in what way an action type which certainly satisfies the plasticity test is subsidiary to a basic or derived goal. To understand it as a means would involve conceptualising the situation in the way the agent himself does. How-ever, allowing for the obscurity of the concept of consciousness, the concept of a conscious goal is not especially problematic for the externalist.

It is simply the concept of a goal that the agent has and knows he has. The fact that he can represent symbolically the fact that he has it no doubt helps him to aim at it more efficiently, and may generate subsid-iary goals which he would not otherwise have had. To that extent, his consciousness may create subgoals. But the whole edifice is rooted in ultimate goals, either basic or derived, which he must already have. According to the externalist, non-conscious goals are logically prior to conscious ones. The theory is reminiscent of Schopenhauer's view that consciousness can do no more than inform us of the biologically based urges that we are destined to obey.[3]

I shall not trace these further developments in detail. Some final

[3] See P. L. Gardiner (1963), pp. 178–9.

remarks are called for, however, concerning the status of the theory and the picture of teleological explanation that it presents.

The ultimate aim of the theory is to provide a recursive definition of 'goal', whose stages match the stages in the development of the organism. The definition looks something like this:

A goal of an individual at a time = df. An action-type which is

(1) a focus of plasticity at that time and is

(2) either (a) a biologically significant kind of action. (Basic goal, ultimate or subordinate)

or (b) a means to a basic goal in the prevailing circumstances. (Subsidiary goal)

or (c) a kind of action that frequently used to be a subsidiary goal in the individual's past life. (Derived goal)

or (d) a kind of action that is performed as a result of a conflict between two or more goals of type (a), (b) or (c). (Displacement goal)

or (e) a means to a basic goal or a derived goal or to a displacement goal, adopted with conscious calculation. (Conscious subsidiary goal)

or (f) . . . etc. etc.

Whereas others would regard it as contingent that an individual's goals develop out of biologically given goals, the externalist regards this as necessary. It is built into his general definition of 'goal'. He sets no absolute limits on what might be aimed at – any type of action can be a derived or subsidiary goal, given the right circumstances. But he does claim that if an action-type is a goal, there must be a story tracing a connection back to a basic goal, which makes intelligible why the organism has it. The position is similar to one proposed by Miss Anscombe in *Intention*, pp. 70–2. She regards a chain of 'Why did you want that?' questions as being appropriately terminated by an answer which characterises the object of desire as inherently desirable.

The externalist account of the way TDs explain is also akin to Miss Anscombe's view of intention explanations. They illuminate the explanandum by fitting it into a pattern which is not a pattern of causal antecedents. The pattern has two dimensions: first, there is the ever-changing pattern of plasticity: second, there is the more stable context of the individual's whole life. The explanandum is transiently a means to something the agent characteristically tends to do given the type of thing he is and the type of life he has led.

TDs are like taxonomic hypotheses, which classify the behaviour by reference to a possible effect that stands out as important. This method of classification is suitable for shifting, evanescent subject-matter. If there were such a thing as a taxonomic chart for actions, it would be an animated model, like a container full of moving bubbles. Each bubble represents an action-type, and lights up when the action-type is instantiated. The bubbles constantly rearrange themselves into different patterns. When a goal-directed sequence of actions occurs, the observer is able to discern for a moment a straight line of bubbles which light up. When the lights go off, the line is lost to view, and the bubbles drift into new arrangements.

We can imagine the teleological connective 'in order to' being grammatically parsed in a way that brings out a connection with biological taxonomy. The parsing goes like this:

in – preposition governing noun 'order'
(the) – definite article (deleted)
order – noun, (from *ordo, ordinis*) as used by Linnaeus to mean
    'category' or 'classificatory group'.
to – particle of infinitive functioning as verbal noun in apposition
    to 'order'.

Thus 'S did B in order to do G' is a truncated version of 'S did B in the order: to do G'. I do not claim that this parsing is etymologically plausible. Indeed, it is not historically correct. But to an externalist it is *suggestive* of the similarity between TDs and taxonomic hypotheses. Asking whether the bird is ruffling its feathers in order to scare away a rival or to attract a mate is like asking 'Does the genus *homo* belong to a separate order of Bimana (as claimed by Blumenbach and Cuvier), or is it included[4] among the Primates?' A further advantage claimed for the taxonomic approach is that it creates a unified theory spanning internal and external teleology, in Kant's sense.

Refutation

Although no philosopher has ever explicitly formulated or espoused externalism, it fits into an Aristotelian-cum-Wittgensteinian tradition. Aristotle's influence is reflected in two ways: first, the concept of goal covers roughly the same range of immanently teleological phenomena as the concept of *telos*; second, the theory makes use of the concepts of normality and biological kind. Wittgenstein's later philosophy is

[4] As Darwin argued in *The Descent of Man*, pp. 149–55.

echoed first in the idea that teleological explanation renders behaviour understandable by locating it into a context; second, in its aversion to hidden mental entities. There is an obvious connection between the Wittgensteinian view of explanation and the Aristotelian emphasis on normality.

Views akin to externalism are to be found in Miss Anscombe's *Intention*, and A. Kenny's *Action, Emotion and Will*, where they discuss restrictions on the possible objects of desire. There are strong parallels with the externalist's restrictions on possible goals. Kenny writes (pp. 122–3): 'Animals lacking language can express wants only by behaviour. It follows that they can want to do only what they can in general do and sometimes do . . . (An individual) can want to do only those things which animals of his kind can do and do.' Again, 'A desired activity must normally be characterisable as desirable by reference to recognised human goods'. Charles Taylor, in *The Explanation of Behaviour*, arrives at similar views connecting goals with what is natural for an animal. This provokes the thought that teleological explanation is a throwback to an Aristotelian kind of explanation in terms of natural tendencies expressive of the essence of the behaving object.

It would be an interesting exercise to trace the historical trends of thought which feed into externalism. I propose, however, to consider it on its own merits, purely as a theory of goals. My arguments against it are intended to prove that it fails to do what it sets out to do.

I think the main objection is that externalism confuses necessary truths with contingent truths about goals. In our world, an externalist can probably identify the goals of an animal quite well, by first using his two criteria for basic goals, and then by applying the 'derivation' tests for non-basic goals. He gets the answers right because of two contingent facts: (a) that innate goals are usually adaptive, hence count as behaviour functions; (b) that acquired goals are often derived from innate goals as a result of conditioning. By defining the key terms 'basic goal' and 'derived goal' by reference to these facts, he can construct a concept of goal which has more or less the right extension. But he gets the intension wrong. If (a) or (b) did not hold, the glue holding the criteria together would come unstuck. The concepts of basic goal and derived goal, so defined, would cease to have empirical application, but animals might still have goals, in the generally accepted sense.

Let us consider basic goals first. It is reasonable to suppose that some animals have innate goals. Calves, for example, are genetically 'pro-grammed' to seek the cow's udder. Almost as soon as they are born, they exhibit plasticity in this respect. It is also generally true that innate goals are biologically adaptive. Calves that have the teat-sucking instinct are more likely to survive than those which do not. However, it is conceivable that an animal might be innately predisposed to strive after goals that are not beneficial at all, such as eating stones, or sucking the cow's tail. Indeed, abnormal offspring do occasionally have non-functional innate goals – or so it appears from the evidence of their behaviour. Since tail-sucking is not a behaviour-function, it cannot be a 'basic' goal in the externalist's sense; nor can it be a 'derived' goal in this example since it is *ex hypothesi* innate. The externalist is forced to say that tail-sucking in such a case cannot be a goal of the calf at all. It seems clear, however, that a calf might well have that as a goal. Evidence of plasticity would positively invite the hypothesis that a calf had this instinctive goal. What this means is, roughly, that tail-sucking is something the calf is aiming at. It is not necessary that what is aimed at should be functional. The argument is the same as the one used in the previous chapter against Theory One: there is no contradiction in the idea that animals might instinctively aim at things which are bad for them, or neither good nor bad.

Whenever an animal strives after some G which is not a basic goal or a means to a basic goal, the externalist is committed to saying that G is a derived goal or a displacement goal. He thus commits himself to a factual claim about the animal's past history, that S acquired the goal G because G used to be associated with a basic goal, or because of a con-flict between basic goals. Many acquired goals do, in fact, arise in these ways. But it is not conceptually necessary that all non-basic goals should be derived from a set of basic goals. One can easily imagine an adult acquiring a new goal for some other reason. He might, for example, undergo an operation which changes his personality. Human beings, certainly can adopt goals for a variety of reasons (e.g. spite, jealousy), which have nothing to do with survival, pleasure, or any other biological end. The externalist tries to analyse the meaning of 'S has goal G' (where G is non-basic), by answering the question 'How did S come to be plastic with respect to G?' But the attempt is bound to fail. There is no limit to the number of possible explanations of why S is plastic, apart from the explanations that are built in to the recursive definition; and some of these explanations sever the desired historical connection between G and basic goals.

The concept of goal allows, then, for (a) innate goals that are not 'basic' in the sense stipulated, (b) acquired goals that are not generated out of basic goals. So it is not impossible for an animal to have the goal of moving its shadow from A' to B', or of going to the north west corner of the room for its own sake, even though these goals are not, and never have been, beneficial to the organism or associated with anything beneficial. I agree, of course, that these would be highly implausible goals, and that we should be at a loss to understand how the animal came to have them. But externalism is no better than a pure plasticity theory at analysing what 'having a goal' *means*.

It can be also argued that externalism is deficient in its account of how the citing of a goal explains why S did B. The explanatory force of a basic TD arises, according to externalism, from the way it glues together two elements: the generality of basic goals, ascriptions of which are implicitly quantified over performances and individuals, and the generality introduced by the transitory class of hypothetical alternatives. These combine to give a classification of B. The TD says that B is a representative of a certain class of actions, all of which are expressive of a contemporary tendency of the individual towards a type of action characteristic of the species. Despite their greater complexity, teleological explanations are in the same group as dispositional explanations, as Ryle conceives them in *The Concept of Mind*, ch. v. They explain why S did B_1 by saying that S is the sort of thing that tends, in a variety of circumstances, to perform actions, like B_1 in these circumstances, which lead to an action G characteristic of S.

But a classificatory generalisation of this kind does not explain what motivated S to do B_1 in these circumstances. Surely the point of saying that S was aiming at G at t is to explain why B_1 actually occurred. Of course, the reason why it was B_1 as opposed to B_2 is that the circumstances were C_1 rather than C_2. But why should any response occur at all? The answer is, I think – 'Because S was moved to action by the state it was in'. Every action in the plasticity range is such that, if it occurred at t, the fact that S was aiming at G at t would explain why it occurred. The goal-hypothesis explains not only each particular response, but also *why S has this general tendency to do whatever is appropriate*. That is, it explains why the synchronic plasticity-conditionals hold at t.

S's having goal G at t cannot *consist in* S's tendency to behave appropriately at t, given that it explains why S has that tendency. Plasticity is itself something that can be explained teleologically, by reference to the fact that S has a goal. The explanans must be distinct from the explanandum; so S's having goal G must be a distinct state of affairs from S's being plastic with respect to behaviour-function G.

The point is emphasised when we consider cases where S has several goals concurrently. Suppose S has goals G_1 and G_2, but does B at t in order to do G_1, not in order to do G_2. In the terminology used in chapter 6, G_1 was engaged, G_2 disengaged at t. I suggest that the only way to make sense of this distinction is to recognise that G_1 is *controlling* the behaviour at t, where this means that the fact that S has G_1 is causally influencing the performance of B. Take Scheffler's example of the cat crouching in front of a mouse-hole in order to catch the mouse. The cat also has the standing goal of drinking cream whenever she gets the chance. Her behaviour while she is crouching is plastic with respect to cream-drinking, since if a bowl of cream were introduced into the room, she would forsake the mouse-hole and go to the cream. But she is not crouching in order to get cream. The reason is that in the actual situation her standing goal of cream-drinking is not *engaged*. While she is crouching, her behaviour is being controlled by the fact that she has the goal of catching the mouse.

In order to explain why any response B was emitted, a TD must assert not merely that B is a manifestation of a disposition to behave plastically with respect to G_1, but also that a manifestation of that disposition occurred because that disposition was actively engaged at the time. If we accept that a teleological explanation does purport to account for the *occurrence* of an appropriate response, we are compelled to recognise that S's having a goal at a time must be an internal state with the power to influence behaviour causally.

Once this step is taken, we can account for certain peculiar features of the 'search' paradigm. It is crucial to the notion of searching that an organism may search for something that is not there. For example, a man may look for a box of matches in a room where there is no box of matches. His behaviour is consonant with a number of different hypotheses – that he is taking an inventory, that he is looking for a piece of string, that he is wandering about aimlessly, and so on. What makes it true that he is searching for a box of matches? According to a behaviourist the criterion would be the truth of a conditional, like, e.g. 'If he were to see a box of matches, he would home onto it.' Suppose, however, that an animal S roams around, comes across some food and starts to home in on it at t. This behaviour is consonant with the hypothesis that S was searching for food prior to t, but it by no means requires it. S might not have been acting on its goal of getting food before it saw the food. For the roaming to count as 'searching for food', S must have roamed in order to find food. The goal of finding food needs to be engaged and in control of S's behaviour *before* S switches over to the aiming paradigm at t.

10

Internalist theories

Remarks on strategy and method

Is there more than one kind of goal teleology? No one doubts that human beings sometimes entertain purposes consciously, and that any account of this kind of teleology must recognise its mental aspect. But the authors considered in Part Two claimed that there exists another kind of goal teleology. It is supposed to be exhibited by systems that do not have minds, and by systems which, although they do have minds, do not necessarily use their minds in exhibiting it. Taking the term 'goal-directedness' as a general name for all goal teleology, I have been trying to determine whether there is such a thing as goal-directedness without mind. Braithwaite, for example, explicitly says there are two separate kinds. The mentalistic kind covers actions regulated by conscious desires and beliefs; the other kind requires a more complex analysis in terms of plasticity.

However, the situation is complicated by the fact that some writers, assuming that there is such a thing as non-mental goal-directedness, *equate* it with the *genus* goal-directedness. They then treat mental goal-directedness as a special case. They assume or argue that a general account of goal-directedness will not commit itself to holding that goal-directed systems have minds, but will leave it open whether mental states are involved. Such writers, by identifying the problematic species with the genus, unintentionally make the genus problematic. Charles Taylor, for example, treats goal-directed behaviour as behaviour requiring explanation of the teleological 'form', but believes that 'there is more to explanation by *purpose* than simply the teleological form; it is, one might say, a form of teleological explanation with special features of its own' (1964, p. 26).

Despite these differences of opinion about classification, the theories I have considered all purport to analyse a concept of goal-directedness which we apply unhesitatingly to animals and perhaps to other things too; my arguments have assumed that we do have such a concept. In chapter 6, I distinguished between the externalist and the internalist approaches; in chapter 9, I showed that the best version of externalism that I could concoct failed to catch crucial features of the intended concept. It remains, then, to examine the internalist approach in the hope that it will lead both to a correct analysis and to a satisfactory resolution of the taxonomic issues.

Some philosophers, however, might urge that the enterprise is misguided, on the grounds that the concept being analysed is inherently tainted by its externalist origins. The term 'goal-directed' was invented by E. S. Russell, and taken up with alacrity by others, precisely in order that there should exist a name for a kind of teleology that complied with behaviourist and verificationist dogmas. If there is no kind for which a behaviourist analysis can be given, the name designates nothing and should be scrapped. It is futile trying to give an internalist analysis of that concept.

Things would be much simpler if this view were correct. Unfortunately, however, it ignores the *dynamic* nature of language. 'Goal-directed' is certainly poorly defined; its introduction and dissemination may well have been motivated by philosophical views that we now see to be wrong; but there is undoubtedly a general concept of goal-directedness *now* in use which is no longer wedded to ancient errors. The ground it covers is roughly indicated by the examples used. The three main paradigms of goal-directed behaviour are *searching*, as illustrated by a rat looking for food, or a man trying to find a box of matches; *aiming*, a heterogeneous category that includes lions running after antelopes, guided missiles homing on to targets, and chicks pecking at grain; and *keeping*, for example, balancing a ball, staying upright on a tightrope, and maintaining a steady temperature. I disagreed with Sommerhoff and Nagel about some of the phenomena they would include, notably certain physiological homeostatic processes, and I shall explain in due course my reasons for this. But borderline disagreements about its extension afford no grounds for doubting that there is a worthwhile concept to be explicated.

'Internalism' is the name of an approach or strategy of analysis. Internalists are people who believe that to call behaviour goal-directed is to explain it causally by reference to some internal state of the agent, the state of 'having a goal'. Every different opinion as to what that kind of internal state is will give rise to a different theory, but all of them will be internalist. Our present task is to select the theory which is also a correct analysis. I use the term 'theory' advisedly. All internalists agree that a TD is an empirical explanatory hypothesis which asserts that S did B because S was in a certain state. Any analysans of a TD must itself be a sentence used to assert a hypothesis, therefore. But in order to be an analysans, it must be a paraphrase that captures the meaning of the original. This means that it must not speculate about the nature of the internal state any more or any less or on any other level than the TD itself does. In particular, it must not be a sentence used to propose a theory about the brain mechanisms responsible for producing that behaviour. If every statement of the form 'S has goal G' were matched to a statement of the form 'S has property P', which had the same truth-conditions, where the expansion of 'property P' involves making references to parts of S's brain standing in certain relations, then for each statement of the form 'S did B *because* S had goal G' there would be a matching statement of the form 'S did B *because* S had property P'. But the physiological explanatory statement is no more an analysis of the meaning of the teleological explanatory statement than the simple statement about S's brain state is an analysis of the simple statement about S's having a goal. Each asserts that S is in an internal state, but whereas the former describes the state as a state of some of S's internal parts, the latter describes the state holistically, without referring to parts.

What kind of internal state descriptions, then, are suitable as candidates for employment in an analysans? I think there are three possibilities. First, the internal state may be described as the basis of a disposition, that is, a state whose intrinsic nature may be unknown, but which is type-identified by reference to certain of its overt characteristic effects. In cases where these effects are functions, the state may be said to be 'functionally defined'. Secondly, it may be described as a mental state, type-identified by reference to its content. Thirdly, it may be described in a variety of ways borrowed from systems theory, control theory, information theory and computer language, provided that such descriptions do not refer to specific internal parts. I take it as a condition on the adequacy of any of these kinds of description that they should mention G, but without containing the word 'goal'. They must be descriptions which reveal perspicuously what is meant when G is said to be a goal.

Although, given a realist view of dispositions, the first possibility does count technically as internalist, the prospects for conducting an analysis on these lines look no better than the prospects for any externalist account. Since the internal state is specified entirely by reference to its behavioural manifestations, the only way in which an internalist dispositional analysis differs from a behaviourist one is by the addition of the existential hypothesis that there is some occurrent basis underlying S's disposition.

The second possibility is that the internal state is a mental state. It possesses, along with other mental states like desires, beliefs and thoughts, the feature of intentionality. However, some philosophers believe that mental states themselves can be given a realist dispositional analysis (e.g. D. M. Armstrong, 1968). For them, the second line of approach would collapse into the first.

The third tactic looks initially promising, given that we do think of servomechanisms as goal-directed systems. Our contemporary concept has been influenced by the development of automata; it might well call for an analysis that is internalist without being mentalist. Such an analysis would have the required generality covering all the relevant systems. If such an analysis were possible, mental goal-directedness would indeed turn out to be a species of the genus. As mental processes are becoming better understood through Artificial Intelligence work, we may eventually be able to interpret statements about the mind in terms of statements about cybernetic systems, and thus, in a sense, map the second approach onto the third.

Still, this is empty talk, in the absence of actual examples of the sort of internal state descriptions that would be employed. Is the third approach really a distinct alternative to the other two? Although the vocabulary might be novel, its deployment might lead merely to *functional* characterisations of the internal state, or to characterisations in terms of the state's *content* or *meaning*. If it characterised states in the latter way, all its plausibility would be derived from the plausibility of a mentalist analysis. Instead of there being a generic concept of goal-directedness of which the concept of mental goal-directedness was a refinement, the true state of affairs would be that there was a core-concept of mental goal-directedness from which the concept of generic goal-directedness was derived by an extension. In such circumstances, the best way to explain why the class of goal-directed systems is as wide as it is would be to stratify its members, and show that the ones that do not have minds are included because they are similar to the ones that do.

I think that this is, in fact, the true situation. I believe, therefore, that the best way to approach the task of analysis is to *hypothesise* that there is a core-concept and a broadened concept, such that the core concept of having G as a goal involves the concept of wanting G, and such that the broadened concept involves the concept of

either wanting G or being in an internal state analogous to wanting
G.

The hypothesised core-concept

When we considered (in chapter 6) the plasticity conditionals that TDs
might be held to entail, we noted that S might suddenly stop aiming
at G in the course of the activity. Such a change would be an obstacle
to responding that is naturally thought of as internal. The externalist
was forced to extremes in his attempt to get rid of such a variable. Now
that we have rejected externalism, we can afford to recognise that
plasticity conditionals covertly rely on many assumptions about the
internal state of S, e.g. that S is alive, switched on, working normally,
etc. In the examples concerning animal behaviour, as distinct from
machine behaviour and physiological processes, certain internal conditions need to hold that are normally described in mental language. I
mean to include under the heading 'mental language' such verbs as
'perceive', 'believe', 'recognise', 'learn', 'remember', etc. The use of
such verbs does not necessarily imply that the subject is self-conscious
or can speak, only that the subject is conscious of, i.e. aware of, things
and facts. These central examples correspond, I suggest, to a core-
concept of goal-directedness.

For example, the rat whose goal is to reach the food on the other side
of a river will swim across for that reason only if he sees where the food
is. His perception of the food controls the direction in which he swims.
The plasticity conditional 'If the food were further to the left, the rat
would swim further to the left' relies covertly on the assumption that if
the food were further to the left, the rat would perceive it as being
further to the left. It is not possible to eliminate reference to perception
by saying that the animal perceives the situation correctly if it behaves
in a way appropriate to its goals. This would be question-begging in
the present context. One can try to give a behavioural analysis of the
concept of perception, taking the concept of goal for granted, or one
can try to give a behavioural analysis of the concept of goal, taking
the concept of perception for granted, but one cannot do both at
once.

In crediting the rat with perceptions, one is already crediting it with
beliefs. In perceiving that the food has moved to the left, the rat
acquires the belief that the food has moved to the left. The rat may also

need to remember what it has perceived. If it loses sight of the food while swimming, yet continues to swim in the right direction, this is probably because it remembers that there is food on the opposite bank. Memories based on past perceptions are continuations of beliefs about the environment. The general point is that conditionals of the form 'If the environment were E_i, S would do B_i (where B_i is appropriate to G in E_i)' are true only on the assumption that if the environment were E_i, S would believe that it was E_i.

They rely also on a further assumption, concerning another, more complex, kind of belief. For it is not always the case that if S correctly believes that the situation is E_i, S performs the response which is in fact, a means to G in E_i. S may be right about the situation, but wrong about the best way to get to G in that situation. S does what he *believes* to be appropriate. Thus any plasticity conditional whose consequent asserts that S does B_i, where B_i is in fact appropriate, must be relying tacitly on an assumption that if B_i leads to G, S will believe that B_i leads to G. The plasticity theorist omits to mention these perceptual and instrumental beliefs because he takes their general reliability for granted. He assumes that these cognitive states are accurate mirrors of reality. They are variables that always have the same value as stimulus-variables, so they drop out of account.

But this assumption is incorrect. The animal may have false beliefs about the environment and/or false instrumental beliefs. Furthermore, we normally pay regard to this fact when we judge the appropriateness of behaviour to a hypothesised goal. For instance, if the rat wrongly believed that the food had moved further to the right, e.g. if two mirrors were so arranged as to make it look as if the food were further to the right, and started swimming to the right, we should certainly judge that behaviour to be appropriate given the rat's belief. We should take that behaviour as corroborating evidence that the rat had the goal of getting the food, provided we knew that the rat had that belief. Similarly, if the rat correctly believed that the food had moved to the left, and started swimming to the left, but happened to be wrong in its belief that swimming to the left would conduce to getting the food (perhaps because of a strong current), we should again probably judge the behaviour to be appropriate in the light of information available to the rat. The concept of appropriateness that we employ is already one that credits S with a point of view. If mental states are necessary anyway, in order to explain how S gets to the goal or why S does the things it does in typical cases such as these, then there is no good reason for denying that having a goal is itself a mental state. There seems to be a core concept that lies firmly within the mental realm.

The most obvious kind of mental state with which to identify the state of having a goal is the state of wanting or desiring. Thus for every statement of the form 'S does in B order to do G' which entails that S has a goal (in the core sense of the word), there corresponds a statement of the form 'S wants to do G'. This schema shows clearly that the goal-description is within the scope of an intensional operator. The core-concept of a goal is the concept of an intentional object of desire. No wonder, then, that the truth-value of a TD is unaffected by whether G occurs or not. The plasticity theorist recognises that 'G' does not refer to a future act-particular. But he does not agree that 'G' occurs non-referentially in the context of an 'in order to . . .' sentence. He thinks that 'G' refers to an act-type enjoying independent existence. His reason for this is that he wants to say that S's goal exists at t. For him G must exist on some level or other, because S *has* it at t. However if we construe 'S has goal G at t' as meaning 'S wants to do G at t', then the temptation to hypostatise act-types fades away. The goal does not exist at t, except as the intentional object of S's state of desire at t. If S achieves G later, then we would say that the goal exists or occurs at that later time; but this is to say that something exists or occurs which was desired, i.e. is a token of a type of action that S wanted to do.

The desire-belief model of explanation

I suggest, then, that teleological explanations of the central kind rest on assumptions that S can perceive, remember, recognise kinds, learn, believe and want. But I still have to distinguish between what a teleological hypothesis actually asserts, and what it presupposes in the way of background. The final analysans of 'S does B in order to do G' aims at being an acceptable paraphrase. It must not assert anything that the TD takes for granted, nor take for granted anything that the TD asserts.

Consider a present tense TD with values assigned to S, B and G, used to make a report on a current situation. If the statement is true, then S has whatever mental capacities are required for behaving in that way and for having that goal. But the statement does not assert, of every capacity that S must have, that S has it. For example, the statement that the rat is swimming across the river in order to get the food may imply, in context, that the rat now perceives or has perceived the food. But the statement does not explicitly assert this, any more than it asserts that the rat has eyes or nose, or knows how to swim. If the statement does imply that the rat perceives the food, it does so in virtue of the specific nature of the goal that it ascribes, not in virtue of the mere fact that it ascribes a goal. If the rat's goal were to *find* food, the ascription of that goal would not imply that it now perceives any food. We want to crystallise out what is essential to teleological explanation in general, abstracting from the things that are implied by specific values of B and G.

I have claimed that in the central case having a goal G involves wanting G. Desires, like goals, may be longstanding or brief. They may also exist disengaged; S might have a desire or goal that he is not acting on at t. A teleological explanation hypothesises that a desire is *engaged*, i.e. that the behaviour at t is caused by a desire for G. However, engaged desire cannot be the whole story. A rat's desire to reach the food may be responsible for expressive and involuntary behaviour, like squeaking and twitching. But the rat does not squeak or twitch in order to reach the food. We have to separate side-effects from main effects.

Although squeaking is not a *means* of getting the food, this cannot be the criterion. In certain circumstances, swimming may not be a means either, yet we might still count the swimming as directed to G, on the grounds that the evidence available to the rat suggested that it was a means. Also squeaking *may*, in peculiar circumstances, be a means to G. The criterion is rather that S *believe* that B is a means to G.

In ascribing an instrumental belief to S, we credit him with the ability to select a response from his repertoire in the light of available evidence, using his own criteria of appropriateness. Normally S does this by using perceptual information. He sees the situation as E_i, and calculates (consciously or unconsciously) that B_i is the best way, or a way, to get to G in E_i. The calculation may draw upon a store of acquired general knowledge about spatial relations and causal regularities, or S may be genetically programmed to select a certain response B_i whenever he perceives a certain configuration of stimuli E_i, or S may have had specific past experience of B_i leading to G. In the primitive cases, we approach the limits of the concept of an instrumental belief. However, it is important to acknowledge the existence of a mediating belief distinct from the belief about the environment E_i, because teleological explanations allow for the possibility that S might perform an inappropriate response despite having a correct belief that the environment is E_i. The inappropriate responses might be due to miscalculation, or to erroneous beliefs about general principles. An instrumental belief is the outcome of a computation that may go wrong for a variety of reasons. But a TD does not go into the reasons why S believes, rightly or wrongly, that B is a means to G. It simply asserts that S does B because S believes that; and it presupposes the beliefs about the environment, if any, that led S to believe that. Thus there is no need to include beliefs about the current environment in the analysans.

I have characterised the content of the instrumental belief as 'that B is a means to G'. One action is a means to another if it causally contributes to it. But I should like to include also the relations that hold when S does G *by* or *in* doing B, or when doing B *amounts to* doing G in the circumstances. A. I. Goldman (1970) invented the term 'level-generation' to cover such cases. For example, S may flip the switch in order to turn on the light (causal-generation); extend his arm out of the car window in order to signal for a turn (conventional generation); and jump six feet in order to outjump George (simple generation). The content of the instrumental belief must be suitably modified to cater for these. A difficulty still remains over the relevant instrumental belief in the search paradigm. Is it not too strong to say, e.g. that Stanley turned left at Lake Victoria because he believed that turning left would contribute to finding Dr Livingstone? He probably believed no more than that the chances of finding the doctor would be higher if he turned left than if he did not. Even this may be an exaggeration. He may have believed simply that the chances would be higher if he carried on looking, but that it did not matter in which direction he looked. What content ought we to assign to the belief in the *general* analysans?

It is worth noting that the analysandum itself reflects this difficulty. Is it really true that Stanley turned left *in order* to find Dr Livingstone? Perhaps it would be more accurate to say that Stanley performed a chain of actions in order to find Dr Livingstone, one component of which was turning left at Lake Victoria. By adjusting the value of B in this way, we can continue to construe the relevant belief as a belief that B will contribute to G. 'Contributing to' sometimes amounts to no more than 'increasing the chances of'. I shall use the notation 'belief that $B \Rightarrow G$' from now on to cover all cases.

Does the TD assert both that S wants G and that S believes B ⇒ G, or does it assert one and presuppose the other? Some philosophers would say the latter, and claim that it does not matter which is said to be asserted, since the two ways round are equivalent. A belief which has the power to motivate is a desire, and a desire which has the power to select a means is a belief. But this is clearly wrong. It implies that an analysans which mentions both the desire and the belief contains a redundant component. However, the fact that squeaking is caused by a desire to eat is not enough to make squeaking goal-directed. Conversely, the fact that a driver lets go of the steering-wheel in panic because he suddenly realises that to do so would make the car go over a cliff, is not sufficient to prove that he lets go in order to achieve that result, for he has no desire to do so. Both components are necessary, therefore, and must be asserted.

Our language could have had a word for the total mental state that results from the conjunction of a desire and a belief. Why is it useful to distinguish two components, instead of regarding the desire/belief composite as a single unit? One reason is that TDs are offered not only of single actions but also of sets. By splitting the explanans into two components it is possible to reveal an underlying structure in the set of actions. If S performs a sequence of actions B, C, D that are directed to the same goal, the elements are bound together by the fact that they are all partly caused by the same unchanging desire, and yet distinguished from each other by the fact that they are partly caused by different beliefs. The changes in belief can be correlated with changes in environmental stimuli, brought about partly by the animal itself as a result of the previous act. During the period of the sequence, the desire is constant and the instrumental belief is variable, mirroring changes in stimuli. Each action is the outcome of an interaction between the desire and an instrumental belief which is itself the outcome of a computation.

Sometimes it is possible to collapse several instrumental beliefs in one. Instead of saying that S did B, then C, then D, because S believed that B ⇒ G, then S believed that C ⇒ G, than S believed that D ⇒ G, we may say that S did B C D because S believed that B C D ⇒ G. In such cases, the elements in the sequence are integrated not only by the desire, but also by the fact that S conceives them as integrated. To-gether they form a plan. As the beliefs reduce to one, so the three TDs reduce to one, and the three actions reduce to a single explanandum (which could be referred to simply as B). By this trick, behaviour se-quences of great length can be given a single TD, provided that S is sophisticated enough to have the required plan. The same process in reverse sets constraints upon the segmentation of sequences into stages controlled by subgoals. It would be true to say that S did B in order to do *D*, for example, only if the cause of S's doing B was the combination of a desire to do D and a belief that B ⇒ D. But S might not have such a belief or desire, since S might not conceive D as a separate action. Thus, segmentation depends on the agent's own conceptualisation of the sequence. It is not up to the observer to define where the 'natural breaks' lie – he has to discover where the agent has put them.

Since the integration of a sequence consists in the fact that each element is caused by the same desire, the problem of how to classify and count sequences depends on the problem of how to count desires. This is certainly a practical problem, especially if S has a multiplicity of different goals. But at least there is no obscurity about what integration *consists in*. A similar criterion could be given for co-ordination, where several actions are performed simultaneously for a common purpose.

So far we have assumed that 'B' refers to a specific action or sequence. But Charles Taylor, from whom the notation is borrowed, treats 'B' as a variable in his analysans, taking a range of values for any single value of *G*. He thinks that teleological explanations rely on a major premiss that the analysans should make explicit: 'S does whatever is required for G (within limits)'. Indeed, all plasticity theorists try to capture the idea that if S is goal-directed to G, S will do any of a range of actions to that end. TDs explain an action, they say, by asserting that it is drawn from a range of hypothetical alternatives.

Now this idea *can* be captured in the desire-belief schema. If B is a variable, it involves assigning a variable content to the belief that B ⇒ G. We could say that the desire-belief explanation relies on a major premiss: 'For every action B within a certain range, if S wants to do G and believes that B ⇒ G, S does B', or alternatively 'If S wants to do G, S does whatever S believes will contribute to G, provided it is within the range'. This law-like statement sustains conditionals: 'If S believed that B_1 ⇒ G, S would do B_1', 'If S believed that B_2 ⇒ G, S would do B_2' etc. (assuming that B_1, B_2 etc. are within the range). Thus the constant desire explains the persistence, the variability of belief explains the plasticity, if there is any.

However, we do not *wish* to build this into the analysans. First of all, many of the objections I raised against plasticity conditionals also apply to these. It is just not true, in general, that when S wants G, S will do anything in his power that he believes will lead to G. He may refrain from doing a certain thing because he believes that it would contribute via another channel to something he does not want. Familiar qualifications about conflicting desires, akrasia, time references, and forgetting, must be made before we can approach a major premiss that is at all plausible. The best that could be said is that a singular TD of B *hints*, (not *entails*) that B would have been different if S had believed that a different action would lead to G, in virtue of the fact that these other conditions often are satisfied.

More importantly, the general statement is not *required* in order to paraphrase the original TD. The letter B cannot be a variable in the analysandum; if it were, the TD would mean 'S does every action in his repertoire in order to do G', which is absurd. The TD puts forward a hypothesis explaining a particular explanandum B. Perhaps the 'complete' explanation is deductive-nomological, and relies on a major premiss; but the singular explanation does not entail it, any more than singular causal statements entail their own generalisations.

I conclude, therefore, that the desire-belief model of explanation can deal with all the objections made against plasticity theories, and that it can provide a deeper insight into their errors. I claim no originality in presenting it as an analysis of purposive explanation – it is the traditional view. Ducasse, for example, stated it explicitly in 1925. But I claim (*contra* Braithwaite) that it is the right model for animal goal-directedness too.

There is no need for an agent to be aware of the operation of his desire and belief when he acts purposively. He need not even know that he has them. His motives may be unconscious or preconscious. Freud gave many convincing illustrations of behaviour done for the sake of goals that his patients did not know they had, until they had been successfully psychoanalysed. Freudian explanations are not incompatible with explanations in terms of conscious purposes; they delve deeper, but do not necessarily discredit the everyday explanations. However, Freud's explanations of *unintentional* acts like slips of the tongue are not purposive explanations. He illuminates such phenomena by showing how they express or reveal hidden desires, but he does not and cannot show that they are done in order$_G$ to satisfy those desires. It remains possible, nevertheless, that slips of the tongue serve some psychological *function*, i.e. that they are done in order$_F$ to satisfy hidden desires, or to relieve psychic tension.

When we explain animal behaviour purposively, we hypothesise that the animal has beliefs and desires. One consequence of this thesis is that goal-directedness proper may be *less widespread* in the animal kingdom than many behaviourists have thought. The teleological descriptions that we give of the behaviour of lowly organisms that have needs but cannot desire, perceive, recognise or believe, should all be construed as functional TDs. But it is well to remember that desires and beliefs need not be conscious. Since human beings can be in certain mental states without being aware that they are, it would be wrong to deny similar kinds of mental states to animals purely on the grounds that they are not aware of them. Minds may be far *more* widespread than some philosophers have thought.

Is this mentalist model logically adequate?

If a driver takes a certain road because he believes it leads to London and he wants to get to London, then according to my account his action is goal-directed to getting to London, regardless of whether or not the road actually leads there. Suppose the man's belief is false, and that he is in fact driving away from London. It is tempting to say that his behaviour is not 'objectively goal-directed' to getting to London. It is tempting to think that a distinction ought to be made between the goal as the agent conceives it and the 'real' goal, just as a distinction is made between the formal object and the material object of perception. This temptation must be resisted. I have tried to show that it is impossible to give an externalist account of goalhood. There is no such thing as a goal to which the agent's behaviour is directed, yet which the agent does not have; and to have G as a goal is to have G as the object or content of a desire. Confusion arises in the example cited because the objector fails to draw a different distinction, namely that between direction and goal-direction. The man may be directed towards Oxford instead of towards London, but he is certainly not goal-directed to getting to Oxford. Another cause of confusion is our tendency to describe actions *in terms of* their goals. If the man were asked what he was doing, he might reply 'I'm driving to London'. On one reading, this is objectively false, but if we understand it to mean 'I'm driving along this road in order to get to London', it is surely true. A clear distinction can be made conceptually between what an agent thinks he is doing and what he really is doing, though we find it convenient to blur this distinction sometimes by characterising actions in the way we think the agent would characterise them. It follows from my analysis that the purpose of an action, as defined by the agent's belief and desire, is the goal that his action *objectively* has, even though his belief that the action will contribute to that goal may be completely wrong.

However, the analysis does encounter certain difficulties of its own. In particular, there is a fairly weighty argument against the claim that the desire-belief model is sufficient. Partly because he was impressed by it, R. Chisholm (1964) proposed that the teleological concept of 'making B happen with an end to making A happen' should be regarded as an unanalysable primitive concept. The argument relies on counter-examples, of which I shall list four. They are all of human desires, but the problem arises for animal desires too.

(1) *Chisholm's example.* 'Suppose a man believes that if he kills his uncle he will inherit a fortune and suppose he desires to inherit a fortune; this belief and desire may agitate him and cause him to drive in such a way that he accidentally kills his uncle . . .' (Chisholm, 1964, p. 616).

(2) *Benacerraf's example.* S wants to offend his host, and plans to grimace when he tastes the soup, believing this to be a way of offending him. 'Oscar, S's practical joker friend, knows about S's desire and S's belief, but he is determined to prevent S from intentionally offending his host.' So Oscar puts foul-tasting medicine in the soup, which causes S to grimace involuntarily when he tastes it. S's desire and belief caused S to grimace, because they caused Oscar to put the stuff in the soup (Quoted by Goldman, 1970, pp. 60–1).

(3) *R. Taylor's example.* 'Suppose . . . that a member of an audience keenly desires to attract the speaker's attention but, being shy, only fidgets uncomfortably in his seat and blushes. We may suppose, further, that he does attract the speaker's attention by his very fidgeting; but he did not fidget *in order* to catch the speaker's attention, even though he desired that result and might well have realised that such behaviour was going to produce it' (Taylor, 1966, pp. 248–9).

(4) *Davidson's example.* 'A climber might want to rid himself of the weight and danger of holding another man on a rope, and he might know that by loosening his hold on the rope he could rid himself of the weight and danger. This belief and want might so unnerve him

as to cause him to loosen his hold, and yet it might be the case that he never *chose* to loosen his hold, nor did he do it intentionally' (Davidson, 1973, pp. 153–4).

Benacerraf's and Davidson's examples are presented as problems for a causal account of *intentional* action, whereas Chisholm's and Taylor's are directed against the Ducasse theory of purpose. Since I am concerned with analysing the meaning of 'in order to' statements, there would be no formal objection to my including the word 'intentionally' in my analysans, thus ruling out these counterexamples. But since I am concerned with what it *is* to act purposively, as well as with the purely semantic problem of paraphrasing TDs, I ought to be able to provide a deeper analysis of the concept of intentional action. It should be possible to provide a general account of goal-directedness which is at the same time an account of acting intentionally.

In case (2), the causal chain from the desire and belief passes outside S through another agent before reaching B. In (3) and (4), the causation is wholly internal; in case (1), the relevant part of the chain, from the desire and belief to the basic action, is internal. The only external conditions are the ones which make it true that S's foot-pressing causes his uncle's death. Thus the answer to the difficulty cannot be simply to stipulate that the causal chain should consist solely of events inside the agent, for the chain still has to be routed through the right internal channel.

Since the source of the difficulty seems to be the indirectness of the causal link in the four cases, some philosophers recommend that an extra condition should be stated in the analysans. Goldman adds to his own analysans '. . . causes *in a certain characteristic way* . . .'. The analysans does not state what that way is. He believes it is a scientific rather than a philosophical task to identify the precise manner of causation, although people can intuitively feel a difference between an involuntary and a voluntary movement of their own. I find this an unsatisfactory position. If we confidently diagnose that what is wrong with the counter-examples is that the manner of causing is wrong, because, e.g. it goes through another person, or through the agent's nervousness, we ought to be able to say in more detail what the right way would be. In any case, a physiologist surely needs this information about the right psychological pathway *before* he can start to pin down its neural basis.

Can the problem be solved *without* appeal to the notion of 'a proper causal route'? One argument might be as follows. The four cases are not genuine counterexamples, because the respective desire-belief explanations turn out to be just as false as the TDs. The crucial point lies in the interpretation of the 'B' that occurs within the scope of the 'belief' operator. A correct analysis of the TD says that the action which S does results from a belief that that particular action will contribute to G. To have such a belief the agent must believe (just prior to doing B) that he is about to do an action of the B-type. None of the four examples meets this condition, not even the mountaineering example. The climber must not only believe 'If I let go, I'll get rid of the weight', he must believe 'This action of letting go which I am just about to perform will get rid of the weight', and it must be the latter belief which causes him to let go. The climber may or may not have such a belief incorporating the thought of an action that he believes he is just about to do. If he does not see himself as letting go, he has no such belief. But if he does have such a belief and yet he lets go unintentionally, it is not *this* belief which causes him to let go. The action which he sees himself as about to do is already causally determined by the nervousness resulting from the thought that if he lets go, he will get rid of the weight.

While he is performing a goal-directed action, the agent might express his belief as follows: 'This action will contribute to G'. The phrase 'This action' refers to a particular action, part of which has occurred. The conviction sustains and guides the act to completion. Just before he acts, the agent might express his belief by saying 'The action I am just about to perform will contribute to G'. His conviction helps to initiate the action. *We* might describe his belief as a belief that the action he believes he is just about to perform will contribute to G. These descriptions need not be construed as making a reference to a particular action that is future. At that stage, what S believes is that he is about to perform *an* action that will contribute to G. In Benacerraf's case, S *does* believe he is just about to make a grimace that will offend his host. But this belief is not a cause of the grimace that occurred.

However, the argument does not work. Modified counterexamples can easily be constructed. Thus (4′): the mountain climber starts off with the same desire and general belief as before, and is not made nervous by them. At first, he does not think it at all likely that he will let go of the rope. But as time goes on, he comes to believe that he will let go, because he thinks, rightly or wrongly, that his muscles won't stand the strain much longer. There comes a stage at which he believes he is just about to let go. He suddenly realises that the action he is about to perform will lead to G. This thought terrifies him, and makes him let go of the rope unintentionally. His specific belief about a particular action causes that very action, but the TD is false because the causation goes along an inappropriate path.

It might be replied in defence that the action performed here is not identical with the one the agent believed he was about to perform, but is another action of the same type. However, the grounds for saying this are very weak. For instance, one ground might be that the criterion of whether or not this B is the one the agent thought he was about to do is its causation. Suppose S would have done B then anyway, even if the belief had been absent. Then in the actual case, although the belief was present, the B that occurred was the wrong one. Either the belief was not a cause of it at all (which makes the case different from the counterexample, hence irrelevant to the defence), or it was a case of overdetermination. Maybe the belief and the muscular strain were separately sufficient in the circumstances for the unintentional action. If so, the letting go that occurred does not count as the letting go which the agent anticipated, because he thought it was going to be an action resulting from muscular strain. However, this ground for the defence is no good.[1] First, it is far from clear that this is a correct way of determining the identity of a future action. Or, to put the point the other way round, it is unclear that the description 'the action he anticipates' refers to a determinate, future act-token. Secondly, this reply does not answer the objection, for an account is still needed of the appropriate causal path. Under what condition, on the proposed view, is the actual B identical with the anticipated B? The criterion has to be that the actual B be caused by the right belief *in the right way*. The whole point of the counterexample is that the act of letting go was caused by the right belief in the wrong way. The defence concedes the main point, but chooses to describe it differently, as a problem of act-identity rather than as a problem about the causal relation.

The main problem, therefore, is indeed to specify the appropriate causal route. Although I cannot do this in adequate detail, I can at least offer a crude model which imposes a few of the necessary restrictions. One strategy for attacking problems of this sort is clear. If an event a can cause an event b by various routes, and we wish to rule out all but one, an obvious way to do so is to single out an event or item c which figures as an intermediate stage in the intended chain but not in the others. The route is then specified as 'the one that goes through stage

---

[1] The objection to it was pointed out to me by Mr D. F. Pears.

c'. But this division of the routes may be too crude. There may be N channels by which *a* can cause *c*, and M channels by which *c* can cause *b*, hence NM routes from *a* to *b* via *c*. So we apply the principle again to the various subroutes in each section, singling out a chain which goes from *a* to *c* via *d*, and a chain from *c* to *b* via *e*. If this specification is still too vague, we can repeat the process, specifying subsections and sub-subsections in greater detail. The problem is to know when to stop. Theoretically, the regress could continue until we reach the most basic causal interactions which science recognises. In practice, however, we stop subdividing when we reach a criterion for determining the intended route which is precise enough for the job in hand. In our present investigation, the criterion has to be precise enough to yield a sufficient condition for the truth of an ordinary TD. Finer discriminations might be theoretically possible, but the analysis will be indifferent to them.

A promising first suggestion is that the chain must go through a desire or intention to do B. Cases (1), (3), (4) and (4') are thereby excluded on the grounds that S had no such desire. Case (2) is not excluded, however. Many other cases can be constructed in which a desire to do B becomes causally relevant yet the action remains unintentional. A well-known example is that of the butler who wants to drop the delicate antique he is holding (because it belongs to his hated employer). The desire makes his hands tremble so much that he drops the antique. Cases like this, where a desire brings about its own object fortuitously, illustrate in its purest form the main difficulty for a causal account of intentional action, since there is no need to bother with the complication of a belief that B $\Rightarrow$ G. The difficulty is that the desire to do B itself has to cause B by the proper causal route. When what is being analysed is a TD, there is also the second difficulty noted by Davidson (1973), p. 154, of specifying how the desire to do G and the belief that B $\Rightarrow$ G cause the desire to do B. The work has doubled now that we have split the chain into two sections. Nevertheless, this is not a drawback. It represents progress. The method of analysis is feeding us with clearly defined problems, ripe for solution.

Let us take the second task first. One thing seems clear, at least. Both the desire and the belief, which we assume to be initially present, must persist right up to the moment at which the desire to do B is first formed. Take the case of a small-time crook in 1973, who wants to steal a lot of money, and believes that one way of getting it is to break into a bank. As yet he does not want to do this, because he doubts his ability. He sticks to smaller jobs, and comes to value crime for the excitement it brings. By 1975, he is skilled enough to do a bank-job, and he starts wanting to. Meanwhile, in 1974, he wins £1 million on the football pools and loses his original desire to steal money. But by 1975 he wants to break into a bank for the sheer fun of it, and he does so in 1976. It is not the case that he breaks into the bank in order to steal money. His desire to steal does not cause his lower-level desire in the right way. He stops wanting money before he starts wanting to break into a bank. A similar story could be told about his partner, whose desire persists, but who changes his belief.

It also goes without saying that the desire and belief must *sustain* the desire to do B throughout its existence. This means they must persist at least until B gets done, if B is done for the sake of G. Let us suppose, adapting the example of Oscar and the soup, that S had dropped the whole idea by the time he sat down at table. He still wants to grimace, though, because he wants to make Oscar laugh, and he does so intentionally before tasting the soup. It is false that he grimaces then in order to insult the host, since he lacks the relevant desire then. His desire to grimace was *initiated* by them in the right way, but by the time of action this desire was being supported by a different plan.

Part of what I have said so far can be captured by introducing time-references. If the desire to do B starts at t_j and lasts until t_m, then a necessary condition of the desire-belief pair's causing it in the right way is that the pair should be in existence by some time t_i prior to t_j, and should persist at least until t_m. This is not a specification of the pathway. It is rather a condition on possible candidates for the right desire-belief pair. I cannot think of any specific intermediate stage which the route must pass through if it is to count as the right route. However, this is not the whole of what I have been saying. I also placed a restriction upon the manner of causation in saying that the desire-belief pair must *sustain* the desire to do B. The motivating pair must not only persist over a period, they must also keep on pushing, so to speak, at every moment within that period. This surely counts as a specification of the manner in which the right cause must operate. Furthermore, it is a corollary of the distinction between initiating causes and sustaining causes that the two segments of the causal pathway cannot be treated in isolation from each other. Whatever is required to make the first segment appropriate will also be required to make the second segment appropriate, given that the items in the first need to sustain one of the key participants in the second. Because sustaining causes accumulate as time goes on, any satisfactory account of the appropriate causation will have to be cumulative.

Perhaps I have not given a sufficient condition for the right pathway in the first segment. Nevertheless, I shall leave the problem in abeyance, and turn to the other task of specifying the pathway from the desire to do B to B. This is the segment which pertains to the intentionality, as opposed to the goal-directedness of B. Clearly, similar time restrictions are needed here as well. If the desire to do B comes into existence at t_j, and the action which it causes starts at t_m, then that desire must persist throughout the period t_j to t_m. But what else needs to happen between t_j and t_m? One fairly obvious reason for the delay is that the agent doesn't act until he judges that the time is ripe. This judgment contains two components, a belief that the outside world offers an opportunity to do B, plus a belief that there is no internal obstacle, such as a handicap or an aversion. It may take a long time before both these beliefs are present together. Let us suppose that t_k is the moment at which both obtain. From t_k onwards, S believes that the time is ripe all things considered, and this belief must sustain the remainder of the process until the action is complete. If he suddenly ceased to believe this in mid-movement, for example, he would stop as soon as he could.

If S is engaged in another activity at t_k, that fact counts as a logical obstacle to his doing B at t_k. But it might also be a physical obstacle to his commencing to do B before a short interval has elapsed. It may take a little time for his limbs to be appropriately redeployed. However, this kind of obstacle is not the sort which figures in his belief that the time is ripe. The content of this belief, more accurately described, is that there is no obstacle to his doing B as soon as is physically possible. Intentional behaviour is controlled by a plan in the way in which a computer's output is controlled by its programme. A switch of plan is like a change of programme. Before the computer can embark on a new operation, its circuits have to be cleared. It takes time for the executive components to revert to a state in which they can respond to new instructions.

In the interval between t_k and the start of the movement at t_m, S's brain receives a barrage of information from afferent nerves about the position and state of the body. Such neural impulses are transmitted continuously, of course. Although people are not directly aware of them by introspection, it is in fact thanks to such impulses that they know immediately how their limbs are disposed. Some of these impulses will be 'All Clear' signals, emanating from the parts of the body that are required for doing B, which 'tell' the brain that the parts are in position and ready to receive instructions.

But is there any other *mental* state which intervenes between t_k and t_m, such as a volition or a decision to do B next? I don't think so. After t_k, whatever else may be going on in the agent's mind, no mental states other than the wanting and believing are needed to produce an intentional action. Certainly, agents don't need to be aware of any others. A normal agent will, no doubt, be aware that he is just about to act, and then, when he acts, he will be immediately aware that he is acting. But these monitoring awarenesses are not causes of the action. They are collateral to it, the former being caused, presumably, by the belief that the time is ripe, and the latter by proprioceptive and kinaesthetic feedback.

Nevertheless, it is necessary to mention one other state into which the agent must be brought, immediately after t_k, by the combining of the desire and belief. Although it is not a mental state, since it has no intentional content, a reflective agent will realise that he must enter such a state before any intentional movement begins, and that it must initiate and sustain the movement. It begins at t_l, where t_l is defined as 'the point of no return with respect to the start of the movement'.[1] Given the empirical facts (a) that it takes time for an efferent impulse to travel from the brain to the limbs, and (b) that mental processes are more closely correlated with brain processes than with processes in the muscles or skin, it follows that there must be a short period before t_m during which the agent, if he were suddenly to stop wanting to do B or believing that the time is ripe, would be physically unable to inhibit the start of the movement at t_m. It would be difficult to identify this moment precisely by psychological experiments, since it is difficult to time changes of mind precisely. But if, in the future, the cortical basis of the state is identified, it will be possible to calculate the time-lag between the onset of the state and the muscle movement, using our knowledge of the speed of neural impulses. Then t_l will be pinpointed, since it is equal to t_m minus this time-lag dt.

If the action B is such that its performance requires the completion of a movement, we may say that the state which begins at t_l sustains the action B. For every instant i at which S is in that state, it is physically impossible for S to inhibit that bit of the movement which occurs at i plus dt. So if the whole movement in which the doing of B consists

[1] This idea is borrowed from D. F. Pears, who has developed it more fully.

lasts from t_m to t_n, then S must be in the relevant state from t_m–dt to t_n–dt, and his being in that state must be causally sufficient in the circumstances for the whole movement, if he is to do B intentionally.

The state in question can best be characterised negatively, as 'the state of the last restraint's having been removed'. It starts immediately after the last 'All Clear' signal has come in, and it persists until either the movement is completed or S changes his mind about making it, whichever is the sooner. Given the psychological background conditions already mentioned, it is the precipitating cause of intentional action. Divorced from this background, it precipitates an unintentional action. That is, if a physiologically normal agent were brought into this state as a result of electrical stimulation of the cortex, and not as a result of wanting to do B and believing that the time is ripe, he would do B, but his action would be unintentional.

In terms of the hydraulic analogy beloved of motivation theorists, desire is like water in a tank connected to a network of channels. The water can be routed in various ways by opening and closing the entrances to different channels. The water exerts continuous pressure. Open any exit from the tank, and the water floods through that channel as far as the next closed door. Coming to believe that the time is ripe is like opening the penultimate door before the water escapes outside. The final door comprises a number of layered panels, which slide back individually in response to 'All Clear' signals from different parts of the system. Whichever is the last to slide back becomes the flood-gate. As soon as that last obstacle is removed, the water flows freely, providing power for the watermill downstream. Opening the flood-gate at t_l, or rather, the obtaining of a state such that it has been opened, is sufficient in the circumstances for the millwheel's starting to turn at t_m. On the assumption that this state of the system persists, the continuation of the effect does not need further explaining, gven that one of the background conditions is a continuously pushing cause.

Although the analogy is crude, the distinction between triggering causes and sustaining causes is important, because it shows that to specify a pathway between a and b by reference to points traversed is not the only way of explaining how a might cause b. One may also explain the *manner* in which a operates, and the manner might be by pushing, or driving, or energising. 'Controlling' is perhaps the best word to describe the type of causation involved here. More will be said about the concept of control in the next chapter.

However, to the extent that one does identify the appropriate causation by specifying essential stages on the pathway, one is committed to saying at some point: 'So long as the route goes through all these stages, it doesn't matter where it goes in between any two adjacent stages.' One can, of course, impose a blanket restriction by saying that each basic stage should cause the next in the 'normal' way. But here 'normal' is like a variable. What is abnormal today may become normal tomorrow. Thus it would be wrong, I think, to rule out the possibility that part of the causal chain might, in some circumstances, pass outside the agent's body, and go via a prosthetic device. In the interstices where the analysis does not penetrate, anything might happen, provided all the conditions remain satisfied.

If my account is correct, then the meaning of the TD, fully spelled out, is something like this: 'S did B because S wanted to do G and believed that B ⇒ G, and this desire – belief pair initiated and sustained a desire to do B, which, after joining forces with a belief that the time was ripe, gave rise to an internal state that controlled the performance of B'. But this is rather cumbersome. It could be abbreviated to 'S did B intentionally because S wanted to do G and believed that B ⇒ G', given that the role of all the extra clauses is simply to convey the information that the explanandum of this kind of teleological explanation is always intentional. However, what I shall do henceforth is to continue to employ the old version as convenient shorthand for the new. That is, I shall leave it to be understood that 'S did B because S wanted to do G and believed that B ⇒ G', while not in itself a correct paraphrase, is nevertheless an elliptical version of something which is a correct paraphrase, and that it does duty as an economical stand-in. Let it serve from now on as a mnemonic for the full statement above. The difference between them will not, in any case, be philosophically exploited in the remainder of the book.

The cybernetical approach

The second version of internalism, the one that characterises the internal state as a pair of mental states having intentional content, seems plausible. But let us investigate the third version to see whether it can offer a better account, of equal or greater comprehensiveness. This kind of internalism claims to analyse the generic concept of goal-directedness straight off by means of concepts borrowed from cybernetics, without postulating a mentalistic core-concept. Its point of departure is the fact that servo-mechanisms are goal-directed, although they do not have desires and beliefs. Since we can explain their behaviour non-mentalistically, perhaps we can give a non-mentalist account of goal-directed animal behaviour too. Some animals do indeed have desires and beliefs, but perhaps there is no need to mention these in the analysis. The key concept, it is suggested, is that of *feedback-control*.

In this chapter I shall argue that feedback is intimately related to goal-directedness, but not in the way suggested by those who try to analyse the concept of the one in terms of the concept of the other. Rather, feedback explanations and teleological explanations are complementary. They cover roughly the same behaviour, but they address themselves to different aspects of it. In fact, cyberneticians do not try to analyse the concept of goal at all, in the philosophical sense of 'analyse'. They *use* the concept, because at a certain level it is convenient. What really interests them is how the system works, what the system must be like in order to be able to behave in that way. In their theories and models they freely exploit in both directions any analogies there may be between organisms and automata. They make use of the most convenient descriptions that come to hand, whether mentalistic or functional or mechanistic. When extremely complex systems are being viewed on a holistic level, teleological explanations of their behaviour naturally go together with mentalistic descriptions of their internal states. Such systems mimic the goal-directed behaviour of animals *because they simulate the animals' mental states and processes*. Workers in AI do not dispense with, or bypass, mental states; they try to illuminate what the mental states are. In doing so they use mentalistic and teleological terms, and *rely on* the meanings these terms already have.

A feedback system is any entity capable of being affected at time t_1, by some of the consequences of what it does at an earlier time t_0, and whose behaviour at a later time t_2 is influenced by that effect. This characterisation makes three main points. First, it assumes a distinction between the system itself and the environment of the system. Second, it assumes a distinction between what the system does and what is done to the system, i.e. a distinction between output and input. Third, it makes it clear that feeding back is a process of reciprocal causation, as objective as causation itself. There are two separate causal chains of events which are mediated by two separate channels: the first chain of events is the process whereby the output at t_0 brings about some change in the environment which affects the input at t_1. This channel passes outside the system. The second chain of events occurs within the system, and is the process whereby the input at t_1 determines the output at t_2. This output then feeds back again via the environment and affects the input at t_3. In many cases, these two processes go on simultaneously, but it is useful to separate them temporally for the purposes of exposition. One can then see clearly that there must be some criterion of whether the system has been affected by an environmental change which is independent of the criterion provided by system's overt behaviour. For if it takes time for input at t_1 to influence output at t_2, it is possible that the internal chain of causes could be broken at some moment between t_1 and t_2. It would be true then that the system had been affected by the environment, i.e. had registered a certain input, although nothing that it had yet overtly done would have indicated the fact. The method of exposition shows that the system must have a 'front end' and a 'back end'. It must contain at least two separate components, a part that is sensitive to environmental changes (sensor), and a part that can produce environmental changes (effector). Furthermore, the parts must be capable of existing in at least two different states each. The sensor must be either being affected or not being affected, and the effector must be either operating or not operating. In between the sensor and the effector there must be a link. The link may be all the rest of the system.

There are many ways of representing feedback systems diagrammatically, and many ways of describing them. The output, for instance, could be measured by rate of activity or by amount of work done. The input could be measured by the intensity or frequency or duration of some stimulus. The sensor and effector could have just two states, or they could have a range. There is a fundamental difference between *positive* and *negative* feedback, however. The former kind is present when an increase in input to the sensor stimulates the effector to increase the output, which in turn raises the succeeding level of the input. Such a system is unstable. Eventually it either breaks down, or reaches an upper limit of output imposed by extraneous factors. In a negative feedback system deviations in rate of output from a certain level are counteracted by the system. Increases in input give rise to decreases in subsequent output, and decreases in input produce increases in output. Rosenblueth, Wiener and Bigelow (1943) called this process 'control by the error of the reaction'. It is now standard in control theory to use what are called 'block-diagrams', which chart the flow of information through the system, rather than the flow of energy. The following block-diagram illustrates the simplest type of feedback control system, as exemplified in the thermostat, Watt's governor, the fantail windmill, and so on.

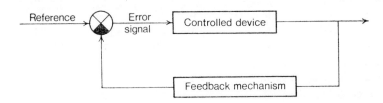

The reference variable or command signal represents an instruction, such as 'Keep the temperature at seventy degrees'. The error signal means either 'Turn on' or 'Turn off', and the feedback signal sends the message 'Too hot' or 'Too cold'.

Although the noun 'feedback' is new, and control theory is a young science, the idea of reciprocal influence is not new. It is implicit in the idea of two people talking to each other. What A says affects what B says in reply, and what B replies influences what A says next. Feedback is present when an inspector checks someone else's work and the other person takes note of any corrections. According to Dr Johnson's dictionary, the word 'control' originates from 'contre rôle': 'a register or account kept by another officer that each may be examined by the other' (sic) (quoted in H. Kalmus, 1966, p. 4). The experimental method in science exemplifies a feedback process. The scientist interferes with nature, observes how nature responds, adjusts his hypotheses, tests again, and so on. The theory of social contract, Grice's theory of meaning (Grice, 1957), and David Lewis's theory of convention (Lewis, 1969) utilise feedback loops, or believed feedback loops. So the notion of 'feeding back' is very familiar in philosophy.

If an observer looks only at the output or end result of a negative feedback system, he will not be able to tell with certainty whether the system has achieved that result by feedback. The steadiness or invariance he sees might have arisen in other ways. Even if he sees that variations in the input are followed by changes in the output, he still cannot conclude that the system is operating by feedback. The net result might be due to a simple physical equilibrium. For example, the temperature of hot water in a tank might remain constant because the heat gained from the electric element is exactly offset by the heat lost through conduction. The observer might hypothesise, on the basis of input and output data, that the system is operating by feedback, but it follows from the way 'feedback' is defined that confirmation of the hypothesis must await an investigation into *how* the system achieves the output. The fact that there must be two causal processes, occurring in separate media, which join to form a closed loop, shows that feedback is a structural notion. It is not reducible to a mere functional relationship between input and output variables, where variations in either one are matched by variations in the other. This point is obscured by the fact that such a relationship is sometimes called 'mathematical feedback' (McFarland, 1971, ch. 2). Rosenblueth *et al.* were confused about this point in their paper, partly owing to their operationalist bias. They stated that feedback is an observable property of behaviour. In fact, feeding back is a process, dependent on structural properties of the system.

Nor is the mere distinctness of the two causal pathways sufficient for feedback. As Wimsatt (1970) points out, a hydraulic system in which water flows from A to B via one channel and is pumped back from B to A via another channel would not count as a feedback system. He does not claim to know what would constitute a sufficient condition, but mentions the view that feedback might not be a wholly objective property. It might be an 'artefact of our mode of representation'. This is quite wrong. What is lacking in the hydraulic system is the appropriate reciprocal causation between sensor and effector. Events occurring in the subsidiary (feedback) channel should both causally depend on the output from the main channel and should causally affect the capacity of the main channel to produce further output. In a feedback system, the output is *controlled* by sensory input in the sense that *changes* in the rate or amount of output are brought about by changes in the input. It is presupposed that there is some source of energy which ensures *that there will be output* in the first place.

The point is important in relation to the question of goal-directedness, because one of the defects in previous accounts was that they failed to exclude simple equilibrium systems from the discussion. However, since feeding back is a process part of which takes place inside the system, any account of goal-directedness that makes use of the concept is bound to be internalist. Moreover, we are forced to assign to a feedback system a minimal internal structure, consisting of a sensor, an effector and a connecting link. This is necessary in order to allow for proof that the system is sensitive to changes in its own output, and that the output is not due simply to the cancelling out of forces within the system. By doing this, we avoid the criticism that anything whatever can count as a feedback system, given long enough time intervals between t_0, t_1, and t_2.

It may now be proposed that the concept of a goal is the concept of an end-state towards which the system tends as a result of the fact that its behaviour is controlled by negative feedback. 'Having G as a goal' amounts to 'being structured, or being in an internal state, such that deviations away from G are compensated for by negative feedback.' The proposition is supported by evidence of machines that can exhibit keeping, aiming and searching behaviour because they are controlled by feedback.

Keeping behaviour is perhaps the simplest to produce mechanically. A thermostat, for example, keeps the water temperature constant because it contains a bi-metallic strip that disconnects the power supply when a certain temperature is reached, and reconnects when the temperature falls. Signs of changes in water temperature feed back via the casing in which the metal strip is housed. The desired water temperature can be adjusted by means of a screw or dial, which fixes the position of the point of contact between the bi-metallic strip and the entry to the electric circuit. It is this part of the system's structure which determines its 'goal'. Having the goal of keeping the water at 70° amounts to being in an internal state such that the contact breaks at 70°.

Sommerhoff's automatic gun provides an example of the aiming paradigm. The gun incorporates a device that is sensitive to the position of the target. Changes in the target's position relative to the angle of the barrel are fed back to an effector mechanism with the power to alter that angle, so that when and if the gun is fired, it is pointing in the right direction. The act of firing is not controlled by feedback. Once the bullet is fired, its trajectory is irrevocable. Strictly speaking, only *processes* can be feedback controlled, since feeding back is itself a process that takes time. Feedback explains why the gun is fired in the right direction, in virtue of the fact that firing is preceded by an aiming process.

Self guided missiles combine the roles of gun and bullet by moving bodily towards the target. Information in the form of light, heat or radio signals is picked up by a sensor connected to a controlling device which adjusts the steering mechanism of the missile so that it points towards the source of the signals. If the target moves, or the missile veers off course, the deviation is corrected. In more sophisticated systems, the controlling device computes the velocity of the moving target and 'predicts' its future positions. The missile is steered at t_1 towards a spot where the target will probably be at t_2, in the light of the information available up to t_1.

Servomechanisms have also been designed to search for a target, as well as to move towards one that has already been sighted. The main additional requirement is a scanning device, such as a revolving radar tower or an echolocator, which samples the environment systematically until it picks up a signal. It then locks on to the signal source, and the homing mechanism takes over.

One of the most sophisticated machines that had at that time been built was the Stanford Mobile Automaton, described by Rosen in 1968. Essentially, it is a computer on wheels with a T.V. camera on top, which can be programmed to perform sequences of actions, the precise form of which is determined by the sensory input. Two notable features are that it can scan the environment for an object satisfying a certain shape and size description, and that it can navigate a path towards such an object. To be able to do this, the computer has to store large quantities of data about the layout of the room and the objects in it. A convenient way of describing the automaton without going into technical details is to say that it starts off with an 'internal representation' of the goal object which it matches against input from the scanner. Meanwhile it pools this input to construct an 'internal model' of the environment. Once it recognises an object of the right sort, it calculates the best route to it; then it moves toward the object following that route, monitoring its own progress and adjusting for changes in the environment that might occur along the way.

The structure of such a machine is extremely complex. It would be misleading to say that feedback was the 'magic ingredient' that enabled it to behave in that way, if by this one meant the feedback loops that are built into its workings. Although there are many feedback sub-systems inside, a number of other engineering principles are embodied in the workings too. However the automaton *taken as a unitary whole* is a feedback system, sensitive to the environmental consequences of its own actions. It is because there exists feedback at that holistic level that the robot can search for an object and home on to it.

This point, that feedback is present on many levels, is important, because it shows how implausible would be the claim that all feedback systems are *ipso facto* goal-directed. The notions of system, subsystem and environment are relative to each other. The identity of a system depends on where one happens to draw the boundaries. One could isolate sets of components in the Stanford Robot and think of each set as a system, existing in the environment provided by the rest of the components. There are indefinitely many ways of doing this, and many of the 'systems' so created would operate by feedback. But these systems would not be said to have goals of their own, any more than radio components linked by a closed loop are said to have goals. Feedback loops are ubiquitous in electronics, but they do not create goal-directedness wherever they appear.

The point also shows that systems that are goal-directed are not goal-directed in virtue of *containing* internal feedback loops. Radios and televisions for example are not goal-directed, though their circuits do embody feedback loops. The term 'feedback system' is ambiguous. It can mean (i) 'system whose output or behaviour is sensitive to feed-back from its environment, or (ii) 'system containing, as one of its components, a system of type (i)'. Whenever there exists a system of type (ii), there exists within it a subsystem of type (i). But only systems of type (i) are candidates for the description 'system exhibiting goal-directed behaviour', assuming that 'behaviour' means *output* of the system in question.

It follows from this that the property of being a system whose behaviour is feedback-controlled couldn't possibly be more than a *necessary* condition of being a goal-directed system, if that. It is diffi-cult to determine precisely what else is necessary. There are a number of characteristics of organisms that may well be *presupposed* by goal-ascriptions in central cases, but which are not part of the meaning of 'goal-directed'. Some especially relevant properties might be that S is mobile, relatively autonomous of the environment, possessed of its own local energy supply, capable of *not* acting on a goal that it has at time t, and so on. These are satisfied by the Stanford Robot, but not by the thermostat or Watt's governor or the fantail windmill. Different people have different intuitions about whether these last can be said to have a goal or not. Since it is unlikely that we shall satisfy everyone if we specify other necessary conditions, let us leave them unspecified. Whatever these other conditions may be, the main suggestion to be considered is that feedback is especially relevant to the system's being goal-directed.

How is one to evaluate this suggestion? I think the first thing to recognise is that feedback is a perfectly familiar phenomenon, even if the term is new. It follows from the definition above that animals are feedback systems of type (i), in the sense that they act, perceive the environment, attend to the consequences of their acts, and adjust their next acts in the light of those consequences. They are also feedback systems of type (ii). Physiologists have discovered many homeostatic processes in the autonomic nervous system, and many feedback loops in the CNS. However, taking animals as whole systems, we *already know* without research that feedback is especially relevant to their goal-directed behaviour. The philosophical problem is merely to state exactly in what way it is relevant. In particular, is there anything here that could provide the materials for a conceptual analysis?

Let us take it as read that all goal-directed systems are feedback systems, and that all feedback systems with properties α, β, γ, (unknown) are goal-directed systems. We can then ask the more discriminating questions: Is every bit of *behaviour* that is goal-directed controlled by feedback? Do feedback explanations and teleological explanations cover the same range of explananda? How are the two types of explanation related? We can ask these questions with respect to the behaviour of any kind of system that we choose to select from within the agreed class. We can, if we wish, deal directly with animals. There is no need at this stage to adjudicate whether machines are literally or metaphorically goal-directed.

The term 'behaviour' is vague. We remarked earlier that teleological explanations can explain single actions or whole sets of actions, but that the difference can be ignored if we let the letter B do duty for both.

Even if B is a single action, it might be either a process or an instantaneous response. We also noted that strictly speaking only processes can be continuously monitored by feedback. Taken together, the two remarks indicate that only a rough coincidence of explananda can be hoped for. For example, I take it that when a cuttlefish ejects its tentacles in order to catch a shrimp, it performs a goal-directed response. But this response is not controlled by feedback. If the shrimp moves after the cuttlefish has started to respond, the cuttlefish cannot compensate (McFarland, 1971, ch. 2). However, the seizing response is preceded by a process of aiming or fixating which *is* feedback controlled, as in the automatic gun example. I take it that aiming would also count as a goal-directed action. The point is that a teleological explanation can be given of each component separately, as well as of the whole process. The question whether continuous or 'on-line' feedback is always involved in goal-directed behaviour amounts, therefore, to the question whether goal-directed instantaneous actions always belong within a context of other actions joned together to form a process or sequence, the precise unfolding of which is guided by perceptions.

I think the right answer is that although they do not *always*, they very often, and typically, do belong in such a context. There is no doubt that the total pattern of behavioural data that calls for a teleological hypothesis is also typically a pattern that invites a feedback hypothesis. Adaptability to environmental changes and convergence upon an end-result are the distinctive signs of feedback-control, and also of goal-directedness. But it is possible for an action to be goal-directed without being part of a process and without being perceptually monitored. For example, an animal caught in a trap may snap and bite haphazardly in order to escape; a man may shout or yell in order to attract attention, and so on. (There are also cases where the animal misperceives the situation or hallucinates. But these are best assimilated to feedback-controlled behaviour which goes wrong on account of some interference with the loop. Analogues of misperception and false belief can easily be found in machine behaviour.)

The fact that the overlap of explananda is loose (taking 'explananda' to mean the behavioural phenomena being explained) rules out the possibility of any direct reduction of one kind of explanation to the other. It suggests that the two kinds of explanation are not trying to answer the same kinds of questions. That is to say, if we take an explanandum to be a *fact* introduced by a why? or how? question, instead of a phenomenon, the two kinds of explanation have *different* explananda.

Imagine the total sequence of behaviour performed by a cat trying to catch a mouse. The hunt takes several minutes, let us say, from the first moment when the cat sees the mouse running across the garden path, to the final pounce. In between there are periods of rapid movement and periods of slow movement. There is no limit to the number of ways in which the sequence could be split up, or to the number of why? or how? questions that could be asked about selected aspects of what went on. Moreover, several different answers could be given to one and the same question. 'Why did the cat leap across the wall at that moment?' 'Because she saw that the mouse was escaping through a hole in the wall', but also 'Because she wanted to head the mouse off'. Variety is present even if we stick to the level of psychological explanations, without touching on physiological ones. At this level, feedback explanations explain primarily *how* the cat managed to perform a certain task, get to a certain place, keep the mouse in sight, and so on. The task is specified by reference to a goal or subgoal that the cat has to achieve in order to achieve the final goal. The most general explanandum of a feedback explanation, then, is *how S gets to G*. The answer will show how the various elements of the process were influenced, with regard to timing, direction, speed, etc. by S's perceptions of the ongoing situation and of the results of the previous response, in such a way that nearly every new response brought S a step nearer to the end-state, or enabled S at least to consolidate her position. A feedback explanation is not so much a single sentence of the form 'S did B (at that time, in that way, etc.) because . . .', but rather a set of sentences describing a sequence of actions, perceptions and changes in the situation. The unifying element is the reference that is made to the fact that the cat is a feedback *system*, i.e. that she has the sensory and motor equipment necessary to control her actions in the way described. That she has the goal of catching the mouse is something that is taken for granted. W. R. Ashby emphasises this central point when he writes: 'Throughout this book it is assumed that outside considerations have already determined what is to be the goal . . . Our concern, within this book, is solely with the problem of how to achieve the goal in spite of disturbances and difficulties' (*Cybernetics*, p. 219).

Just as feedback explanations take goals for granted, so teleological explanations take it for granted that the cat has all the perceptual and locomotor capacities required to perform the sequence of actions. They aim to explain why the cat did any or all of them by citing some underlying, unifying goal. Of course, they do not explain why the cat had that goal, any more than feedback explanations do. If B is a part of a feedback-controlled sequence, then there are two complementary answers to the question 'Why did S do B at t_2?' A 'feedback' answer locates B as an element in the sequence, e.g. 'S did B at that moment t_2 because S perceived at t_1 that the situation was E, and the situation was E at t_1 partly because S did A at an earlier moment t_0'. The teleological answer is indifferent to whether B is part of a sequence or not; e.g. 'S did B at t_2 because S believed that B at t_2 would contribute to G and S wanted to do G'. No doubt there are many other possible answers, each selecting one little aspect of the complete sufficient condition for B at t_2. The reference that is made in the feedback explanation to the earlier action A and the perception of E indicates that there may be a tie-up between this explanation and an explanation of why S believed that B at t_2 would contribute to G. But the teleological explanation does not go into the cause of the belief, nor does its truth require that there be any such tie-up. There may be a tie-up with medium-term feedback too (i.e. the reinforcing effects of past connections between B-type and G-type actions).

It would appear, then, that only careless and superficial thinking would lead a philosopher to claim that the concept of feedback control wholly or partially *explicates* the concept of goal-directedness.

Let us now reconsider artificial servomechanisms and homeostats. These things are commonly said to be goal-directed. In what does their goal-directedness consist? It consists in the fact that they behave as if they had desires and beliefs in virtue of the fact that they are feedback systems. The last clause is important. Boulders rolling down a hill behave as if they had a desire to get to the bottom and a belief that rolling would contribute to getting to the bottom, but they are not said to be goal-directed. Feedback systems are special because the 'desired' end-state is encoded in their internal structure. They minimise the difference between the actual state of affairs and the desired or optimal state of affairs in the same way that animals do, by 'comparing' the one with the other and making the next action contingent upon the results of the comparison. This means that there is something about *them*, as well as something about their behaviour, in virtue of which they are said to have a goal. The goal that they have can be identified in advance of behavioural observations; if they fail to reach the goal, the identity of the goal can still be discovered by examining the internal workings.

My hypothesis, that when we describe servomechanisms as goal-directed we are employing a mentalistic analogy, is supported by the fact that other descriptions of them on the same explanatory level are often clearly mentalistic. This emerges most clearly with machines that can search. The Stanford Automaton, for example, is said to *recognise* objects of a certain kind. It is programmed to subject the raw input-data to a series of tests. The tests are satisfied only if the input fits the hypothesis that an object of a certain kind gave rise to it. If the tests are not satisfied, the Automaton points its T.V. camera in a new direction. It is also said to *learn* about the environment, because it can store infor-mation and use it adaptively at a later time; and it is said to *plan* strategies for achieving subgoals in the light of that information. Its most pertinent feature which makes these descriptions appropriate is that the Automaton has the ability to *represent* or *model* aspects of the outside world within itself. Differentiations between states of the computer correlate with differentiations between states of the outside world in a way that makes it convenient to type-identify the internal states by reference to their external correlates. This mode of identifica-tion is analogous to the identification of perceptions and ideas by reference to what they are *of*. The relations between a perception and its object is similar to that which holds between a description and an object when that object *satisfies* the description.

Desires, too, are type-identified by reference to the things that satisfy them. A desire to eat cake is satisfied by eating cake. Satisfaction here involves a number of elements, e.g. the feeling of pleasantness upon attainment of the object, the fact that the desire normally ceases upon attainment. But it also connects up with satisfaction in the semantic sense. Consciously desiring to eat cake paradigmatically involves hav-ing the idea of eating cake, which means being in an internal state that pictures cake-eating symbolically. When we describe a machine as having goal G, we describe its internal state by reference to that which satisfies it, in the quasi-semantic sense, while cancelling the implication of feeling or emotion that would be present if we had said that the machine 'wanted' G. In order for an internal state of a machine to be so described, it is not sufficient that the state should cause the machine to behave in a way that characteristically leads to G. Additional features are required in order to justify its being called a *representation* of G.

I do not think that my conclusion would be denied by most AI workers. They do not conceive of themselves as philosophical analysts of the concept of goal. M. Arbib (1972) remarks that goals are the 'phlogiston' of cybernetic discussions. There is widespread recognition that the concept of goal is primarily mentalistic, and is in many cases inappropriate. R. A. Hinde, for example (1966, pp. 38–41), prefers to avoid mentalistic overtones by using the German word *Sollwert* to cover the set-point or optimal value of physiological feedback systems like the proprioceptive muscle-control mechanism, the temperature regulating system and the blood-sugar homeostat.

If my hypothesis about the meaning of 'goal-directed' is correct, the constraints it imposes ought to be mirrored by the extension that the word actually has. However, it is very difficult to tell whether we normally count as goal-directed any systems which would not count if my hypothesis were right. I claim that the literal meaning of 'goal-directed' is built on top of a mentalistic metaphor. There are no clear rules for deciding when an internal state is sufficiently similar to a desire to count as the state of 'having a goal'. I have claimed that it must *represent* G, but have not attempted to give necessary and sufficient conditions for representing. Still, it may be said that certain simple goal directed systems like thermostats ought not to count, according to my analysis. It may be said that in this case there is no hint of a submerged mentalist metaphor, nor do we describe any other states of the thermostat mentalistically. What plausibility does my account have here, if there are no signs that any metaphor is retrievable?

I would reply, first, that thermostats are not immediately ruled out by my analysis. It is a matter for further discussion whether the setting of the dial at 70° represents the optimum temperature in a way sufficiently similar to that in which a desire to keep the water at 70° would represent it. Nor am I asserting that one should have an intuition of metaphor when one calls thermostats goal-directed. My thesis is that the epithet now applies literally, but that an explication of its meaning has to refer back to a metaphorical *origin*. Secondly, if it were felt that the similarity is not great enough for my analysis to apply here, I could point out that at least the thermostat behaves *as if* it were goal-directed. That is, I could pile a second analogy on top of the first. But thirdly, if neither of these explanations of why we call thermostats goal-directed proved satisfactory, I should assert that we do so wrongly. There is a very plausible explanation in reserve that could account for the error, namely that we are confused about the difference between goal-directedness and functionality.

Thermostats are artefacts designed to fulfil the function of keeping water at the temperature which their users desire. Their functionality by itself licenses teleological descriptions, e.g. 'They turn the current on and off in order to keep the water at a constant temperature'. They are no different in this respect from sparking plugs, which spark in order to ignite the petrol vapour in the cylinder. The step from saying their function is to do this to saying their goal is to do this may be the result of our projecting the goal of the designer or user on to the thermostat itself. However it need not be due to animistic projection. It might be due simply to the mixing up of two elements: first, the fact that the end-state or outcome is a function; second, the fact that the system performs this function by means of feedback-controlled behaviour. These two elements define a kind of hybrid category of teleological systems which includes items with *organic* functions as well as artefacts. Anything with a *Sollwert* that was functional would come into this category, which is perfectly valid and objective.

But consider how shaky is the rationale for calling items in this category 'goal-directed'. If the fact that an end-state is brought about by feedback is not sufficient *by itself* to prove that the end-state is a goal, how can the addition of the fact that the end-state is a function possibly provide a sufficient condition? The examples that were cited in support of the first point, such as the steady states and constancies of output brought about by electronic feedback-subsystems, already *are* examples of functions performed by such subsystems. But I take it that no one would wish to call these components goal-directed in their own right. The plausibility of the present proposal depends largely on the tacit assumption that we should include only items which have further unspecified properties α, β, γ etc. That is, it is assumed that there are certain additional conditions which rule out radio and T.V. components and the like. But now consider what is left. Everything in the category is a feedback system with properties α, β, γ etc. This is precisely the class of entities which my analysis claims to be goal-directed for the reason that they behave as if they had beliefs and desires. If there is any doubt about the eligibility of certain peripheral members of this class, then that doubt will remain even after it has been established that they serve a function. Functionality is simply irrelevant as a criterion of inclusion.

According to my definition, physiological homeostats ought not to count as goal-directed, nor ought artificial thermostats to count, unless some material difference can be shown between them on the one hand and 'systems' consisting of electronic feedback circuits on the other, such that this difference provides a reason to analogise in the one case and not the other. If no such difference can be cited, my analysis has the effect of tightening up the class of goal-directed systems. The systems that are left out belong within a special subcategory of items with functions, namely items that perform their functions by means of feedback-controlled behaviour. It is easy to confuse this category with the category of items with goals, because there is a great deal of empirical overlap. Many goals are functions and all goal-directed systems operate by feedback. But the *concepts* of function and of goal are quite different.

It is remarkable how easily one can be bewitched by superficial similarities between teleological phenomena that are in fact quite distinct. A blatant, yet common example of false assimilation is the view that the convergence of behaviour upon a G-state is an instance of the same phenomenon as the synergism of functional components in a system. This view amounts to a failure to see any essential difference in the following two diagrams.

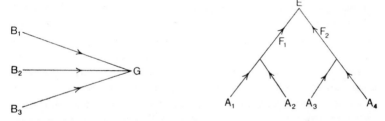

In the fan-diagram on the left-hand-side, each line represents a possible pathway of behaviour through time. The convergent pattern conveys the idea that there is a variety of alternative ways to G, only one which actually occurs on a given occasion. In the pyramid-diagram, time is frozen, and the lines do not represent hypothetical alternatives. They represent actual activities of parts of a system which contribute to an End. It is a structural picture, showing how these activities co-operate to produce higher-level activities, which in turn combine to maintain a single state of the whole, such as survival. In an integrated system of functioning parts, it is not necessarily the case that if one component were to stop functioning, another one would take over, thus keeping the system in an E-state. Although living things are plastic in this way to some degree, this plasticity is no part of what is meant by saying that their organs have functions. Moreover, although some of the components of living systems regulate their activity or output according to the prevailing circumstances (e.g. the heart, the glands), other components (e.g. the bones), are not sensitive to circumstances in this way, yet they have functions too. So *this* kind of adaptability is not part of the meaning of 'function' either.

Recent discussions of feedback have promulgated false assimilations of a particularly subtle kind. The concept has often figured in non-teleological explanations of the facts that underlie teleological phenomena. Psychologists often say 'The apparently purposeful character of such and such behaviour can be explained away without resorting to teleologism. It is really due to Skinnerian reinforcement, i.e. medium-term feedback'. And biologists frequently say 'The adaptation of an organism to its surroundings, which gives rise to the impression that its parts have been designed to fulfil a purpose, can be explained by natural selection, which is a long-term feedback process'. Feedback thus comes to be seen as the empirical thread running through both kinds of natural teleology. It then becomes tempting to regard feedback as a unifying concept in terms of which teleological concepts can be analysed. This move is similar to the one made by Sommerhoff, who thought that we could achieve greater understanding if we moved to a higher level of abstraction, from which we might regard both functionality and goal-directedness as manifestations of a single, generic system-property. But abstraction can be taken too far. Superficial similarities can blind us to deep essential differences, which then get obliterated by new terms, diagrams and other conceptual apparatus.

Statements like the ones above foster confusion in at least two ways. First, they imply that if a scientific explanation of a teleological phenomenon can be given, this proves that the teleology was not real, but only apparent. Secondly, they blur the distinction between explaining the same facts in a new way, and offering a reductive analysis of the old explanation. To say that S did B in order to do G does not *mean* that S did B because B has been rewarded by G in similar circumstances in the past. Similarly, to say that X does A in order to do F does not *mean* that X does A because past doings of A have led to F, and that the consequences of this are now feeding back. The first of these is an *alternative* explanation of why S did B, compatible with the TD, and very often true. But it has quite different truth-conditions from the TD. The second is a filling-out of what was previously an explanation-sketch. It asserts some of the background conditions against which the

TD was set. The patterns of underlying regularities which these explanations exploit are not what teleology *consists in*, but are like empirical *schemata*, in the Kantian sense, of purposeful and functional teleology respectively. (This illuminating Kantian comparison was first noticed by J. Watling (1973, p. 107)).

Finally, the biological statement commits a further error in calling natural selection a feedback process. Strictly speaking, evolution is not a process which consists of a system's being influenced by the consequences of its previous behaviour. This is merely an analogy, which derives from our regarding a species as a unitary system which persists over time, and which 'responds' to ecological pressures in such a way as to issue changes in its own composition as 'output'. In reality, there is no single continuing entity which does things and is influenced by what it does, when a species changes its characteristics over time. Only the organisms which make up the species do things. What actually happens is that individuals of one generation reproduce differentially, and the consequences of this, when aggregated, determine the composition of the next generation. The way in which the distribution of characteristics throughout a population alters as a result of natural selection will depend on haphazard environmental changes. The parents do not foresee the changes, or reproduce differentially in order that the next generation will be fit. It just so happens that, as a result of natural selection, the offspring that get born do tend to be well-adapted to the prevailing environment, just as their parents were. Species-survival (when it occurs) is not a goal, therefore, but a *de facto* result of the evolutionary process. Species are neither goal-directed systems nor feedback-controlled systems. Indeed, to be accurate, they are not *systems* at all.

PART FIVE

I 2

Unifying theory of teleological description

It is now time to draw the strands of the argument together. First I shall summarise the view about goals that was proposed in the previous two chapters, and say a little more about desires. Then in the next section I shall set out systematically the fruits of the various analyses, exhibiting their points of similarity and difference. This marks the stopping-point of the semantic enterprise, as far as the present work is concerned. Finally, I shall attempt to show that the theory, incomplete though it is, can help to clear up some of the puzzling questions about teleology which were raised in chapter 1.

Further remarks about goals and desires

In order to analyse our present notion of goal-directed behaviour it was found necessary to postulate a mentalistic core-concept, and to hypothesise that our present concept, which applies to machines as well as to animals, was derived from it by an analogical extension. It had been discovered earlier that no behaviour of a system could be goal-directed unless it was the result of the system's being in a certain kind of internal state. It followed from this that only certain kinds of system were capable of goal-directed behaviour, namely, those capable of being in the relevant internal state. The class of goal-directed systems is not, however, a class of equals. The members of it can be arranged in a rough sort of order according to their degree of sophistication.

The class has expanded in the last few decades as a result of a shift in the meaning of the words 'purposive' and 'goal-directed'. The shift has been due to the technological advances which made it possible to build new, sophisticated machines, and which in turn created the need for an appropriate vocabulary in which to talk about such machines. The language responded to this need by stretching its old resources. Human beings and higher mammals had always provided the paradigm cases of goal-directedness, while lower organisms had qualified as goal-directed partly on the basis of analogies between them and the more central cases. However, since the development of servomechanisms, certain kinds of inanimate systems have been allowed to join the club. Their claim to be sufficiently similar to the central cases was felt to be at least as good as the claims of some lower animals which were already members. Originally, the fact that they were inanimate was thought to be a strict bar to their joining. To call them goal-directed was felt to be metaphorical, however similar in behaviour they might be to existing members. But as time went on, the metaphor became moribund, because it was used so frequently by the people who worked with such machines, so that it is now not felt to be metaphorical at all. As yet, the servomechanisms that have been built are fairly primitive, and are comparable to the sorts of organism that lie near the periphery of the original class of purposive systems. But these mechanisms are now in the class, because, as it were, the rules have been altered so as to admit associate members.

The essential feature that full members possess is the capacity to have, and to act on, desires and beliefs. Whether a system wants to do G is an objective matter, a matter of whether it is in a certain kind of internal state. At present, our methods of telling if a system wants something are mostly indirect, and very complex. We draw upon evidence from many sources: past and present behaviour, the environment, the life-history of the organism, from comparisons with other organisms of the same kind, and from analogies with ourselves. When it concerns the desires of human beings, it is sometimes possible to use the more direct, though not infallible method of asking them. Although in a given case our evidence may not be conclusive, we think that there is a right answer to the question 'Did S want to do G then?', and that possibly new evidence might come to light, or even new methods of obtaining evidence, which could help to determine the right answer. Since it is also an objective matter whether a given piece of behaviour was caused by a desire, goal-directedness is a perfectly objective relational property of behaviour, according to this account.

I have been free with the terms 'want', 'desire' and 'intention', switching from one to the other as if they meant the same. A soldier may intend to carry out an order that he wishes he did not have to carry out. In one familiar sense of 'want', he does not want to carry it out. But in the sense in which I use the word (which is also familiar), he does want to, all things considered, in so far as he intends to. I construe 'want' and 'desire' broadly. For me, wanting or desiring is the most generic kind of motivational state. Perhaps the word 'desire' has a rather narrower connotation, and ought not to be used in this way. Goldman illustrates the broad sense by saying that 'to want x is to find the prospect of x attractive, nice, good, appropriate, fitting, etc. (1970, p. 94).

A desire to do G, in the broad sense intended here, is much the same as a belief that to do G would be a good idea. There are various ways in which an agent can come to view an action as a good one to do, which parallel the various different reasons for wanting to do it. He may regard doing G as intrinsically pleasurable or virtuous, or as a means to some other end, or as the least unpleasant of the alternatives open to him. His evaluation may be ill-founded, of course, but desires may be ill-founded too. One may regard an action as good to do even though one has no reason, or very poor reasons, for so regarding it. It is a familiar fact that one often wants to do things which are neither pleasurable nor advantageous, and which, when performed, bring no enjoyment or satisfaction at all.

The close parallel between desire and evaluative belief brings out just how general the relevant concept of desire is. It also suggests a way of simplifying the analysis of the TD by reducing the desire-belief pair to a single, even more generic mental attitude, whose content contains an evaluative component and a factual component. It will be a belief that G is a good thing to do and that $B \Rightarrow G$. But several qualifications are needed here.

It is well-known that an agent may want to perform an action, like smoking a cigarette, which he does not believe to be *good for* him. He may know full well that smoking does him no good. So if we are to equate desiring with believing good, we need to specify the intended sense of 'good' more precisely. This is no easy task, for the word 'good' is notoriously slippery. The agent need not believe that doing G is good *for* anything or anyone. He simply has to welcome the prospect of doing it. 'Good' is the most general adjective of commendation in English. The kind of commendatory attitude we are after is entirely subjective and non-moral. It is the sort of attitude which is expressed by a person who replies 'Oh good!' to a suggestion about what to do.

The suggested action could be anything: helping a blind man, going for a drink, or beating up an old lady.

Another qualification concerns the word 'believe'. It denotes an attitude which is too cognitive. The synthetic beliefs of a rational being are sensitive to what goes on in the world, because he tries to make his beliefs match the truth. Possibly it is part of the concept of belief that this should be so. The term 'evaluative belief' could be misleading, therefore, because it denotes an attitude which has the duty of matching the truth about what is good, whereas this feature does not seem to be essential to the concept of wanting. The person who believes that G would be a good thing to do, in the sense I am after, need not feel that there is a right answer, which someone else could tell him perhaps, about whether G really is a good thing to do. Perhaps the expression 'see as good' is better than 'believe good'. 'Seeing as' is the nearest thing that the English language has to an all-purpose psychological verb that does duty for both cognitive and affective mental attitudes. The TD could then be analysed as 'S did B because S saw G as being a good thing to do, and saw B as being a means to G'. However, I don't think much hangs on this. I propose, therefore, to go ahead and substitute 'S believes that G is good' for the clause 'S wants to do G' in my analysans, intending it to be interpreted in the light of the above qualifications.

I should emphasise that there is no hidden moral message in this proposal. I do not claim to be analysing the word 'good', nor do I believe that we always desire the good. I am, if you like, stipulating a use for the word 'good' in this special context. All that is meant here by 'S believes that G would be good to do' is that S wants to do G. I stick by my arguments for the thesis that having G as a goal (in the 'core' sense) involves being in the mental state of desiring G. My only reason for offering the new locution is so that I can bring to light certain analogies in the next few pages.

Since I do not analyse the concept of desire further than this, some philosophers might be inclined to say that I have relocated the problem of teleology without solving it. Goal-directed behaviour is behaviour motivated by the having of a goal. Having G as a goal amounts to having G as the intentional object or content of desire, and type-identifying an internal state as 'a desire to do G' involves, they would say, classifying it on the basis of a teleological taxonomical principle. Instead of explaining observable behaviour straightforwardly by reference to a future goal, I am (they would say) explaining it by invoking an internal state which has a reference to the future goal built into it. The problematic forward orientation is still there.

This line of criticism rests on a serious misapprehension. Desires are not type-identified retrospectively, according to their outcomes. If a desire to do G does reach fruition, this is a contingent fact which in no way enters into the definition or classification of it as a desire to do G rather than H. That it is a desire to do G was true beforehand.

It is terribly tempting to think of a goal as a concrete future event, and to think of the present desire as involving a conception of that future event, with the conception of the goal being in some sense logically or ontologically derivative from the goal itself. But this is the wrong way round. A goal just *is* the intentional object of the relevant kind of conception. Admittedly, in a loose sense of 'refer', a man's desire to do G tomorrow does refer to a future time, and to an act-type G. The man may envisage a possible future doing of G. But the description of the desire does not make a reference to a particular action in the actual future. There is indeed a problem about understanding what it is for a desire to have a certain content, but it is not specifically a problem about teleology. It is part of a much wider problem about what it is for an internal state to point outside itself and to represent reality symbolically. It arises not only with desires to do G, but also with thoughts of doing G, memories of doing G, perceptions of doing G, and so on, through many other kinds of mental states. It is beyond the scope of this book to offer a general theory of intentionality.

The pattern of the analyses

I now set out the final results of my analysis of TDs, illustrating the similarities and differences between the schemata. Their structural similarities are striking enough, I think, to justify the conclusion that the different types of teleological explanations are variations on a single theme. This theme is, to put it simply, the idea of a thing's happening *because it is good*. More exactly, the TDs I deal with convey the idea that the thing happens or exists because it leads or is believed to lead to something which is good. This idea is central in the philosophy of Leibniz. It will naturally appeal to anyone who believes that ours is the best of all possible worlds, as Leibniz did, and also to anyone who believes that, though this world may not be the best, it is getting better. However, as we have seen, there are several ways of interpreting teleological explanations, not all of which require the assumption of a benevolent God or of natural progress.

The idea is also to be found, not surprisingly, in Aristotle. In *Physica* Book II.3, he says that final causes are 'causes in the sense of the end or the good of the rest; for "that for the sake of which" means what is best and the end of the things that lead up to it. (Whether we say the "good itself" or the "apparent good" makes no difference.),[1] Except for the sentence in brackets, this thought could almost serve as a motto for my account. The results of the analyses are set out in the following chart.

TABLE OF ANALYSES

ANALYSANDUM		ANALYSANS			
Explanandum	*Explanans*	*Explanandum*	*Explanans*		
				Intensional Causal	*Evaluative*
S does B	in order to do G	S does B	because	S believes (B $\Rightarrow$ G & G is good).	
S does B	in order to do F	S does B	because —		B $\Rightarrow$ F & F is good.
X does/has A	in order to do G	X does/has A	because	S believes (A $\Rightarrow$ G & G is good).	
X does/has A	in order to do F	X does/has A	because —		A $\Rightarrow$ F & F is good.

From this chart it can be seen that together the essence of teleology lies in welding a causal element and an evaluative element to yield an explanatory device. The causal clause identifies an actual or envisaged effect of a certain event, the evaluative clause says that this effect is good from some point of view, and the whole TD says that the combination of these elements provides *raison d'être* of the event. The central difference between natural function 'in order to' and purposive or artefact function 'in order to' is that the latter relies on a mind to weld the elements. The presence or absence of 'believes that' in the analysis determines the way in which a TD is explanatory, the way it must be tested, and so on. But although functional and purposive explanations are assessed by completely different criteria, the similarity in their underlying grammatical structures explains why they are bracketed together under the same label.

In the purposive TD 'S does B in order to do G', the letter S stands for a system, i.e. an integrated whole with the capacity to act

[1] *Physica* 195a, 24–6. See also *Metaphysica* 1013b, 25–7.

in and on its surroundings, and possessed of a point of view. S may be an animal or a group of animals, like a tribe or a society. The TD means 'S does B because S believes that (B $\Rightarrow$ G and G is good)'. 'B $\Rightarrow$ G' means that B contributes to G in some way or other, 'G is good' is interpreted as meaning that G is good to do, so that the belief that G is good amounts to a desire to do G. Brackets indicate that both clauses are within the scope of 'believes that'. S may be an artefact, like a robot. Assuming that such systems do not literally have desires and beliefs, TDs of them would not be objective statements, according to this analysis. However, it is not realistic to say that purposive or goal TDs are always metaphorical in such cases. They may have been figurative originally, but many people would say that the metaphor is now dead. I suggested that a TD like 'The robot turned left in order$_G$ to get back to base' should be interpreted to mean that the robot turned left because the robot 'believed' (quasi) that (turning left would contribute to getting back to base and getting back to base would be a good thing to do). It is not the job of the analysis to decide *when* it is appropriate to identify machine-states in terms of intentional content. My claim is simply that a purposive 'in order to' statement presupposes such a mode of identification. If that mode is felt to be unjustified in particular cases, then the TD can only be construed as an 'artefact function' TD, implying that the robot turned left because its *designer* wanted it to (be able to) get back to base.

I shall not list a separate analysans for purposive TDs of inanimate systems, but shall leave it to be understood that S's internal state can be either a belief or a belief-analogue. Equally, then, I must allow that purposive behaviour can occur among living systems that don't have fully-fledged beliefs, but only belief-like states.

Purposive explanations are normally given in the past tense, since they normally answer 'Why?' questions about particular events that have already occurred. Within the scope of the belief operator, verbs have to obey the rules about the sequence of tenses in indirect speech (e.g. 'S believed that B *would contribute* to G . . .'). A purposive explanation of a particular event in the present tense would typically say 'S *is doing* B because S believes that (B *will* contribute to G and G is good)'. The simple present tense, 'S does B', might convey the undesirable impression that the statement is a general law, 'Whenever S does B, S does B in order to . . .'. However, I ignore these subtleties over tense in my schema, leaving the reader to make appropriate adjustments for particular cases.

The other three kinds of TD shown on the Table are *functional* ones. The schema appropriate to *biological functions* is 'X does A in order to do F', where X stands for some organ, part, or internal mechanism of a system S, A stands for a characteristic activity of X, and F stands for an activity of X which is caused or causally generated by A. It answers the question 'Why does X do A?' The schema can be generalised a bit more if we allow A to stand for properties of X as well as activities, and write 'S does/has A in order to . . .'. This copes with questions of the form 'Why does X have A?' (e.g. 'Why are peacocks' tail-feathers so brightly coloured?').

I take this TD as the normal form. But it is just as common to ask for a functional explanation of the item X as it is to ask for a functional explanation of X's activities or properties (e.g. 'Why does the pineal gland exist? What is it for?'). Admittedly, many physiological components are defined by what they do, so the questioner is in effect asking 'Why do things which do/have A exist?' But quite often, he may not know that X does A, and may be satisfied by being told that X exists because it does A. Function-statements are often of the form 'The function of X is to do A', where no mention is made of any further activity F. The corresponding TD would be 'X exists in order to do A'. It is easy to extend my analysis of three-termed TDs to cover two-termed ones like this.

The standard analysis I offer is 'X does/has A because A ⇒ F and F is good'. 'A ⇒ F' means 'A characteristically and normally contributes to F', where A and F are types; 'F is good' is understood to mean that F is good for S (in normal circumstances), either intrinsically or because it characteristically contributes to some further good. A certain amount of interpretation and supplementation is needed before this can be regarded as a valid explanation of why X does/has A. Standardly, the TD is a tenseless general statement about *types* of organs. 'The heart beats in order to circulate the blood' is about hearts in general, of whatever individual of whatever species; 'Peacocks' tail-feathers have bright colours in order to attract peahens' is about the tail-feathers of peacocks in general. But it is possible to ask functional 'Why?' questions about individual specimens. This heart beats because *other* hearts have beaten in the past and have contributed to the blood circulation of their owners who were the ancestors of the owner of this heart. Furthermore, it is possible to give an 'ontogenetic' functional explanation of why a particular heart beats. The TD would say that this heart beats because its own past beating has benefited the owner by helping him to survive. Functional TDs sum up a number of historical facts by fudging time-references, thereby creating the illusion that the cause of the present beating is the fact that it will have a beneficial effect.

We may now turn to TDs assigning *behaviour-functions*. If the behaviour-pattern is innate, it is part of the organism's natural equipment. The logic of the explanation is the same as above. The only difference is that the item with the function is an activity of the whole instead of an activity of a part. (We can extend this also to cover *properties* of the whole if necessary.) The standard behaviour-function TD is 'S does B in order to do F', a general statement answering the question 'Why does S (a species or an individual) characteristically do B (in these circumstances)?'. It therefore has a different explanandum from the purposive TD, which typically explains a particular doing of B. The analysans is 'S does B because B $\Rightarrow$ F and F is good'. Once again, it is understood that F is good *for S*, either *qua* individual agent, or *qua* species, in case F promotes reproduction, survival of offspring or of conspecifics. Birds, for example, sit on their eggs because sitting on their eggs contributes to hatching their young, and hatching young is good (for the species).

Statements to the effect that a social practice or institution has a 'latent' social function (Merton, 1949) receive exactly the same analysis, but here S stands for a social rather than a biological group. For example, 'The Navaho persecute witches (in certain circumstances) in order to lower intra-group hostility' means 'The Navaho persecute witches (in certain circumstances) because persecuting witches contributes to lowering intra-group hostility and lowering intra-group hostility is good (for the Navaho)'. Assuming that the Navaho are not aware that this is why they do it, and that their proclivity for witchcraft persecutions is not genetically determined, anthropologists might explain the phenomenon on the hypothesis that tribes which hand down the tradition of persecuting witches in certain circumstances have been favoured by natural selection. A tribe which practises this custom is more likely to survive external threats to its existence than a tribe which does not, because the process of casting out witches makes the remaining members more loyal to the tribe and more willing to strive to preserve it.

Kluckhohn (1944) observed, however, that the frequency of persecutions increased when the tribe underwent pressure from the outside world, and diminished when the threat was overcome. This suggests that the Navaho resort to this custom when they perceive that things are going badly for the tribe. Perhaps they are conditioned by the reinforcing effects of persecutions in the past. This suggests that they remember what happened, and believe in some hazy and inexplicit way that a collective witch hunt helps them to regain their cohesion. If this is the case, then lowering intragroup hostility is a goal which happens also to be useful. The TD should be construed as purposive, though the Navaho would probably not describe the goal in the way the anthropologist does, and perhaps would not even recognise it.

Alternatively, the religious law that witches should be cast out might be a social institution designed by Navaho elders in the past to serve what Merton would call a 'manifest' social function. This brings us to the topic of *artefact-functions*. I use the term 'artefact' widely so as to include both material objects like baskets, bowls and sparking-plugs, and abstract objects like institutions, created by some organism or group of organisms for some purpose. There are as many variants of 'artefact-function' TDs as there are of 'natural function' TDs. We say, for example, 'Knives exist in order to cut', 'Knives have blades in order to cut', 'Knives are used in order to cut' and so on. As before, I select a standard form of TD for artefact-functions and treat other forms of TD as variants whose meaning is illuminated by the analysis of the standard form. The standard is 'X does/has A in order to do G', and its analysis is 'X does A because S believes that (A ⇒ G and G is good)', where S refers to a system or kind of system that designs, creates and uses X. Here X may be either an individual or a type, which may or may not be functionally defined. It may be understood that S has to make X do A, and that X does A in certain circumstances only. These are degrees of freedom that the analysandum and the analysans both share. It is clear that the 'theological' analysis of the meaning of biological function statements is a special case of this model for artefact-functions, where X is the organ and S is God.

I think that every true 'in order to' sentence is equivalent in meaning to a sentence exemplifying one or other of these schemata, or can be assimilated to a standard form that is. Quite a bit of variability is allowed for by my notation. On the chart, 'X' and 'S' stand sometimes for individuals and sometimes for kinds; A and B may be either actions or properties; 'S does B' is a general statement in the behaviour-function schema, a singular statement (normally) in the purposive schema. 'F' and 'G', however, are always names of act-*types*, and 'G' always appears within the scope of an intensional operator. Before we can know whether the verb following 'in order to' in a given sentence should be represented schematically by 'G' or by 'F', we need to know which kind of TD is being made by the sentence. We cannot tell from the nature of the action named, since the same action, e.g. mating, might be either a behaviour-function or a goal. Similarly we may need to know whether the whole sentence is a goal or function TD before deciding whether its subject term should be represented by 'S' or by 'X'. Systems capable of having goals of their own are sometimes assigned functions within some wider whole. Such explanations are often used by sociologists. But their ambiguity can be confusing. How, for instance, is the following TD to be taken: 'Psychiatrists exist in order to help deviants conform to society's norms'? If the TD assigns a natural function which is a behaviour-function that benefits the social group rather than the agent, it hardly matters whether we use the 'S does B' or the 'X does A' schema, since the individual S can be regarded as a useful 'part' of the group. But if not, then it does matter, since the TD could be ascribing either a goal or an artificial function to psychiatrists, and it is important to know which.

Despite the degrees of freedom within each schema, the differences between them are too great to allow them to be subsumed under one grand, abstract form. The presence or absence of the psychological verb 'believes' marks a crucial dividing line. This factor determines the 'logic' of the explanation offered. TDs which do not have this psychological verb in their analysans rely for their validity (a) upon their generality, the fact that they are loosely quantified over past and present items and events, (b) upon supplementation by various other premisses. TDs which rely on their subject's having an attitude are straight-forward causal explanations in terms of mental antecedents. It is interesting to speculate whether the former developed out of the latter. Perhaps biological function statements started out as artefact-function statements, but dropped the implicit 'God believed/intended that . . .' at some stage in history. However, it is clear that they are separate in meaning now, and that they provide logically distinct modes of explanation.

When Aristotle said that it didn't matter whether a teleological end was actually good or apparently good, he encouraged the conflation of two quite different conceptions of what an end is. If the end is actually good for a being, it is what I call a natural or biological end. If the end is an action that a being regards as good to do (i.e. an action which appears good to that being), then it is a goal. Natural ends are states of affairs that obtain, or can obtain, in the real world. Goals, on the other hand, are mental entities, living permanently inside intentional brackets. I agree that if a goal is achieved, we say that it exists or has been actualised. But this teetering from intensional to extensional usage is a loose *façon de parler*. Intentional objects can never break free of their shackles, for they can never become real objects. What is actualised, strictly speaking, is always some action or state of affairs that *matches* the goal by satisfying a goal-description.

People still confuse functional explanations with purposive explanations, just as Aristotle did. Why is this such a perennial temptation? Is it because we are unable to break free from *our* shackles, the shackles of our Aristotelian intellectual heritage? I think there is a better explanation, which appeals to a general feature of linguistic communication. When people speak, they tend to drop intensional operators, or teeter in and out of them, when they think that no ambiguity or confusion will result. We do not preface all our utterances with 'I think that', because the fact of our uttering a thought is normally taken to show that we think it. It is unnecessary to say so explicitly. Similarly, if the context makes it clear that the speaker is projecting himself into another person's position and describing things as they appear from that position, then the intensional operator 'He thinks that' may be left unspoken. A person will often leave it to be understood, when calling a thing good, that he is speaking as the mouthpiece of conventional opinion. What he means is that the thing is regarded as good.

This tendency to peel off intensional operators in conversation may overreach itself, however. Sometimes the audience is not sure whose point of view the speaker is expounding. Sometimes the speaker himself is not sure what thought he is thinking. This is exactly what often happens when we think about teleology. We get confused, for instance, about the differences between a thing's being good, our thinking it good, and someone else's thinking it good. Hence we fail to distinguish between (a) a thing's having a purpose antecedently, before anyone thought it was good for anything, and (b) a thing's having a purpose for someone antecedently, before *we* thought of it as being good for anything. These and similar confusions, resulting from careless use of intensional operators, are the source of the teetering between different meanings of 'in order to'.

The point of fitting all TDs into a single general table with headings for the separate sentence-components is to show that they have structural similarities despite their logical diversity. It enables one to see that teleological explanations have a sort of unity. The fact that the explanandum event has, or is regarded as having, a good effect is presented as a reason for its occurrence. Given that there are these various components, the question arises whether they could not be combined in different ways to yield new explanation-schemata which are autonomous of the ones listed. No doubt some grammatically possible arrangements of clauses would simply fail to provide valid forms of explanation. But might there not be some variations that could be interpreted as possible explanations or explanation-sketches? If so, would they not deserve to count as teleological explanations in virtue of their fitting into the general matrix?

In chapter 2, I said that my initial criterion of teleology was linguistic – the field of study was roughly demarcated by our actual use of sentences containing 'in order to' and 'in order that' – but that my real interest lay in discovering what it was about the world which made true teleological statements true. The various objective relationships have now been teased out and sorted into types. The matrix reveals, however, that the various TDs are unified at an abstract level. To a realist, this suggests that there might be a unifying pattern in the facts themselves. Any set of appropriate objects and events causally related in a way that exhibited the same pattern ought to count as an example of objective teleology, whether or not we happen to describe their relationship by means of an 'in order to' sentence. If there are any other valid explanation-schemata that fit into the table, in one sense they count as teleological explanations in virtue of the facts which make them true. But they would not count as analyses of any existing form of teleological explanation, since we don't happen to use teleological sentences to mean what they mean. They would be aspiring analyses that lacked analysanda.

I do not think, however, that there are any genuine alternative schemata. All coherent variations that I can imagine rely on the truth of teleological explanations of the familiar types. Consider, for example, the schema 'S does B because $B \Rightarrow G$ and S believes that G is good'. This is a hybrid, with 'G' occurring once inside and once outside the scope of 'believes that'; it is neither a pure goal TD nor a pure function TD. The clause '$B \Rightarrow G$' is about act-types: it means that B generally and characteristically leads to something that S wants. It might be supported by evidence that B has led to G in the individual's past. The explanation can be validly interpreted on Skinnerian lines to mean that S does B now because S has been conditioned to do B by the reinforcing effect of past performances of B. Now the fact that B has led to G in the past would be causally irrelevant unless it had left some trace on S. If S had ever perceived or been aware of B's reinforcing effects, this would have made some mark on S's mind. S would remember or believe, perhaps unconsciously, that B leads to G. In that case, the schema is parasitic on the analysis I offer of standard purposive TDs. We must assume that 'B $\Rightarrow$ G' is within the scope of an intensional operator that has been left out. If, on the other hand, S had never been aware that B led to G, then presumably the conditioning would have taken place even if S had not regarded G as a good thing to do. Doing G is evidently rewarding to S, not because it satisfies a desire with G as its intentional object, but simply because it fulfils a need, and is thus good *for* S. G has the explanatory role of a function, not a goal. Responses that promote G are stamped in during ontogeny by a process analogous to natural selection.

Similar remarks apply to another hybrid, 'S does B because G is good and S believes that B $\Rightarrow$ G'. How is the fact that G is good causally relevant to S's doing B? Either it registers on S's mind via a perception that G is good which generates a desire for G, or there must have been selection pressure on S to develop a tendency to do things that contribute to G. If the former, then 'G is good' is within the scope of an implicit intensional operator; if the latter, then it is not causally necessary for S to believe that B $\Rightarrow$ G. Provided it is true that B $\Rightarrow$ G, S would have an innate or acquired tendency to do B in any case. So the explanation is either true but dependent upon a standard purposive TD, or it is false, the true one being a standard functional TD.

Since my analysis of artefact-function statements also contains an intensional operator, hybrids can again be constructed. But these too are either incoherent as explanations, or parasitic upon standard schemata. For instance, 'X does/has A because A $\Rightarrow$ G and S believes that G is good' may be true, but only in virtue of the fact that S correctly *believes* that A $\Rightarrow$ G, and creates an X that does A because of this belief, plus his desire. In the reverse schema 'X does/has A because G is good and S believes that A $\Rightarrow$ G', there is no obvious connection between S's belief and the fact that G is good for S. Either the designer must have some conception that G is good which inculcates a desire, as in the standard artefact-function schema, or his making an X that does A must be the expression of a creative urge which S would have whether or not he believed that A $\Rightarrow$ G, just as bees have an innate tendency to build hexagonal cells. If that were the situation, the object X, though an artefact, would have a natural function in the same way that organs have functions. The cells are hexagonal because their being hexagonal contributes to their fitting together to form a stable honeycomb and their fitting together stably is good (for the bees). But this functional explanation relies on another functional explanation in the background, namely one of the form 'S does B (i.e. makes an X that does/has A) because B ⇒ F and F is good (for S)'.

It is evident that things could get more complicated. A belief that (A ⇒ G and G is good) could itself result from natural selection of ancestors innately programmed to have that belief. So the fact that S has a certain goal could be given a functional explanation in terms of the beneficial consequences of having that goal. Thus here we can give a functional explanation of goal-directedness to G. There may be other mutant schemata that can be interpreted as valid explanations, but I believe their logic will always turn out to be basically the same as one of my standard forms.

Does everything I have said hold equally for 'in order that' sentences? The grammatical difference between the two teleological connectives is that 'in order that' is followed by a whole sentence, while 'in order to' is followed by an infinitive. The verb following 'in order that' has to have a subject. This subject may be different from the subject of the main verb. To convert a TD like 'Peter ducked in order that Paul might score' into a TD containing 'in order to' we need a complement which names an action of which Peter is the agent. It is often possible to construct appropriate infinitives by judicious use of causal verbs like 'bring it about that', 'let', 'help' and so on, for example, 'Peter ducked in order to allow Paul to score'. In my schematic analyses, it has to be understood that such transformations have already been made. It would have been quite possible to make the subjects of all predicates explicit in the analyses. The TD 'Peter did B in order that Paul might do G' could have been rendered as 'Peter did B because Peter believed that (Peter's doing B would contribute to Paul's doing G and Paul's doing G would be good)'. But in the examples I have used it was unnecessary to lay bare that much structure.

Nevertheless, there exist TDs which have a more complex grammatical structure than my standard schemata, and it must be acknowledged that the 'in order that' form often reveals that structure more clearly. For example, in the sentence 'Peter persuaded Paul to go with him to the station in order to help carry the luggage', the implied subject of the verb 'help' is not Peter but Paul. It does not exemplify the standard form. Any attempt to paraphrase it straight off in the standard way will yield wrong results. But the sentence 'Peter persuaded Paul to go with him to the station in order that Paul might help carry the luggage' exhibits the structure better, because it states Peter's aim more precisely. It indicates that the analysis must refer to Peter's desire that Paul might help. In general, TDs containing 'in order that' describe the situation more perspicuously, when S wants someone else to do G.

This example raises several other difficult points. There are, in fact, at least three dimensions of complexity that have been ignored in my account. First, there is the question of TDs that contain references to two or more persons. This is a minor problem. Second, there are problems raised by TDs containing terms which are themselves covertly teleological. The verb 'persuade' is a case in point. To say that Peter persuaded Paul to go to the station is to say that Paul agreed to go to the station as a result of Peter's saying or doing something in order to achieve that result. Thus there is at least one other TD in the background. In this case, all the covert teleology can be carried over wholesale into the analysans without being unpacked; but perhaps this is not so in all cases. Thirdly, there is a range of problems raised by the presence in TDs of words which introduce intentionality. Typical among these are psychological verbs and verbs naming speech acts, which create intensional contexts. The teleological connective, which is itself an intensional operator, may interact with other intensional operators in unexpected ways, and give rise to ambiguity. Indeed the present example is ambiguous for that reason, for it has an alternative interpretation: 'Peter persuaded Paul that Paul should go to the station in order to help'. Here we have a standard TD, with Paul as its subject, embedded within a 'that' clause. On this interpretation, the sentence taken as a whole is not really a TD at all, because 'in order to' does not have the whole sentence as its scope.

A clearer example of the third problem, untainted by the first and second, is 'Mary wants to go shopping in order to buy a present'. The verb 'wants' is an intensional operator which may take either wide scope: 'Mary wants it to be the case that (she goes shopping in order to buy a present)', or narrow scope: 'Mary wants (to go shopping), in order to buy a present'. The former interpretation creates no special difficulty. The embedded TD is of the standard form, hence it can be analysed in the standard way. But the second reading presents a problem for my account. Although the teleological connective now has the wider scope, and so the whole sentence is a TD, the other intensional operator interferes with it. On my account, this TD ought to mean 'Mary wants to go shopping because Mary wants to buy a present and believes that *wanting* to go shopping will contribute to buying a present'. But it does not mean this. It means 'Mary wants to go shopping because Mary wants to buy a present and believes that going shopping will contribute to buying a present'. Mary's reason for wanting to go shopping is exactly the same as her reason for going shopping, if she goes in order to buy a present.

Of course, she might well believe that her desire to do B will induce her to do B which will in turn contribute to G. But this belief cannot be the one that is entailed by the TD, as the following cases show. A person may want to stumble *unintentionally*, in order to make people laugh. Yet he does not believe that his desire to stumble unintentionally will contribute to his making people laugh, for he does not believe that this desire will help bring about an unintentional stumbling. The point is even clearer in a two-person case. Peter wants Paul to have an accident, in order that Peter may win a race. (Here 'in order that' has the wide scope. It isn't that Peter wants it to be the case that Paul has an accident in order to let Peter win the race.) Peter believes that if Paul has an accident, Peter stands a better chance of winning. But he does not believe that his desire that Paul has an accident will improve his chances of winning, for he has no intention of acting on this desire.

The upshot is that TDs of the form 'S wants to do B, in order to do G' are not yet catered for in my scheme, because they are not of standard form. Wanting cannot be construed as just another kind of acting, a value of the variable B. How, then, should such TDs be treated? The rule for translating them seems to be as follows. First, peel off the verb 'wants', i.e. substitute 'S does B' for 'S wants to do B'. Then translate the resulting TD in the standard way. This will give the correct explanans. Finally, replace the verb 'wants', making sure that it binds the explanandum only. Similar rules could no doubt be formulated to deal with complex TDs that contain other psychological verbs. But such rules are merely *ad hoc*. I should prefer to give a deeper explanation, in terms of general principles, of why TDs behave this way when the explanandum is S's wanting, intending, deciding, etc. Why is it that only the action which figures in the *content* of the desire is mentioned in the explanans, even though what is being explained in the desire itself? In all other cases, the explanandum itself was mentioned again in the explanans as part of the content of the relevant belief. I don't know the answer. What is going on here seems to have some affinity with the 'teetering' phenomenon mentioned earlier. Teetering was, of course, a mistake, a symptom of confusion, whereas this phenomenon is evidently rule-governed, and built into our language. But both seem to involve the shedding and donning of intensional operators. They are probably the tip of a large iceberg of problems, but they have more to do with intentionality than with teleology. I think the essence of teleology is adequately captured in standard TDs.

Some applications of the theory

Clarity about the logical structure of teleological explanations is surely an intrinsically desirable thing, especially for psychologists, sociologists and anthropologists, whose theoretical literature retains traces of serious conceptual errors on this topic. At the end of chapter 1, however, I claimed that my analysis would help to answer substantive questions, like 'Does the universe have a purpose?', and 'What is the purpose of life?'. Ordinary people often get perplexed about such matters. The questions seem important, but it is hard to think clearly about them. I shall now try to make good that claim, by dissecting a couple of specimen questions and showing how to disentangle the issues. What follows is just a sketch. I leave it to the reader to fill in the details.

Does the universe have a purpose? The question is ambiguous. 'Purpose' can mean (1) goal, (2) natural function, or (3) artificial function. Let us assume that the question is concerned with the universe as a single, integrated unit, and not about things *in* the universe. As regards (1), it is doubtful whether it even makes sense to suppose that the universe has a goal of its own. But if it does make sense, it is undoubtedly false, since the universe has no mind of its own, hence it cannot want anything.

The universe taken as a whole cannot possibly have a purpose in the sense of 'natural function within a wider system', since there is no wider system. Nor can it be good for any other system which is distinct from it, since all other systems are its own parts, hence not distinct from it.

Whether it has an artificial function depends on whether any being with a mind designed it or uses it for a purpose. The only candidate for the role of designer is God. Some people would regard it as being true by definition that God designed the universe. But this immediately raises the question whether there exists anything that answers to their definition of 'God'. If, on the other hand, 'God' is defined in some other way, or not defined at all, the proposition is a synthetic one whose truth or falsity depends on the prior question of whether God exists. Either way, the important question is whether there exists something that designed the universe. The claim that there does is unfalsifiable, being a contingent existential claim. Nevertheless, it has not yet been verified or rendered probable by evidence. Although it *might* be true that the universe was designed, there is no reason for thinking that it *is* true.

The universe could conceivably have acquired an artificial function through being used by some being as an instrument to further his purposes. It would not matter if that being were embodied, and existed in some part of the universe. Political parties, after all, can be used as instruments by individuals who belong to them. But to manipulate the whole universe in the way that politicians manipulate social institutions would require power of a different order of magnitude from that possessed by anyone living today. Perhaps in a few years the universe will have a function for someone. For the time being, however, it has no function in this sense. The short answer to the original question is that in no sense does the universe have a purpose.

Let us next consider whether a person's life can have a purpose. If someone comes up to you and asks 'Is there really any purpose in my life?', the chances are that he is depressed and is appealing for help. He would not intend the question to be answered in the way I do here. I am after the sober truth. I treat it as a factual question to which there is an objectively right answer. For ease of exposition, let us imagine that the question has been raised with respect to a particular person called Dave. Dave is a biologically normal male of twenty-five, fairly average, who works in a garage maintaining motorcycles. The question 'Does Dave's life have a purpose?' is three-ways ambiguous, like the previous one. But it requires a more complicated answer.

Dave has a purpose in sense (1) just so long as he has at least one desire. It doesn't matter what the desire is for. It could be to commit suicide. That would be enough to make it true that he had a goal in life. However, the original question was not so much about Dave as about his life. A life is a different category of thing from a person. Lives, as distinct from their owners, are not capable of desiring, or of goal-directed behaviour. I think that what is normally meant when we say that a person's life has a goal is that the person has devoted his or her life as a whole to some *overriding* goal. That is, the life is lived in such a way that nearly everything the agent does is aimed at one object, say a political ideal. To do this involves subordinating one's more immediate desires to the long-term goal. If one spent large chunks of one's life doing things that were not directed to this goal, it would be wrong to say that one's life, taken as a whole, was directed to it. Few people are so single-minded as this. Dave certainly is not. Like most people, he devotes sizeable chunks of his life to the achievement of a relatively small number of dominant goals, but these dominant goals vary in an aimless fashion as his life continues.

Far more interesting is the question of whether Dave's life has a purpose *already*, independently of his will. This matter is not up to him. He may be genuinely unsure about it, since he has to discover the truth by looking outside himself. What needs to be determined is whether Dave plays a role in any natural or artificial scheme.

In so far as he is a biological organism, he does indeed have a part to play in the scheme of nature, hence a purpose in sense (2). For example, he has reproductive functions which contribute to the survival of the human species. It is irrelevant whether he ever performs them. Also, if it is the case that the species *homo sapiens* has functions within nature, then Dave has them *qua* member of the species. But this is a tricky area. Man's presence is essential for the survival of many species, e.g. a certain kind of flea. But these fleas are parasites. It is not man's function to harbour them. What we need to look for is a species with which man is related symbiotically, such that the two species together constitute a natural unit. Biologists have, in fact, discovered species of bacteria which are related to man in this way. There seem, then, to be natural systems of which man is a functional part. It is a purely contingent fact that we do not yet have names for them.

It seems certain, given that Dave has a job, that he or his life has a purpose in sense (3). Very probably he has many other artificial and social functions as well. Let us split the class of beings whose plans could involve a role for Dave into God versus the rest. If God exists, then quite possibly he intends Dave's life to serve some purpose of His. But there is no way of discovering if this is so, and certainly no way of finding out which particular purpose it might be, except by divine revelation. A lot of people believe in God, and believe that He has given their lives a purpose. They try to live their lives so as to serve whatever purpose they think God had in mind for them. But such cases are of type (1), not type (3). They devote their lives to an overriding goal of their own, to serve God's (hypothesised) purpose. In a genuine type (3) case, there must be an S, an A and a G such that Dave does A because S believes that (Dave's doing A will contribute to G, and G is good).

There are probably many human beings who stand in the relevant relations to Dave. One such is his employer. Dave's characteristic work activity of maintaining motorcycles serves a useful function for his boss, and that was the reason why he hired Dave to do it. Whether Dave realises this or not, the fact is that in his capacity as an employee he is there in order that the company should prosper. Of course, a lot of other background conditions hold too. By working, Dave earns money for himself, and he works partly with this goal in mind. I am not trying to provide an exhaustive description of the employer/employee relation, but simply focussing upon one aspect of it.

A clearer case would be one where Dave is used purely as an instrument like a corkscrew, his own desires and beliefs being irrelevant. Suppose that gangsters kidnap Dave in the hope of extorting a ransom from his family. If the money is paid, they say, they will release him unharmed; if not, they will kill him. By turning Dave's life into a bargaining counter, the kidnappers endow it with a purpose in sense (3). A noteworthy feature of this case is that the gangsters exploit the mere fact of his being alive. His life has a purpose for them, but not because of anything he does.

Thus a person's consent is not required in order for it to be true that his life has an intended function, any more than the consent of a corkscrew is required before it can be said that the corkscrew has a function. It is not even necessary that he should know about it. However, human beings *can* become aware of one another's schemes, and *can* consent to play their allotted parts. People confer purposes upon one another mutually, and through consenting they acquire new goals for themselves into the bargain. The 'bootstrap' effect comes about because a person will often start wanting to perform an activity as a result of learning that he has been assigned it as a function by someone else. His reasons for consenting may be purely self-interested: he likes the role, or sees that it will benefit him in some way. Alternatively, he may consent out of a general willingness to co-operate with others. That is, he has a non-specific desire to fall in with plans which assign a role to him, which is then focussed by a specific plan into a desire to perform that specific role. So people with ideas and plans not only give Dave functions to perform, they also stimulate him to develop new goals of his own.

Does Dave, in the very act of falling in with someone else's plan, confer back a new purpose upon the *planner*? Robert Nozick, in a lighthearted article called 'Two philosophical fables' (1971), has suggested that this is so. In the fable about teleology, a neurotic god who feels that his existence lacks purpose tries to cure this disease by creating a world. The therapy doesn't work at first. Viewed coldly, his world appears worthless. The god starts to think that the creation was a pointless exercise. Then he hits upon the following solution.

> 'If I were to create a plan, a grand design into which my creation would fit, in which my creatures, in serving the pattern and purpose I had ordained for them, would find *their* purpose and goal, then this very activity of endowing their existence with meaning and purpose would be *my* purpose, and would give my existence meaning and point.'

But although this solution might make the god think that his life was worthwhile, it doesn't show that he has a new purpose in life that he didn't have before. To get this result, we need an extra step. The creatures have to build the creator into their own plans.

Recently, human beings have started to build teleological machines which perform their humanly intended functions by acting on goals of their own. Perhaps in the future man will create robots which rejoice in the fact that they have functions for man, and take up their jobs willingly. But such developments would not, by themselves, be enough to give a new purpose to human existence. Even if the robots knew they were man-made and felt a kind of filial gratitude, the value which they confer upon their creators would be backward-looking, not teleological. They would prize human beings for having done something good. The only automatic way in which the robots can give their creators new purposes in life is by devising plans of their own in which human beings have a role. It is also possible, of course, that they will excite new desires in people, either unintentionally, through their beauty or the force of their magnetic personalities perhaps, or intentionally, through communication. But this is not logically guaranteed to happen.

Similarly, a person might want Dave to fulfil a role, and he might also want to encourage Dave to take up a new goal of his own, the goal of fulfilling his allotted role. Both of these objects might be achieved.

But neither of them gives the planner a new goal in life which is different from the two he already had. Nevertheless, Dave can confer new functions upon other people by devising roles for them in his own plans, and if he does so, that fact may in turn encourage them to develop new goals, once they learn about it. Any readers of this book who are suffering from the same complaint as Nozick's god will be pleased, therefore, to know that their lives have a purpose, bestowed by me, and that they have actually been serving this purpose up until now.

Select Bibliography

Anscombe, G. E. M. (1957), *Intention*, Oxford, Blackwell, 1957

Arbib, M. (1972), *The Metaphorical Brain*, New York & Toronto, Wiley-Interscience, 1972

Aristotle, *De Caelo* (trans. J. L. Stocks). *The Works of Aristotle Translated into English*, ed. W. D. Ross, vol. II, Oxford, 1930

Aristotle, *De Partibus Animalium* (trans. W. Ogle), W. D. Ross edition, vol. V, Oxford, 1911

Aristotle, *Ethica Nicomachea* (trans. W. D. Ross), W. D. Ross edition, vol. IX, Oxford, 1925

Aristotle, *Historia Animalium* (trans. D'Arcy Wentworth Thompson), J. A. Smith & W. D. Ross edition, vol. IV, Oxford, 1910

Aristotle, *Metphysica* (trans. W. D. Ross), J. A. Smith & W. D. Ross edition, vol. VIII, Oxford, 1908

Aristotle, *Physica* (trans. R. P. Hardie & R. K. Gaye), W. D. Ross edition, vol. II, Oxford, 1930

Armstrong, D. M. (1968), *A Materialist Theory of the Mind*, London, Routledge & Kegan Paul, 1968

Ashby, W. R. (1956), *Cybernetics*, London, Chapman & Hall Ltd., 1961

Ayala, F. J. (1970), Teleological explanations in evolutionary biology, *Philosophy of Science*, 37, 1970

Bacon, F. *Works of Sir Francis Bacon*, vol. VII, London, W. Baynes & Son, 1824

Beckner, M. (1959), *The Biological Way of Thought*, University of California Press, 1968

Beckner, M. (1969), Function and teleology, *J. History of Biology*, 2, 1969.

Bernatowicz, A. J. (1958), Teleology in science teaching, *Science*, 128, 1958

Bertalanffy, L. von (1933), *Modern Theories of Development*, (trans. J. H. Woodger), Oxford U.P., 1953

Braithwaite, R. B. (1946), Teleological explanation, *Proc. Aristotelian Society*, XLVII, 1946–7

Braithwaite, R. B. (1953), *Scientific Explanation*, Cambridge U.P., 1953

Broad, C. D. (1925), *The Mind and its Place in Nature*, London, Kegan Paul, Trench, Trubner, 1929

Butler, J. (1726), *Sermon XI*, in *British Moralists*, ed. L. A. Selby-Bigge, vol. I, Oxford, Clarendon Press, 1897

Canfield, J. (1963), Teleological explanation in biology, *Brit. J. Phil. Science*, 14, 1963–4

Canfield, J. (1966), (ed.) *Purpose in Nature*, New Jersey, Prentice-Hall, 1966

Chisholm R. (1964), The descriptive element in the concept of action, *J. Philosophy*, LXI, 1964

Cohen, G. A. (1974), Consequence-laws and functional explanation, unpublished, read at Oxford Philosophical Society, February, 1974

Cohen, L. J. (1950), Teleological explanation, *Proc. Aristotelian Society*, LI, 1950–1

Dampier, W. C. (1929), *A History of Science*, Cambridge U.P. (4th edition), 1948

Darwin, C. (1859), *The Origin of Species*, Penguin edition, 1968

Darwin, C. (1871), *The Descent of Man*, London, John Murray, 1871

Darwin, F. (1888), (ed.) *The Life and Letters of Charles Darwin*, (3 vols.) vol. II, London, John Murray, 1888

Darwin, F. (1908), Presidential Address in *Report of the 78th Meeting of the British Association for the Advancement of Science, Dublin 1908*, London, John Murray, 1909

Davidson, D. (1973), Freedom to act, in *Essays on Freedom of Action*, ed. T. Honderich, London, Routledge & Kegan Paul, 1973

Dobzhansky, T. (1969), On Cartesian and Darwinian aspects of biology, in *Philosophy, Science and Method*, (ed.) S. Morgenbesser, P. Suppes & M. White, London, MacMillan, 1969

Ducasse, C. J. (1925), Explanation, mechanism and teleology, *J. Philosophy*, XXII, 1925

Frankfurt, H. & Poole, B. (1966), Functional analyses in biology, *Brit. J. Phil. Science*, 17, 1966–7

Galileo Galilei (1623), *The Assayer*, in *Discoveries and Opinions of Galileo*, (trans. Stillman Drake), New York, Anchor Books, 1957

Galileo Galilei (1631), *Dialogue on the Great World Systems* (in the Salusbury Translation), ed. G. de Santillana, Chicago U.P., 1953

Gardiner, P. L. (1963), *Schopenhauer*, Penguin Books, 1963

Goldman, A. I. (1970), *A Theory of Human Action*, New Jersey, Prentice-Hall, 1970

Grice, H. P. (1957), Meaning, *Phil. Review*, LXVI, 1957

Grice, H. P. (1968), Utterer's meaning, sentence-meaning, and word-meaning, *Foundations of Language*, 4, 1968

Gruner, R. (1966), Teleological and functional explanations, *Mind*, LXXV, 1966

Hempel, C. (1959), The logic of functional analysis, in *Symposium on Sociological Theory*, ed. L. Gross. Reprinted in Hempel, *Aspects of Scientific Explanation*, ch. 11, New York, Free Press, 1965

Hinde, R. A. (1966), *Animal Behaviour*, New York, McGraw-Hill, 1966

Johnson, S. (1755), *Dictionary of the English Language*, London, 1755

Kalmus, H. (1966), (ed.) *Regulation and Control in Living Systems*, London, John Wiley & Sons, 1966

Kant, I. (1790), *Critique of Teleological Judgement*, (trans. J. C. Meredith), Oxford U.P., 1928

Kenny, A. (1964), *Action, Emotion and Will*, London, Routledge & Kegan Paul, 1964

Kluckholn, C. (1944), *Navaho Witchcraft*, Boston, Beacon Press, 1944

Lehman, H. (1965), Functional explanation in biology, *Phil. of Science*, 32, 1965

Leibniz, G. W., *Philosophical Papers and Letters*, 2 vols. ed. Leroy E. Loemker, Chicago U.P., 1956

Lewis, D. K. (1969), *Convention: A Philosophical Study*, Harvard U.P., 1969

McFarland, D. J. (1971), *Feedback Mechanisms in Animal Behaviour*, London, Academic Press, 1971

McFarland, D. J. & Sibly, R. (1972), 'Unitary drives' revisited, *Animal Behaviour*, 20, 1972

McFarland, J. D. (1970), *Kant's Concept of Teleology*, Edinburgh U.P., 1970

MacKay, D. M. (1972), Formal analysis of communicative processes, in *Non-Verbal Communication*, ed. R. A. Hinde, Cambridge U.P., 1972

Mackie, J. L. (1965), Causes and conditions, *American Phil. Quarterly*, 2, 1965

Mackie, J. L. (1973), *Truth, Probability and Paradox*, Oxford, Clarendon Press, 1973

Merton, R. K. (1949), Manifest and latent functions, in *Social Theory and Social Structure*, ch. 1. Revised edition, Illinois, Free Press of Glencoe, 1956

Nabokov, V. (1964), *The Defence*, London, Panther Modern Fiction, 1967

Nagel, E. (1953), Teleological explanation and teleological systems, in *Readings in the Philosophy of Science*, ed. H. Feigl & M. Brodbeck, New York, Appleton, 1953

Nagel, E. (1956), A formalization of functionalism, in *Logic Without Metaphysics*, Illinois, Free Press of Glencoe, 1956

Nagel, E. (1961), *The Structure of Science*, London, Routledge & Kegan Paul, 1961

Nissen, L. (1971), Neutral functional statement schemata, *Phil. of Science*, 38, 1971

Noble, D. (1967), Charles Taylor on teleological explanation, *Analysis*, 27, 1966–7

Nozick, R. (1971), Two philosophical fables, *Mosaic*, XII, Spring 1971, Harvard-Radcliffe Hillel Societies, Cambridge, Mass.

Pears, D. F. (1971–2), Ifs and cans, parts I and II, *Canadian J. of Philosophy*, 1, 1971–2

Pears, D. F. (1973), Rational explanation of actions and psychological determinism, in *Essays on Freedom of Action*, ed. T. Honderich, London, Routledge & Kegan Paul, 1973

Rosen, C. A. (1968), Machines that act intelligently, *Science Journal*, 4: 10, October 1968

Rosenblueth, A., Wiener, N., & Bigelow, J. (1943), Behaviour, purpose and teleology, *Phil. of Science*, 10, 1943

Ross, W. D. (1923), *Aristotle*, London, Methuen University Paperbacks, 1964

Ruse, M. (1971), Functional statements in biology, *Phil. of Science*, 38, 1971

Russell, B. (1921), *The Analysis of Mind*, London, Allen & Unwin, 1921

Russell, E. S. (1945), *The Directiveness of Organic Activities*, Cambridge U.P., 1945

Scheffler, I. (1959), Thoughts on teleology, *Brit. J. Phil. Science*, 9, 1958–9.

Scheffler, I. (1963), *Anatomy of Inquiry*, London, Routledge & Kegan Paul, 1964

Sommerhoff, G. (1950), *Analytical Biology*, London, Oxford U.P., 1950

Sommerhoff, G. (1969), The abstract characteristics of living systems, in *Systems Thinking*, ed. F. E. Emery, Penguin Modern Management Readings, 1969

Sommerhoff, G. (1974), *Logic of the Living Brain*, London, John Wiley & Sons, 1974

Sorabji, R. (1964), Function, *Phil. Quarterly*, 14, 1964
Sprigge, T. L. S. (1971), Final causes, *Aristotelian Soc. Suppl.*, vol. XLV, 1971
Taylor, C. (1964), *The Explanation of Behaviour*, London, Routledge & Kegan Paul, 1964
Taylor, C. (1967), Teleological explanation – A Reply to Denis Noble, *Analysis*, 27, 1966–7
Taylor, C. (1970), The explanation of purposive behaviour, in *Explanation and the Behavioural Sciences*, ed. R. Borger & F. Cioffi, Cambridge U.P., 1970
Taylor, R. (1966), *Action and Purpose*, New Jersey, Prentice-Hall, 1966
Waddington, C. H. (1968), The basic ideas of biology, in *Towards A Theoretical Biology*, vol. 1, ed. C. H. Waddington, Edinburgh U.P., 1968
Watling, J. (1972), Teleology and functional explanation, unpublished, lunch-time lecture given at University College, London, March 1972
Watling, J. (1973), 'Causes or reasons?'. *Inquiry*, 16, 1973
Wertheimer, R. (1972), *The Significance of Sense*, Cornell U.P., 1972
Wimsatt, W. (1970), Some problems with the concept of feedback, in *Boston Studies in the Philosophy of Science*, vol. VIII, PSA 1970, ed. R. C. Buck & R. S. Cohen, Dordrecht, Reidel, 1971
Wimsatt, W. (1972), Teleology and the logical structure of function statements *Studies in History and Philosophy of Science*, 3, 1972
Wittgenstein, L. (1921), *Tractatus Logico-Philosophicus* (trans. D. F. Pears & B. F. McGuinness), London, Routledge & Kegan Paul, 1961
Woodfield, A. (1973), Darwin, teleology and taxonomy, *Philosophy*, 48, 1973
Wright, L. (1968), The case against teleological reductionism, *Brit. J. Phil. Science*, 19, 1968–9
Wright, L. (1972), Explanation and teleology, *Phil. of Science*, 39, 1972
Wright, L. (1973), Functions, *Phil. Review*, 82, 1973

Index